Learning English

Parts of this book were published previously as:

Mercer, N. and Swann, J. (eds) (1996), *Learning English: Development and Diversity*, London, Routledge/Milton Keynes, The Open University.

Titles in the series:

Book 1 *Changing English* (edited by David Graddol, Dick Leith, Joan Swann, Martin Rhys and Julia Gillen)

Book 2 *Using English* (edited by Janet Maybin, Neil Mercer and Ann Hewings)

Book 3 *Learning English* (edited by Neil Mercer, Joan Swann and Barbara Mayor)

Book 4 *Redesigning English* (edited by Sharon Goodman, David Graddol and Theresa Lillis)

Series editors: Joan Swann and Julia Gillen

Learning English

Edited by Neil Mercer, Joan Swann and Barbara Mayor

Published by

Routledge
2 Park Square
Milton Park
Abingdon OX14 4RN

in association with

The Open University
Walton Hall
Milton Keynes MK7 6AA

Simultaneously published in the USA and Canada by

Routledge
270 Madison Avenue
New York NY 10016

Routledge is an imprint of the Taylor & Francis
Group

First published 2007

Edited and designed by The Open University.

Typeset in India by Alden Prepress Services,
Chennai.

Printed and bound in the United Kingdom by CPI,
Glasgow.

This book forms part of an Open University course
U211 *Exploring the English language*. Details of this
and other Open University courses can be obtained
from the Student Registration and Enquiry Service,
The Open University, PO Box 197, Milton Keynes,
MK7 6BJ, United Kingdom: tel. +44 (0)870 333 4340,
email general-enquiries@open.ac.uk

http://www.open.ac.uk

A catalogue record for this book is available from
the British Library.

Library of Congress Cataloging in Publication Data
A catalog record for this book has been requested.

ISBN 978 0 415 37686 0 (hardback)
ISBN 978 0 415 37687 7 (paperback)

1.1

Contents

Preface to the series

The books in this series provide an introduction to the study of English, both for students of the English language and the general reader. As Open University course books, they constitute texts for the course U211 *Exploring the English language*. The series aims to provide students with:

- an understanding of the history of English and its development as a global language
- an appreciation of variation in the English language across different speakers and writers, and different regional and social contexts
- conceptual frameworks for the study of language in use
- illustrations of the diversity of English language practices in different parts of the world
- an understanding of how English is learnt as a first or additional language, and of its role as a language of formal education
- introductions to many key controversies about the English language, such as those relating to its position as a global language, attitudes to 'good' and 'bad' English, and debates about the teaching of English
- explorations of the use of English for new purposes and in new contexts, including multimodal texts.

Parts of these books were published previously as:

Graddol, D., Leith, D. and Swann, J. (eds) (1996) *English: History, Diversity and Change*, London, Routledge/Milton Keynes, The Open University.

Maybin, J. and Mercer, N. (eds) (1996) *Using English: From Conversation to Canon*, London, Routledge/Milton Keynes, The Open University.

Mercer, N. and Swann, J. (eds) (1996) *Learning English: Development and Diversity*, London, Routledge/Milton Keynes, The Open University.

Goodman, S. and Graddol, D. (eds) (1996) *Redesigning English: New Texts, New Identities*, London, Routledge/Milton Keynes, The Open University.

The editors for the previously published books were listed in alphabetical order. The list of editors for the present series retains this original order, followed by the additional editors who have worked on the present series. Production of this series, like that of the previously published books, has been a collaborative enterprise involving numerous members of Open University staff and external colleagues. We thank all those who contributed to the original books and to this series. We regret that their names are too many to list here.

Joan Swann and Julia Gillen
Series editors

Biographical information

Book editors

Barbara Mayor is a Lecturer in the Centre for Language and Communication at The Open University. Her research interests include bilingualism and the use of English as a global language of education. Recent publications include 'The English language and "global" teaching' (with Joan Swann) in *Distributed Learning* (2002, Routledge Falmer) and *A Story in Every Word* (2005, in connection with BBC Voices).

Neil Mercer is Professor of Education at the University of Cambridge. He is a psychologist with a special interest in the role of language in the classroom and the development of children's thinking. His books include *Common Knowledge* (with Derek Edwards; 1987, Routledge), *The Guided Construction of Knowledge* (1995, Multilingual Matters) and *Words and Minds* (2000, Routledge).

Joan Swann is currently Director of the Centre for Language and Communication at The Open University. She has extensive experience producing teaching materials on linguistics and English language studies. Her research interests include language and gender and other areas of sociolinguistics. Recent publications include *The Art of English: Everyday Creativity* (co-edited with Janet Maybin; 2006, Palgrave Macmillan) and *A Dictionary of Sociolinguistics* (2004, Edinburgh University Press).

Additional contributors

Dennis Bancroft is head of educational research for the British Educational Communications and Technology Agency (BECTA) in Warwick. He has written on children's cognitive and language development and edited a book on implications of work in developmental psychology for the lives of children.

Douglas Barnes was formerly a Reader in Education at the University of Leeds. His central research interest has been the role of language in school learning, and since retirement he has been an advisor to the National Oracy Project. Books include *From Communication to Curriculum* (2nd edn, 1992, Heinemann), *School Writing* (1991, Open University Press) and *Communication and Learning Revisited* (1995, Heinemann).

Jill Bourne is Professor of Primary Education and Head of the Centre for Research on Pedagogy and Curriculum at the University of Southampton. She has published extensively on teaching English to speakers of other languages and on raising the attainment of bilingual students. Publications include *World Yearbook of Language Education* (co-editor; 2003, Routledge Falmer) and *English in Urban Classrooms* (co-author; 2004, Routledge Falmer).

Pam Czerniewska, at the time of writing, was a Lecturer in the School (now Faculty) of Education at The Open University. From 1985–89 she was Director of the National Writing Project. She has written and contributed to books and journals on children's language and literacy. She is now a practising speech and language therapist specialising in autistic spectrum disorders.

Julia Gillen is Chair of the Open University course U211 *Exploring the English language*, and a member of the Centre for Language and Communication at The Open University. She is author of the book *The Language of Children* (2003, Routledge). Her interests include discourse analysis, the history of literacy research and children's communication skills.

Ann Hewings is a Senior Lecturer in the Centre for Language and Communication at The Open University. She worked on the COBUILD project, researching and contributing to English dictionaries and reference material. Her research focus is academic writing in disciplinary contexts, particularly at tertiary level and in electronic environments. Recent joint publications include *Grammar and Context* (2005, Routledge) and *Applied English Grammar* (2004, Hodder-Arnold).

Theresa Lillis is a Senior Lecturer in the Centre for Language and Communication at The Open University. She has published research on academic writing, including *Student Writing: Access, Regulation and Desire* (2001, Routledge), and articles on multilingual scholarly publishing in *TESOL Quarterly* and *Written Communication*. She is co-author of *A Dictionary of Sociolinguistics* (2004, Edinburgh University Press).

Frank Monaghan is a Staff Tutor in Education at The Open University. Previously he taught English and English as an Additional Language in a multilingual comprehensive school in London. He is an executive member of the National Association for Language Development in the Curriculum (NALDIC) and author of *Practical Ways to Support New Arrivals* (2004, National Centre for Language and Literacy).

Introduction

Barbara Mayor

The most casual observer cannot fail to be impressed by the rapidity, and apparent facility, with which young children learn language. The topic has also fascinated academic researchers from a range of disciplines, shedding light both on learning processes and on the nature of language itself – how language works and how it is used. In this book we examine the acquisition of English, tracing its development from the earliest years, through its formal teaching in schools, to its use as a language of higher education.

English is now taught to many millions of primary-school children on all six continents, and bilingualism and multilingualism in which English plays a vital role has become a fact of daily life in face-to-face transactions and electronic communications across the world. Our focus here is on how learners of English, from infancy to adulthood, *learn* what it means to be an English speaker across such different contexts.

Although the chapters cover different topics, and the authors themselves have differing academic backgrounds and interests, there are some common threads that run throughout the book. Children in the home, and students in formal education, are all seen as active learners, making hypotheses about the structures of English and how the language is used. The book as a whole also takes a broadly functional approach to language learning, suggesting that learners at all stages of development are not simply acquiring linguistic structures, but also an ability to use these to perform social acts. This has implications for the formal teaching of English: debates across many contexts often centre on the extent to which students should be taught linguistic forms independently of their use in social situations.

Two further points derive from this functional perspective. First, language learning is seen not as an individual matter but as a collaborative enterprise, involving interaction between the learner and family members, friends, teachers and others. Second, children and adults necessarily learn how to behave as a certain kind of person (a child, girl or boy, student, business person, waiter, etc.) through their acquisition of English in specific interactions – in other words, they take on a set of identities as they learn different aspects of the language. This link between language, interaction and identity lies behind many of the more controversial aspects of the English curriculum. English teaching is not a neutral activity. It can be seen either as a mechanism for keeping learners firmly in their social place, or as potentially empowering through giving learners access to powerful language varieties or ways of using the language.

- Chapter 1 considers how young children learn English as their first language. It sees such learning primarily as a collaborative, social activity, in which children learn to use the linguistic structures of English to achieve certain ends.

- Chapter 2 discusses how bilingual and multilingual children learn English alongside other languages; and how all children acquire different varieties of English. Children, in effect, acquire a 'repertoire' of language varieties to express different personal and social identities.
- Chapter 3 focuses on children learning to read and write. It suggests that literacy, from the earliest years, involves much more than an understanding of the writing system: children are actively engaged in working out the meaning of literacy in social contexts.
- Chapter 4 is about the use of English as a classroom language, a role in which it can have a powerful influence on children's language development. The chapter considers the choice of English as a classroom language against or alongside other languages, as well as the characteristic patterns of classroom interaction.
- Chapter 5, through accounts of experience in various English-speaking countries, looks at the way in which the nature of 'English' as a school subject has been shaped according to political contexts and pedagogical fashions.
- Chapter 6 discusses the teaching of English to speakers of other languages: how English has been taught in different contexts; what social positions students are invited to take up through their learning of English; and the effects of English teaching on other languages and cultures.
- Chapter 7 turns to the growing use of English as a language of higher education across the world. It considers the extent to which the English of different academic disciplines may need to be explicitly taught, as well as exploring the implications for students of entering into such disciplinary discourse communities. It also questions whether the nature of 'academic English' may ultimately be challenged by its diverse global users.

Each chapter is accompanied by at least one reading, which represents an additional 'voice' or viewpoint on one or more of the principal themes or issues raised in the chapter.

Each chapter includes:

activities to stimulate further understanding or analysis of the material

text boxes containing illustrative or supplementary material

key terms which are clearly explained as soon as they appear in order to increase the reader's familiarity with the subject.

Like most academic enterprises, this book reflects the input of many colleagues whose names do not directly appear as editors or as chapter authors. I am particularly grateful to Diana Honeybone, who drew on many years of teaching a previous version of the material in order to edit parts of

Chapters 3 and 4; to Neil Mercer and Elizabeth Hoadley-Maidment for material incorporated into Chapter 7; and to Graham Frater and Elizabeth Jackson for comments on the new material in Chapters 5 and 7.

A note on representing the sounds of language

This book is about spoken and written English, and so from time to time it deals with the sounds of speech as well as the letters of the alphabet. The distinctive sounds of a particular language, or more precisely of a particular variety of a language, are known as phonemes, and phonemes are conventionally signalled by being enclosed in diagonal brackets / /. The sound of each phoneme is always clearly explained or illustrated by placing it in a familiar context. The important thing to remember is that when you see diagonal brackets, the symbols inside represent sounds and not letters. Hence the (written) word *cool* would be transcribed by the sequence of phonemes /kul/.

You will also (more rarely) come across instances of symbols inside square brackets [ ]. These symbols are from the International Phonetic Alphabet and are meant to convey an accurate transcription of speech sounds from potentially any language, allowing comparison of subtle differences in pronunciation between different accents or different speakers.

A fuller account of the speech sounds of English is to be found in Graddol et al. (2007).

A note on representing children's ages

Since the development of children's language is very rapid in the early stages of life, it is conventional to represent ages very precisely, not only in terms of years but of months and even days. Where age is represented in the text of this book, it is in the form 1;2 or 1;2,15 indicating one year, two months and fifteen days. Occasionally, in quoted material, the forms 1:2 and 1.2 are also found.

English as a first language

Dennis Bancroft, with contributions from Julia Gillen

1.1 Introduction

What does it mean to learn a language such as English? The task is such an ordinary one that it's easy to forget it's also quite a remarkable achievement. David Crystal (1995) outlines the knowledge that young language learners need to acquire in order to speak English:

- The 20 or so vowels and 24 or so consonants of a spoken dialect of the language, and over 300 ways of combining these sounds into sequences (such as /s+k+r/ into *scr*eam, and /m+p+s/ into ju*mps*).
- A vocabulary which can evidently reach 50,000 or more active words, and a passive ability to understand about half as many again.
- At least a thousand aspects of grammatical construction, dealing with all the rules – some very general, some very specific – governing sentence and word formation.
- Several hundred ways of using the prosodic features of pitch, loudness, speed, and rhythm, along with other tones of voice, to convey meaning: 'it's not what you say, it's the way that you say it'.
- An uncertain (but large) number of rules governing the ways in which sentences can be combined into spoken discourse, both in monologue and dialogue.
- An uncertain (but very large) number of conventions governing the ways in which varieties of the language differ, so that the linguistic consequences of region, gender, class, occupation, and other such factors can be assimilated.
- An uncertain (but even larger) number of strategies governing the ways in which all the above rules can be bent or broken in order to achieve special effects, such as in jokes and poems.

(Crystal, 1995, p. 426, italics added)

What is all the more remarkable is the speed with which such knowledge is acquired. Crystal comments that by the time they attend their first school 'most children give the impression of having assimilated at least three-quarters of all the grammar there is to learn' (Crystal, 1995, p. 428).

This chapter describes the development of young children's ability to speak English and considers how this development is influenced by specific linguistic and cultural factors. The particular perspective on language development that I take in this chapter is this: when young children acquire

English, or any other language, they are acquiring a tool for social action. They learn language in social situations where they, and other people, are trying to get things done.

ACTIVITY 1.1

Allow 5–10 minutes

Consider, for example, the case of Susie, recorded at the age of 4 years 7 months talking to her babysitter (Crystal, 1986). What does Susie seem to have learnt to *do* in English? What skills has she acquired in order to take part in a conversation and tell a story? (Note that '–' indicates a pause.)

SUSIE	Oh, look, a crab. We seen – we were been to the seaside.
BABY-SITTER	Have you?
SUSIE	We saw cr – fishes and crabs. And we saw a jellyfish, and we had to bury it. And we – we did holding crabs, and we – we holded him in by the spade.
BABY-SITTER	Did you?
SUSIE	Yes, to kill them, so they won't bite our feet.
BABY-SITTER	Oh.
SUSIE	If you stand on them, they hurt you, won't they.
BABY-SITTER	They would do. They'd pinch you.
SUSIE	You'd have to – and we put them under the sand, where the sea was. And they were going to the sea.
BABY-SITTER	Mhm.
SUSIE	And we saw some shells. And we picked them up, and we heard the sea in them. And we saw a crab on a lid. And we saw lots of crabs on the sea side. And I picked the – fishes up – no, the shells, and the feathers from the birds. – And I saw a pig.
BABY-SITTER	Gosh, that was fun.
SUSIE	Yes, and I know a story about pigs.
BABY-SITTER	Are you going to tell it to me?
SUSIE	One – one day they went out to build their houses. One built it of straw, one built it of sticks, and one built it of bricks. And he – the little busy brother knowed that in the woods there lived a big bad wolf, he need nothing else but to catch little pigs. So, you know what, one day they went out – and – the wolf went slip slosh slip slosh went his feet on the ground. Then – let me see, er – now I think – he said let me come in, you house of straw. And

he said, no no by my hair of my chinny-chin-chin, I will not let you come in. Then I'll huff, and I'll puff, and I'll puff, and I'll blow your house down. So he huffed, and he puffed, and he puffed, and he puffed, and he blew the little straw house all to pieces. Then away went the little brother to his brother's house of sticks ...

(Crystal, 1986, pp. 9–10)

Comment

As you may have observed, Susie is clearly a competent conversationalist, able to *take turns, involve her interlocutor, respond* to prompts and questions, etc. In addition, she has developed some specific skills to do with storytelling. Crystal comments on her retelling of *The Three Little Pigs* as follows (we have italicised some of the key words and phrases in his account, and to distinguish these we have placed Susie's original words in quotation marks):

The story-line ... comes from one of her favourite bed-time sagas, and she has evidently been a keen listener. She *reproduces* several of its phrases very accurately – not only the wolf's words, but some of the story-teller's style, such as 'Away went ... '. She also *dramatizes* the narrative – though you can't tell from the above transcription: 'big bad wolf' is said with long, drawn-out vowels; and the huffing and puffing is accompanied by a great puffing out of the cheeks, and an increased presence, as Susie draws herself up to her full height – all 42 inches of it. You can easily tell, from her version, how her parents must have acted out the story.

On the other hand, this is definitely Susie's story, not the book's. If you compare her words with those of the original, there are all kinds of partial correspondences, but *hardly anything is repeated exactly* as it was.

For instance, the book does not begin with that opening line; the phrase the 'little busy brother' isn't used there; and she puffs far more than the wolf does. Susie may have learned the events of the story off by heart, and several of its words and phrases, but it is largely *her own grammar* which is stringing them together. It is also very much *her style*: at the time, the use of the 'you know what' and 'let me see' were definite 'Susie-isms'.

As you can tell from the pauses and the rephrasings, Susie's speech isn't perfectly fluent. It's rather jerky at times, and sometimes it comes out in such a rush that it's difficult to follow. Her pronunciation, too, is somewhat immature – she says [kwab] for *crab*, for instance, and [bwʌvə] for brother [you will find a brief note on the use of phonetic script representing language sounds in the Introduction to this book]. And she has the child-like preference for joining sentences using 'and' – the commonest linking word among children, from around age 3 onwards. She is also still sorting out some points of grammar, especially in relation to the way verbs are used: she says 'knowed' instead of 'knew', 'we seen' alongside 'we saw', 'we did hold[ing]' instead of 'we held', and there is the interesting 'we were been', with its confusion of tenses.

But the overwhelming impression we receive from the story, as from the whole dialogue, is one of great *competence and confidence*.

(adapted from Crystal, 1986, pp. 10–11)

The linguist Michael Halliday was one of the first to develop an understanding of language development based on analysis of the functions of utterances (summarised in his seminal 1978 book, *Language as Social Semiotic*). In particular, he introduced the valuable, but difficult, notion that a functional approach to the development of meanings (i.e. looking at what children learn to *do* with language) implies a *social foundation* for the development of language. This perspective is very influential among developmental psycholinguists and it has informed the selection of materials in this chapter.

This seems to me to be a plausible start to our journey since it does not constrain us to an investigation of children's language use from the moment they begin to speak recognisable words, but allows us to explore the possibility that the basis of later language development rests in children's early, preverbal, efforts to make their wishes known.

The chapter has four main sections, dealing in turn with the development of the sounds of language, a child's first words, the beginnings of grammar and finally, as examples of sophisticated usage, the development of humour and narrative skills.

1.2 Sounds and exchanges

Many psycholinguists have investigated stages in the development of communication in infants. A flexible vocal system over which one has control seems to be an essential attribute of all spoken language users and, during the first year of life, infants produce a range of sounds and begin to indulge in vocal play. However, this is not all that they are learning to do. Table 1.1 shows the generally agreed sequence of communicative milestones, as summarised by Lauren Adamson (1995).

Table 1.1 Milestones of early communication development

Milestone	Average age (in months)	Typical range (in months)
Eyes open	0	
Eye-to-eye contact	2	
Social smile	2	
Coos and goos	2	
Laughs	4	
Squeals, raspberries, growls, yells, etc.	4	
Canonical babbling (e.g., [bababa])	7	
Comprehends a word	9	
Comprehends 10 words	10.5	
Variegated babbling	11	
Onset of pointing	12	
Comprehends 50 words	13	
Produces first word	13	9 to 16
Produces 10 words	15	13 to 19
Produces 50 words	20	14 to 24
Produces word combinations	21	18 to 24

(Adamson, 1995, p. 17, Table 2.1)

Notes on some of these terms:

'cooing' – often high-pitched vowel-like sounds that can be combined with [g] or [k]

'babbling' – repetition of well-formed syllables constituted of a vowel and at least one consonant. Usually the same sound is reduplicated, e.g. [ba ba]. Develops into 'variegated babbling' where a number of varied syllables are combined together

'raspberries' – these too can be described in linguistic terms! Adamson (1995, p. 90) explains they are 'labial trills and vibrants'.

Psycholinguists such as Adamson are careful to explain that such charts must be interpreted flexibly. Children do vary hugely in rates of development, and occasionally they may omit a stage such as babbling. Also, of course, many of these milestones may be defined in different ways by observers. It is clear, however, from psycholinguistic research that physiological maturation has an important role in speech development.

Figure 1.1   Early vocal play

ACTIVITY 1.2

Allow about
5 minutes

If you are able to enlist the aid of friends and family, do so; but this demonstration works quite well as a solo effort. Choose some typical sounds produced by an infant, such as *mmm* or *ooh* or *dada*, and try saying them to convey the following:

- pleasure
- disgust
- resignation
- a request.

Listen carefully to yourself or your friends/family while the task is being done.

Comment

This exercise should have shown you how it is possible to have a one-word vocabulary and yet be capable of expressing a range of different meanings, or performing a range of linguistic acts, by varying the **intonation**. This serves to multiply the value of each item in a limited vocabulary. When infants acquire control over their sound-making equipment in the first months of life, they are taking control of a system which may later be useful to them in communicative exchanges.

Crucial also to communication is the *context* in which children are growing up: research over the last few decades has shown that babies' early interactions might be far more important to their development of communication capacities than was previously thought. The remainder of this section, therefore, will focus on two key questions:

- Are the early sounds made by children universally the same? Or do the sounds produced vary with the language community into which the child is born?
- What part do caregivers (the usual term for those people who spend most time looking after and interacting with the child) play in an infant's early language development?

Are the early sounds made by children universally the same?

Many psycholinguists have investigated whether young babies can and do perceive differences between languages and also whether the early sounds produced by infants are universally the same or affected by being in, say, an English-speaking environment. However, despite the considerable effort which has been put into research in this field, there is no clear agreement among researchers about the answer to this question.

Some researchers take a 'universalist' line and state that infants start life able to make all the possible speech sounds that a human can make and then cease to make those sounds not found in their particular linguistic environment. In complete contrast, others claim that infants begin with no ability to make sounds other than cries and rely on the environment to provide sounds to learn and copy. Others uphold what is sometimes called the 'attunement' theory which states that infants start with a basic set of sounds common to all but then build up a repertoire of other sounds found in their own particular environment.

In principle, the validity of each of these conflicting views ought to be testable through observational and experimental research – that is, if suitable data of the sounds infants make were collected from children across a range of different language communities, it would be possible to evaluate the competing theoretical positions. But one of the reasons why there is continuing disagreement is that analysing speech data from young children is difficult, and interpretations of the evidence differ. It may help you to understand the nature of this research if we look at one study in more detail.

Andrea Levitt and Jennifer Aydelott Utman (1992) conducted a longitudinal study (i.e. one that involves researching changes or developments of a subject over a period of time) which compared the sounds produced by one US English-speaking child and one French-speaking child. This study was intended to identify some of the differences between the two languages. Recordings were made of these children at 5 months, 8 months, 11 months and 14 months. In analysing their results, Levitt and Utman used both phonetic transcription and the spectrograph (which produces a visual representation of sound signals).

The reason for comparing a child from a French-speaking community and a child from an English-speaking community was that there are specific and known phonemic differences between the two languages, as well as differences in terms of prosody (rhythm and intonation). For example, of the twenty-one vowel sounds in these varieties of English and French, eight are shared, five occur in English but not in French, and eight occur in French but not in English. These differences suggest that if the language environment has an influence on infant babbling then this influence might become apparent in different sounds made by the two infants. Alternatively, if children's physical development is the main influence on the types of sounds produced, then the sounds made by the two infants should be quite similar.

The detailed findings of this study are quite complex; in summary, the analyses show evidence of similar developmental patterns *and* of the influence of adult language. The sounds produced by the infants were similar in terms of the *range* of consonants and vowel sounds they produced and in terms of the *kinds* of consonant sounds they used (i.e. how and where in the mouth they are produced). This similarity is consistent with the idea that infants from different language communities pass through the same stages of phonological development. But Levitt and Utman also report that effects specific to the language environment began to be identifiable within the recordings made at 11 months. They observe that 'Each infant's phonetic inventory began to resemble that of the adult language both in composition and frequency, so that over the course of time, the two infants' phonetic inventories, in particular their consonantal inventories, diverged' (Levitt and Utman, 1992, pp. 46–7).

This finding is consistent with other evidence which points to language-specific influences becoming identifiable towards the end of the first year of life. On the basis of such research, then, a tentative answer to our first question would be that there is a relationship between the language environment and a child's early sound-making. The distinctive sounds of a language – those which help to distinguish different meanings – are known as **phonemes**. The number of phonemes varies from one language to another, and between different varieties of a language. (For instance, one phoneme, the sound at the end of the word *loch,* is found in Scottish English but not in most other varieties of English.) Children need to learn the set of phonemes that make up their own language variety, as well as how these are pronounced.

Gradually the distinctive sounds produced by the child will come to resemble more closely those of their language community – though the acquisition of the full set of phonemes of any variety of English takes several years.

Learning English phonemes

To master English phonology the child must acquire many different [phonemes], and one salient characteristic of child phonology is that different phonemes are acquired at different rates. By the age of three children tend to have mastered the vowels, and certain consonants such as plosives (e.g. /p, b/) and nasals (e.g. /m, n/), but they may be in their seventh year before a few troublesome consonants such as the 'th' (/θ/) in *th*ing and 'ch' (/tʃ/) in *church* are acquired. Children vary greatly with regard to the rate of acquisition of the different phonemes. [Table 1.2] shows the progress of acquisition, and while the order and particular time schedules may vary, it's unlikely that you will find a child who (for example) masters *sh* (/ʃ/) before *p* (/p/).

Table 1.2 Acquisition of English phonemes

Phonemes	Median age
p, b, m, h, n, w	1;6 (years; months)
k, g, d, t, ŋ	2;0
f, v,	2;6
r, l, s	3;0
t', ʃ	3;6
z, dʒ	4;0
θ	4;6
ð	5;0
ʒ	6;0

(Sanders, 1961, p. 62; adapted by Aldridge, 1991, p. 15)

A variety of factors determine the rate at which phonemes are mastered. Visibility is one such factor: sounds produced by visible movement such as front labial sounds like /p/ (where the lips are brought tightly together) are acquired before invisible sounds produced at the back of the mouth like /k/. Another factor is complexity: some sounds are harder to pronounce than others. For example, /t/ is a relatively easy phoneme to articulate since it involves only one movement of the tongue with the alveolar ridge [just behind the top front teeth]; in contrast 'ch' (tʃ) is a complex phoneme involving two movements, where the tongue must come into contact with the alveolar ridge but there must also be simultaneous contact of the tongue with the hard palate. Children are therefore likely to acquire /t/ before (tʃ). Similarly, single consonants will be mastered before consonant clusters, so we would anticipate that the child will correctly articulate /r/ in *red* before /r/ in st*r*eet.

(adapted from Aldridge, 1991, p. 15)

[Note: as explained in the Introduction to this book, we show phonemes in diagonal brackets. This convention differs from that in the original article.]

Various researchers have found that infants are extraordinarily good at identifying features of specific languages, differentiating one from another, and indeed even at recognising characteristics of individual speakers; for example:

> ... human infants begin to become familiar with the speech sounds they hear around them – in terms of the types of sounds of their language and the voices of particular speakers such as their mothers – while they are still [in the womb] ... By the time they are near their first birthdays, infants have already begun to zero in on the particular sounds they need to know to speak the language they are born into – in terms of both perception and production – to the extent that they are beginning to lose the ability to perceive and produce the sounds of other languages ...

(Tomasello and Bates, 2001, p. 2)

What is the role of a caregiver in early language development?

We can now move on to consider our second question, which concerns the role of a child's caregivers in influencing the sounds made by the child. It has been the practice in much research in this area to focus on the pair, often termed a **dyad**, consisting of the child and the child's main caregiver. The evidence from this research points to a clear role for the immediate circle of people with whom the infant has contact. They provide, both in speech addressed to the child and in speech to others, the language environment that the infant is able to sample.

Providing experience of the *sounds* of a language is not the only kind of linguistic modelling that adults provide for children. Many caregiving routines, such as feeding and bathing, give opportunities for predictable *exchanges* involving language. Even though infants of this age cannot reply, adults and others speak to them as though they can and, by this means, introduce them to a world in which language accompanies and complements most of our doings.

One particular kind of exchange between caregiver and child merits more detailed discussion. This involves a very common game (sometimes called 'peek-a-boo') played between infant and caregiver in Western cultures. The game has many variants but will often involve an adult attracting the infant's attention and then 'hiding' their eyes behind a book or a hand or something similar. Then follows a sort of dialogue in which the adult may say 'Are you ready?' to which the infant's movements or vocalisations are interpreted as a reply. The question-and-reply sequence is repeated several times until, with the tension becoming almost unbearable, the adult removes the book or hand and says 'Boo!'. The Social Baby Project (Murray and Andrews, 2000) documents many such games with the aid of video stills.

ACTIVITY 1.3

Allow about 5 minutes

Trevarthen and Aitken (2001) have proposed that games such as 'peek-a-boo' might be termed 'protoconversations'. In what ways is this kind of interaction similar to a conversation?

Comment

- It involves turn-taking. (It is not clear in the early months that infants *intend* to make a contribution, but adults interpret their behaviour as though they do.)
- It is contingent. In other words, each person's turn depends on the prior contribution of the partner. (Indeed an initiative can be made by the infant and taken up by the adult, not just the other way round.)
- The partners share the same purpose and understand the sequence.
- It is pleasurable.

This sort of interaction therefore introduces young children to many of the formal characteristics of conversations long before they are able to speak and, in Trevarthen and Aitken's view, serves to motivate the journey towards language: '[The] natural sociability of infants, engaging the interest, purposes and feelings of willing and affectionate parents, serves to intrinsically motivate companionship, or cooperative awareness, leading the infant towards development of "confidence, confiding and acts of meaning", and, eventually, to language' (Trevarthen and Aitken, 2001, p. 4).

But how universal is this kind of experience for infants across the world? Psychologists have often collected data from children in their own and related communities (usually middle-class communities in countries such as the UK and the USA). Reasoning that 'children are children wherever they are', the psychologists have then commonly made an assumption that the processes they observe are a universal feature of early language experience.

One of the common observations made about the sort of speech addressed to children by adults is that it is different from the kind of speech addressed to other adults. Caregivers often modify their speech in various ways – for example, by giving it a higher pitch, exaggerated intonation and a slower delivery. It has also been noted that older children modify their speech to younger children in a roughly similar way. Observations of this kind are so common in Western literature that it has been suggested that this speech style, previously referred to as 'motherese' and now usually termed **child directed speech (CDS)**, plays an essential role in language acquisition. However, if it could be shown that there are cultures where children develop their language successfully and where these Western observations do not hold true, then it could not be claimed that CDS is essential for language development.

Relevant here is the work of Clifton Pye (1986), who describes some of the cultural practices of the Quiché people of Central America, who speak one of the indigenous Mayan languages. Pye found that the Quiché caregivers do not modify their speech in the way that Western caregivers do, and he notes other differences in the amount and kind of vocal interaction:

> The mothers are quick to interpret any movement or vocalisation as a signal to feed their babies, which they accomplish without interrupting their own activities. Vocal interaction between infants and parents is minimal, although there is some variation between parents in this regard. They certainly lack any concept of talking with their children for the sake of stimulating their linguistic development. ...
>
> I did not observe Quiché parents engaged in any special games with their children. When I asked them if they knew of any games similar to nursery rhymes or finger games, they said they did not. Children five and over had a large repertoire of games (marbles, string figures, football), but these were not played with younger children.

> (Pye, 1986, pp. 86, 91)

Despite this cultural variation in parent–child interaction, Quiché children grow up to be perfectly fluent speakers of their mother tongue.

A classic piece of research by Shirley Brice Heath (1983), who observed the language practices of parents and children in different English-speaking communities in south-west USA, is also relevant here. She found that adults in black working-class communities were less likely to use 'baby talk' in their interactions with young children. (Heath's work is discussed further in Chapter 3.)

It seems, then, that the exchanges often described as characteristic of caregivers and infants and the distinct vocal style that the caregivers adopt are not a universal, or a necessary, feature of early language experience. However, it is possible that such language practices can *contribute* to language development without being *essential* to it. One reason for an interest in the existence and role of CDS is that, if the language addressed to young children can be shown to be structured in a consistent and helpful way and infants can be shown to make use of this language, then we will have moved closer to understanding an aspect of the context of language development. However, the fact that cultural practices can be shown to vary challenges the argument for the importance of CDS.

Figure 1.2   An everyday communicative exchange within the extended family

1.3 Words and meanings

Our story so far takes us to the point at which an infant has control over a range of sounds and may be using this control selectively – that is, meaningfully. The infant may also have some experience of being a partner in social, communicative interactions. The scene is set for the appearance of a child's first word. But this raises the question of what counts as a word. The first word produced by a child may resemble a word to be found in that child's language environment but, equally, it may not.

Children's early words

At one level, a word is a sound or set of sounds produced consistently and with a consistent meaning. These sounds must be recognised as having significance by at least one other person. In these circumstances, any sound produced by an infant on a regular and consistent basis and recognised by the child's caregiver could be considered a word, although these 'words' may be unrecognisable as words outside the specific contexts created by the child and caregiver. Establishing the idea of sound-to-meaning correspondence is an important breakthrough in developing language – although a child may produce a meaningful sequence of speech (such as the phrase *what that*, quoted in the box on children's vocabulary development) before being able to analyse it into its components.

Children's early vocabulary development

We can say quite confidently that initially vocabulary development is slow, with children producing about 50 words in the first eighteen months (they may understand five times as many). But from around 21 months a vocabulary growth spurt occurs and during that period the child may acquire about 10 new words per week, making the task of word counting increasingly difficult. Thus, rather than talking about the rate of vocabulary growth, it is perhaps more interesting to examine the type of words that are first acquired.

[Listed below are] all the utterances produced by Dewi (19 months) in a twenty-minute recording of his spontaneous speech.

> Blue, book, that, see this, what that, look, blow, bubble, want, quack, drum, in there, down, here bubble, boot, no, big, yeah, car, baby, dog, slide, coat.

These utterances are typically one-word structures, and the lexical items produced are short and concrete, that is to say they denote physical objects (*book, car*), actions (*look, blow*), spatial relations (*in, down*), and attributes (*blue, big*), whereas grammatical words such as determiners (*the, a*), pronouns (*I, he*) and modal verbs (*can, may*) are systematically absent. Clearly, children's early vocabularies contain words that pertain to things and actions that are of immediate relevance to their lives. Why are these concrete words first acquired? Among the many explanations which have been proposed, two points are of particular importance. Firstly, in the speech children hear it is these concrete words which carry the stress, thus perhaps the acoustic salience of these items helps the child to acquire them early. Secondly, the child's main aim is to communicate, and it is precisely these concrete words which carry meaning. For example, we can all understand the meaning of the word 'dog' or 'run' but what does 'can' or 'a' mean? Another example is the use of pronouns. Names are stable: 'Jane' is 'Jane' whoever is talking; in contrast, the meaning of pronouns changes from speaker to speaker: 'a person who is you when I speak, becomes I when he [*sic*] speaks!' Thus the child's early vocabulary consists of concrete words, and it is only gradually, from around the age of two years onwards, that abstract, grammatical words emerge.

(Aldridge, 1991, pp. 16, 17, italics added)

Once a child has started to produce words and phrases, a repertoire is accumulated, slowly at first but with increasing speed as the child grows – see the box on early vocabulary development. (Note that linguists commonly distinguish between **lexical** or **content words** – including the 'concrete' words referred to by Aldridge below – and **grammatical** or **function words,** such as *it* or *does*.) Developmental psychologists, particularly those from English-speaking countries, have been very interested in children's accumulation of vocabulary and have used language records, among other things, to investigate aspects of children's understanding of language itself, as well as children's understanding of the meanings of the words they use, and to study some of the factors which may contribute to language development.

In the remainder of this section we will look at two issues. The first is the need to establish a description of early vocabulary development in terms of rate and age of acquisition. The second issue concerns the role, if any, that caregivers have in the development of vocabulary.

The acquisition of vocabulary: comprehension and production

There have been many descriptive accounts of the acquisition of vocabulary, dating back to William Preyer's work in 1882 on the acquisition of German (an English translation appeared in 1889). The great majority of these accounts, however, are based on studies of language acquisition in English-speaking communities. Except on points of detail the accounts tally quite well, so here we consider a representative account by Benedict (1979) which traces the vocabulary development of eight children over a six-month period. This might seem a small number of children to study, but the amount of data which an observational study of this kind can gather from just one child is extremely large (Preyer's account was of the development of a single child, his son Axel). Benedict chose a large enough number of children to allow for individual variation and yet small enough to avoid being swamped by large amounts of language data. Table 1.3 summarises what Benedict found regarding the children's apparent ability to *comprehend* words and to *produce* words, between the ages of about 10 months and about 1 year 9 months. For example, the second entry in the table indicates that the average age at which the children had a comprehension vocabulary of twenty words was 11 months and 15 days (see also the note on representing children's ages in the Introduction to this book).

Table 1.3 Mean age of acquisition (comprehension and production) of twentieth, thirtieth, fortieth and fiftieth words

Comprehension (no. of words)	Mean age (years;months,days)	Production (no. of words)
0	0;10,14	
20	0;11,15	
30	1;0,3	
40	1;0,19	
50	1;1,5	
	1;1,21	0
	1;3,6	20
	1;4,14	30
	1;5,16	40
	1;9,15	50

(Benedict, 1979; adapted by Ingram, 1989, p. 142, Table 6.1)

ACTIVITY 1.4

Allow about
10 minutes

Look carefully at the information provided in Table 1.3. What is the relation between comprehension and production indicated by these data? Is there a difference in the rate of acquisition between comprehension vocabulary and production vocabulary?

Comment

One obvious interpretation is that the onset of comprehension is about four months in advance of production on these figures. This is consistent with the general developmental phenomenon that perception advances before production and the widely held parental view that infants understand more than they can say. The second point is that, in this early stage of development, it takes longer to acquire words in production than it does in comprehension. Before we leave these data we should note that averaging the data from eight children in the way presented here can disguise individual differences among the children. Although there was a gap between comprehension and production for all the children, the size of this gap varied considerably between individual children.

ACTIVITY 1.5

Turn now to 'Understanding words' by Lauren Adamson (Reading A). This should enrich your understanding of the processes involved in the comprehension and production of vocabulary and the relationship between the two, as well as some of the methods by which researchers have investigated the language of infants. As you read make notes on the following:

- the typical difference in extent between infants' receptive and productive vocabularies
- the relationship that often obtains for infants between words and actions
- how and why infants may overextend the meaning of a word
- typical infant reactions to nonsense words and implausible statements
- four different ways in which researchers have studied such phenomena.

The role of caregivers in the development of vocabulary

I want to conclude this section with a brief consideration of the uses that children make of words and the impact of caregiver speech on this usage. My focus is on the role of the *primary* caregiver – although, as we know, children experience communicative exchanges with different people. The variety of these exchanges may have useful consequences for a child's language development by increasing the range of talk to which the child is exposed. For example, Barton and Tomasello (1994) described evidence which shows that (in US English-speaking families where the mother was the primary caregiver) the input of other members of the family may be less conversationally supportive to the child and, in the case of siblings, more competitive.

Relevant research was conducted in the UK by Barrett et al. (1991). They looked at the first ten words produced by each of four children growing up in English-speaking families, and tried to determine the uses to which these words were put. This use was compared to the most frequent maternal use of the same term. There are two points to make. First, there was a very close relationship between the child's first use and the child's mother's use of the words in the great majority of cases (92.5 per cent). 'This finding suggests that linguistic input may play an important role in early lexical development, with children deriving their initial use of a word from the most frequently occurring use which is modelled for them in their environment' (Barrett et al., 1991, p. 22).

Overextensions and underextensions

A striking aspect of many children's early vocabulary development is the way they overextend a word to refer to objects that lie outside its normal range of application for adults. For example, a child might use the word *doggy* to refer not only to all dogs but also to cows, horses, sheep and cats. The overextension of a particular word may last for some months, but often it occurs only briefly before the child learns the correct names of the objects. Furthermore, the child may overextend only some ... words; others will be used appropriately from the beginning.

The list of overextensions reproduced here is taken from early diary studies in which linguists kept a record of children's words and the first referents of those words.

Child's word	First referent	Extensions	Possible common property
bird	sparrows	cows, dogs, cats, any moving animal	movement
mooi	moon	cakes, round marks on window, round shapes in books, tooling on leather book covers, postmarks, letter O	shape
fly	fly	specks of dirt, dust, all small insects, his own toes, crumbs, small toad	size
koko	cockerel crowing	tunes played on violin, piano, accordion, phonograph, all music, merry-go-round	sound
wau-wau	dogs	all animals, toy dog, soft slippers, picture of old man in furs	texture

In many cases it seems that the child has identified the meaning of the word with only one property of the object: its shape or sound or size. He [*sic*] then uses the word to refer to all objects sharing that property. As the child learns more words, he adds other defining properties to his word meanings to distinguish them from one another. When a child who overextends *doggy* to all four-legged creatures comes to learn the word *cow*, he may add to the property of four-leggedness the requirement that things called *cow* be relatively large and things called *doggy* relatively small. ...

Whereas the overextensions of words are most noticeable in early language, children also underextend some words. The word *animal* is typically applied only to mammals at first. Two-year-olds will deny that some birds, fish and insects are animals or that people can also be called animals. In this sense the range of application of some early words needs to be narrowed down, but the meaning of other words needs to be expanded in the child's vocabulary development.

(de Villiers and de Villiers, 1979, pp. 35–7, 40)

Second, Barrett et al. went on to look at the children's subsequent usage of the same words, and here they found an interesting change. In subsequent use, the link between the child's usage and the maternal example was greatly weakened, dropping to 58.6 per cent. This suggests that children rapidly move on from the support provided by caregiver speech and begin to deploy their new linguistic resources on the basis of their own understanding.

The phenomena described by Barrett et al., point to the active nature of children in taking control of language. This active involvement in language will become more apparent as we move on to consider children's ability to assemble words into grammatical utterances.

1.4 Stringing it together

Figure 1.3 Language in action

In this section I begin with a description of the early stages of grammatical development and go on to examine some of the factors which contribute to that development. Some of this discussion is relevant to children's acquisition of any language; but I also consider the particular consequences of learning English rather than any other language.

The development of children's grammar

I use grammar in this section in the sense of **descriptive grammar** – an attempt to describe the structure and organisation in a child's speech which may or may not coincide with grammatical structures used by adults. Descriptive grammars simply describe what is there. They have nothing to say about how people *should* speak, or about what counts as 'correct' English. It follows from this that it is possible to write a grammar (that is, to describe the system) for any stage of a child's language development. We are not concerned here with much of the detail of such grammars. The important point is that identifying and understanding a system that is being used by a child can be very revealing about what that child understands.

Researchers studying children's grammar have attempted to distinguish a series of developmental stages. Crystal, for instance, identifies several stages running from infancy through to the teenage years, as you'll see from the box on 'Grammatical development'.

Grammatical development

Grammar learning is a continuous process, but it is possible to spot certain types of development taking place at certain stages, as children grow up in English.

- The earliest stage is hardly like grammar at all, as it consists of utterances which are just one word long, such as *Gone, Dada, Teddy,* and *Hi*. About 60 per cent of these words have a naming function, and about 20 per cent express an action. Most children go through this stage from about 12 to 18 months. It is often called a *holophrastic* stage, because the children put the equivalent of a whole sentence into a single word.

- The next stage looks more like 'real' grammar, because two words are put together to make primitive sentence structures. *Cat jump* or *Cat jumping* seem to express a Subject + Verb construction. *Shut door* seems to express a Verb + Object construction. Other sequences might be more difficult to interpret ([for instance,] what could *mummy off* mean ...?), but on the whole we are left with the impression that, by the end of this stage (which typically lasts from around 18 months until 2), children have learned several basic lessons about English word order.

- The next step is the 'filling out' of these simple sentence patterns – adding extra elements of clause structure ... and making the elements themselves more complex. The 3-element *Daddy got car* and the 4-element *You go bed now* show this progress, as does (at a more advanced level) *My Daddy put that car in the garage*. To get to this point, and to be able to ring the changes on it (such as by asking a question – *Where daddy put the car?*) takes up much of the third year.

- At around 3 years, sentences become much longer, as children start stringing their clauses together to express more complex thoughts and to tell simple stories. *And* is the word to listen out for at this stage ... Other common linking words at this stage are *because* (*'cos*), *so*, *then*, *when*, *if*, and *before*. This stage takes six months or so for the basic patterns of clause sequence to be established.

- This takes us towards the age of 4, when children typically do a great deal of 'sorting out' in their grammar. A child aged 3½ might say *Him gived the cheese to the mouses*. By 4½ most children can say *He gave the cheese to the mice*. What they have done is learn the adult forms of the irregular noun and verb, and of the pronoun. As there are several dozen irregular nouns and several hundred irregular verbs, and all kinds of other grammatical irregularities to be sorted out, it is not surprising that it takes children the best part of a year to produce a level of English where these 'cute' errors are conspicuous by their absence.

- And after 4½? There are still features of grammar to be learned, such as the use of sentence-connecting features ... and complex patterns of subordination ... The process will continue until the early teens, especially in acquiring confident control over the grammar of the written language – at which point, the learning of grammar becomes indistinguishable from the more general task of developing an adult personal style.

(Crystal, 1995, pp. 428–9)

We look first at just two stages of early grammatical development which correspond closely to the second and third of the stages in the box: a stage in which children use short utterances of two to three words containing no grammatical markers; and the next stage, when children start to add these markers to the words they produce in the form of, for example, verb inflections (such as *I eat*, *she eats*), plural markers (*one cat*, *two cats*), use of the possessive -s (*Anne's book*), tense markers (*I played*) and auxiliary verbs (*is*, *do*). As mentioned earlier, research evidence on language acquisition tends to come from a restricted range of social and cultural backgrounds. Evidence of early grammatical development in English has come mainly from speakers learning a standard variety of the language, in which all these markers are present. Other varieties may mark plurality, possession, etc., differently, and children will have a different set of distinctions to learn.

At Crystal's second stage, children will not be using grammatical markers. Children at this stage will use nouns, verbs and adjectives and also temporal adverbs (words such as *now* and *soon*). The expression **telegraphic speech** is often used to describe the language of children at this stage. All the detail and 'frills' are stripped away, leaving only the essential material. It is also reported that children's imitation of adult speech has this telegraphic character; for example, asking a child to repeat *I am playing with the dogs* is likely to be met with *I play dog*. In this example, the adult utterance contains six words and includes the plural *-s* marker (after *dog*) and the progressive *-ing* ending (to the main verb *play*). All of these refinements are stripped away in the child's imitation. There is also the intriguing question of why these three particular words appear in the child's reply, apart from the fact that only one of them – *I* – appears in the adult's original. Perhaps you might argue that a child of this age has some memory limit that means only three words can be retained. If this is the case, why does the child not remember just the first

---

Plurality in English

Within any variety of English, aspects of grammar such as plurality and tense are marked in different ways. The notion of **morpheme** is useful here. Morphemes may be defined as the minimal meaningful units of analysis of sentence and word structure. A morphemic analysis would divide the word *cats*, for instance, into two morphemes: *cat* (a 'free morpheme', which can stand alone); and *-s* (the plural morpheme, which cannot stand alone as it needs to be 'bound' to other morphemes – *cat**s***, *dog**s***, *horse**s***, etc.).

We often think that, to make such words plural we 'add an *s*'. But this applies only in the written language. The plural morpheme takes different forms in spoken English: /s/ in *cats*; /z/ in *dogs*; and /ɪz/ in *horses*. Children need to learn such differences.

Children also need to learn that plurality may sometimes be signalled by a change of form (*mouse* becomes *mice*); or by no change at all (*sheep* stays as *sheep*). Young children often overextend their use of the plural *-s*, giving rise to forms such as *sheeps*.

three – or the last three – words? The child's answer supports the view that the child is able to scan the whole sentence and to abstract the crucial elements of meaning. The child evidently has this ability even though unable to duplicate the production of the sentence.

Imitation or creativity?

Any record of children in the second of Crystal's stages is likely to contain examples of the following kind:

allgone sticky; *baby drink*; *a more water*

The point to note about these examples is that they do not appear to be the kind of utterances that the children will have heard an adult say. If this is so, then these utterances cannot be said to be 'imitations'. The meaning of such examples will be clear enough in context, so they can be described as novel and successful utterances.

The evidence I have discussed is consistent with a view that, even at this early stage of language development, children are being creative. Does this mean that there is no role for imitation as a means whereby children gain access to language? The answer has to be a guarded 'no'. Almost all parents will have heard their children repeat – complete with intonation – adult expressions that they would prefer had not been overheard at all! Clearly children do imitate, and adults often think that this imitation is a primary route into language. The evidence from children's creative use of language allows us to see imitation as only part of the process.

There have been attempts to map formal grammatical structures on to children's early two-word utterances. However, a purely structural analysis of decontextualised utterances may not do justice to children's linguistic sophistication. There is a much used example in the literature which comes from the work of Lois Bloom (1973). The child that Bloom describes used the expression *mommy sock* on two separate occasions. On one of these occasions the utterance was produced as the child's mother was putting a sock on the child. On the other occasion, the child had picked up one of her mother's socks. The child used the same simple construction on each occasion, but for rather different purposes. The uses seem to have been, first, to indicate the mother's role as the person fitting the sock to the child and, second, to indicate the ownership of her mother's sock. This shows us that to understand the extent of a child's communicative competence we need to have access to the contexts in which utterances are used.

A conversation

Naomi (N) at 22½ months is in discussion with her mother about a storybook that they have just been reading. Notice here that, as often happens in such conversations, Naomi's mother (M) expands her daughter's telegraphic utterances. (Although the examples here are of a child in Stage 2, in fact Naomi was already using the progressive *-ing* form and the plural *-s* and so was moving into Stage 3.)

M   I go fast asleep

N   Fast asleep

M   Yes he's fast asleep isn't he? What's he got in his bed with him?

N   Elephant

M   An elephant yes and what's this here?

N   Teddy bear

(Bancroft, original data)

ACTIVITY 1.6

Allow 5–10 minutes

Consider some of the possible meanings that might be attributable, depending on context, to the following child utterances. Try to express them in 'adult' grammar.

Car go vroom!
Mommy hat.
No more soup.

Comment

Each utterance has several potential grammatical expansions, depending on contextual clues such as intonation and gesture. You may have noted some variations on the following patterns:

All cars go vroom./This car goes vroom./This car went vroom./Make this car go vroom!
Mommy has a hat on./That's Mommy's hat./Mommy, please put my hat on!/Mommy, look at that hat!
I have no more soup left./You have no more soup left./There's no more soup in the pan./I don't want any more soup.

However, not all meanings are equally likely. The box below describes some of the most frequently recurrent meanings expressed by young children.

Some meanings attributed to telegraphic speech

English-speaking children express a limited range of meanings in their first sentences. They talk about actions, what happened to what and who does what:

> Me fall.

> Bump table.

> Car go vroom!

They are concerned, not to say obsessed, with the relationship of possession:

> My teddy.

> Mommy hat.

> Daddy hair.

Equally prevalent is the relationship of location:

> Cup in box.

> Car garage.

> Mommy outside.

Among other early meanings that find frequent expression at this stage are recurrence:

> More milk.

> Tickle again.

nomination, or labelling:

> That Teddy.

> This steamroller.

and nonexistence:

> Beads all gone.

> No more soup.

Comparatively rare in the earliest word combinations, but still occasionally expressed, are relations involving experiences that are not actions:

> See that.

> Listen clock.

and relations involving states:

> Have coat.

> Daddy [is a] policeman.

Children learning many different languages, among them Samoan, German, French, Hebrew, Luo (in Kenya), and Russian, seem to encode the same limited set of meanings in their first sentences. This lends credence to the notion that the meanings depend on, and are restricted by, the two-year-old's understanding of the world.

(de Villiers and de Villiers, 1979, pp. 48–50)

Children's developing concept of time

The rate of language development varies from child to child, but we can say that a new stage has arrived when the child begins to use any of the grammatical items that were so obviously absent before. The appearance of *tense* and *aspect markers* in English has been a rich source of material for those interested in the development of children's understanding of concepts of time and, more importantly, for those interested in language development itself. Obviously different languages have different solutions to the problem of locating an event in time using language. These alternatives may have some impact on speaker's concepts of time as well as the length of time needed to acquire particular aspects of language. In English, the tense and aspect systems are closely related. Tense refers to the location of an event in time with respect to the moment of speech – contrast the present tense, *I eat*, and the past tense, *I ate*. Aspect refers to the duration or type of temporal activity denoted – for example, *I run* versus *I am running*.

The sequence of development of the Standard English tense and aspect systems, which seems consistent over a range of longitudinal studies, is as follows:

- At first there are no tense or aspect inflections, such as the progressive -*ing* suffix (e.g. *he's play**ing***), past tense inflections on regular verbs (e.g. *she play**ed***) or the use of irregular past tense forms (e.g. *she **slept***).
- First to appear on the scene are the past tense forms of irregular verbs. For example, one might find both *sleep* and *slept* in a child's language. Both of these forms will appear to be used appropriately.
- At some later point in development the past tense forms of regular verbs appear. From this moment on, it is reported that *all* references to the past will use verbs with a past tense inflection, even those irregular verbs which had been in the child's vocabulary before this time. So, for example, *slept* becomes *sleeped, came* becomes *comed, went* becomes *goed, held* becomes *holded*.

Actually the picture seems to be more complex than this, with appropriate and inappropriate usage co-existing for some time before adult usage is established. In any case there is some evidence from my own work (Bancroft, 1985) that children are able to locate events in time using language well before they use the Standard English system of verb inflections. There are, in fact, several means available to a speaker of English to refer to the temporal location of an event, including temporal adverbs such as *before*, *after* and *soon*. Some of these alternative means are included in children's earliest vocabularies. It seems that temporal reference is achieved by locating the event referred to and then, having established that this knowledge is shared, the use of the present tense becomes adequate.

An explanation consistent with the description of the development of the grammatical tense and aspect systems is that when children begin to use, for instance, irregular past tense forms, these are treated as though they were new words and not particularly related to the present tense form. When children begin to use regular past tense inflections, they have discovered that it is possible to make a great number of past tense forms by this simple addition. The children, however, do not immediately realise the existence of exceptions to the rule.

The crucial point is that this language behaviour is consistent with the idea that children are trying to discover the *rules* of language. The rule systems they try out are sensible and plausible but they are *not* necessarily the rule systems of adult English. The business of discovering or generating rules is a much more sophisticated activity than the rote learning of new words and expressions. Children who produce *comed* and *goed* are making creative use of the rules they have learnt, rather than copying what they hear adults saying.

1.5 Later language, narratives and jokes

Figure 1.4 Just joking

Much of the psycholinguistic research effort investigating language development has concentrated upon the, admittedly interesting, early stages. Indeed, it is sometimes thought to be the case that nearly all the problems facing the language learner have been solved by the time the child is 4 or 5 years old. While my own focus so far in this chapter has been on early development, I have also indicated ways in which language development continues in older children.

Children's vocabulary obviously greatly increases during their school years; indeed, this development is part of a process that never really stops. Adults can have the experience of learning new words, although the rate at which this happens is very much slower than for children in school. Similarly, children develop their grammatical skills, producing more complex constructions as they hear them used by others or come across them in books, magazines, etc.

In addition to these developments, children have to learn more of the skills needed to maintain a conversation, to be aware of their partner's progress in understanding the communication, and to be able to repair it if it breaks down. In other words, to be an effective communicator a person needs to know much about language but also much about other people and the things that they know and understand.

In this section we look at some of the other skills children need to develop in order to become effective communicators, skills beyond the basic ones of being able to take turns in conversations as described in Section 1.2. I focus on research which has investigated the development of the skills needed to maintain a dialogue and to tell stories. I conclude by looking at some work on the nature and development of children's ability to make jokes.

Sensitivity to the listener

Anne Anderson and her colleagues, working in Glasgow, Scotland, have investigated one particular aspect of communicative skill: introducing new information into a dialogue (Anderson et al., 1991). This is illustrative of the kind of skill we are discussing. In their study eighty-five pairs of children aged between 7 and 13 years were given a map-reading task. Pairs of children sat at a desk with a small screen between them, each having a map of an imaginary location. The maps were quite similar but not identical, and one of them had a 'safe' route through various dangers while the other did not. The child whose map had the safe route on it had to pass on this information to their partner. Giving all the children the same task in this way allowed a more direct comparison of their dialogue styles on this particular task than would have been possible through informal observation. The conversations of the children were recorded and transcribed and then analysed in terms of the ways in which new information was introduced.

The researchers' major interest was in the extent to which new information was introduced in a question form as opposed to a statement. The use of the question form (e.g. *Have you got a palm beach?*) checks up on what the listener knows in a way that the statement version (e.g. *It's by the palm beach.*) does not.

There were two major outcomes from this study, one concerning the speakers and one concerning the listeners. The latter is important since we should not forget that effective listening is itself a conversational skill. In the study, the younger children used question introductions much less than the older children did.

> It seems as if children only become fully aware of the INTERACTIONAL aspects of successful communication as they grow older. Young speakers behave as if the prime responsibility for introducing entities in the dialogue is theirs, with the listener's task being to interpret their messages. They rather infrequently directly seek their listener's involvement by checking on his or her knowledge state and hence on his or her ability to interpret what is being said.
>
> (Anderson et al., 1991, p. 682)

With respect to listener behaviour, Anderson and her colleagues found that, for the children of all the ages studied, the introduction of new information by using a question form was the most effective means of eliciting a useful response. Introducing information in the form of a statement resulted in effective responses only from children of 12 years and older. Although rather beyond the scope of this chapter, we should note that these findings have implications for both educationalists and parents.

Telling a good story

Studies like that of Anderson et al. allow us a glimpse of the development of conversational strategies and the development of increasing sensitivity to the needs of listeners. To tell a good story, rather different skills are needed in addition to those involved in making sure your listener is following you. One needs to be able to organise material in such a way as to preserve a sequence, explain motives and purposes, and maintain the interest of the listener. Children developing storytelling and narrative skills will need to learn a set of conventions, which may differ across different English-speaking communities.

ACTIVITY 1.7

Allow about 5 minutes

This joke was told to a friend by my (Dennis Bancroft's) daughter Anna, who was 12 years old at the time.

> A man was running to catch a moving bus but when he got there the conductor refused him entrance and he was ... he fell off the bus and was run over by a car. The conductor was taken to court on trial for murder and was sentenced to be electrocuted. And the day when he was electrocuted his last request was a bowl of mashed bananas and milk ... and he sa ... and he had this bowl of mashed bananas and milk

and then they switched the current on and it didn't work, so they tried again and again the last request was a bowl of mashed bananas and milk. And they put a higher current on that time but it still didn't work and the third time ... after the third time it's meant to be you have to free the prisoner. And so they tried again and the last request was again a bowl of bananas and milk. And it still didn't work even though they switched the power up. And the con ... and they asked the conductor how he did it and the conductor said maybe it's just because I'm a bad conductor!

What is the crucial item of information about the English language that Anna was relying on her listener to know, in order for the joke to be successful?

Comment

The joke is constructed so that listeners are likely to think that the condemned man's choice of food was related to the malfunctioning of the electric chair. But for the punch line to be effective, it is of course crucial that listeners are aware of the alternative uses in English for the term 'conductor', so that they would recognise they have been misled. (You might also need to know that your friendship was strong enough to survive after inflicting this grievous 'joke' upon your friend!)

We can use Anna's joke to consider some aspects of effective communication, in relation to specific audiences. When we tell jokes we are often intending to amuse or surprise by manipulating our listener's expectations in a way that makes the punch line a violation of those expectations. Jokes are a special case in so far as they involve an element of deliberately misleading information. More often in dialogues and in narratives, speakers are at pains to ensure that their listeners *do not* misunderstand or get lost. In order to do this, speakers need to be aware of what their listeners know on the basis of the story so far, and what they can be expected to know on the basis of their sharing the same cultural knowledge as the speaker. As well as this knowledge, speakers need to be able to use a range of linguistic devices for developing stories and dialogues in a way that ensures their listeners' continued understanding.

The ability to tell jokes is an extremely sophisticated form of verbal behaviour requiring, as we have seen, both knowledge of language and the ability to identify and manipulate the mental state of another person. Playing with language demonstrates both the development of language skills and the development of **metalinguistic awareness**, which refers to the ability to think about and reflect on language itself. The ability to reflect on language is a more sophisticated one than the ability to produce language.

Joke making, as with other aspects of language that we have considered, seems to have its roots in very early exchanges between child and caregiver. Dianne Horgan (1981; and reproduced in Franklin and Barten, 1988) reported a study of the development of joke making by her own daughter Kelly. Horgan describes Kelly's joking in terms of a four-stage progression. As each new stage appeared it was added to the preceding stage and did not replace it. The first stage involved the deliberate violation of semantic categories. For example, when Kelly was 16 months and had a vocabulary of about twenty words she added the word *shoe* to her list. Horgan reports: 'Several days later, she put her foot through the armhole of a nightgown, saying *Shoe*, accompanied by shrieks of laughter' (Horgan, 1981, p. 218). In Horgan's view semantic violations of this kind can be a very useful device for a language learner to explore the boundaries of the concept represented by the word.

Horgan's second category of joking consists of games based on phonetic patterns. For example, at 20 months, Kelly said, '*Cow go moo. Mommy go mamoo. Daddy go dadoo. Ha ha.*' (quoted in Horgan, 1981, p. 219). In Horgan's view, the child must have begun to treat the sounds of a word as 'arbitrary symbols for the objects and not as essential properties of the objects' (Horgan, 1981, p. 221) in order that she is able to 'bend' the sounds to make a rhyme or fit into a regular pattern. You may recall an aspect I noted previously: in the early stages of development children seem to be developing a mastery of their ability to make sounds which are recognisable parts of their language.

The third kind of joke described by Horgan appeared in her daughter's speech early in her third year. Kelly produced a more sophisticated version of the earlier humour by introducing new words into established sequences. The new words were related in some way to the words that had been replaced. For example, Kelly produced '*Little Bo People had lost her steeple*' (quoted in Horgan, 1981, p. 219). In this case the syntax is preserved and the introduced words are real words and make (a sort of) sense.

Rather later in the third year, Kelly began to produce jokes which had a regular discourse format. This form was something like that of a riddle although her parents reported that Kelly had never heard a riddle. For example:

K   How do aspirins make?

M   Huh?

K   How do aspirins make?

M   I dunno, how do aspirins make?

K   They make you feel better.

(quoted in Horgan, 1981, p. 220)

By the end of the third year, Kelly was able to make up jokes which still retained this format although they were also used to set up a linguistically misleading context. For example:

K   Do we kick Mary?

M   No, we don't kick Mary!

K   Do we kick Jennifer?

M   No, we don't kick Jennifer!

K   Do we kick the swimming pool?

M   No, we don't kick the swimming pool!

K   We kick IN the swimming pool. Ha, ha!

(quoted in Horgan, 1981, p. 221)

The purpose of describing these jokes is, first, to illustrate how children become able to manipulate the English language in order to achieve surprise and amusement and, second, to show how learning to use English creatively in this way depends in part on the learning of certain conventional discourse structures or formats.

When children begin to go to school they already know something of the potential of language to amuse. However, there is still much to learn. As children become a little more aware of jokes the humour becomes more apparent – although the joker may feel the need to explain the joke, not being sure that the listener has understood. For example, the following exchange was collected by a colleague of mine:

What do you get if you cross a kangaroo and a sheep?

I don't know.

A woolly jumper!

[Pause] ... because the sheep gives the wool and the kangaroo is the jumper.

In summary, the development of joking is an area where the development of linguistic skill and social awareness are very closely entwined. In order to be amusing, children deploy their knowledge of language, of its sounds and meanings, in concert with their understanding of other people. In a rather similar way, dialogue and narrative skills depend on an awareness of what listeners know or can be expected to deduce.

1.6 Conclusion

In this chapter I have traced briefly the developmental history of children learning English as their first language. I have tried to describe the essence of what is learnt during each phase of development, from the earliest stages of babbling through to the early development of grammar and up to the creative use of certain discourse structures (as in telling jokes). Throughout the chapter, I have drawn attention to the contexts in which children are using and learning English, and to the role of other people in children's language development.

Although the focus has been on the acquisition of Standard English, I have also indicated the variety that exists in human language learning by noting the significant ways in which children's early language experiences can differ according to the particular language variety and culture of their homes and communities. The next chapter continues and extends this discussion, examining children's learning of different varieties of English, and English alongside other languages in bilingual and multilingual communities.

READING A: Understanding words

Lauren B. Adamson
(Lauren B. Adamson is a Member of the Developmental Psychology Program,
and Dean, College of Arts and Sciences at the University of California,
Berkeley.)

Source: Adamson, L.B. (1995) *Communication Development during Infancy*, Madison, WI, Brown and Benchmark, pp. 176–9.

The timetable for milestones in comprehension has been fairly well established. The first inklings of verbal understanding appear at about 9 to 10 months of age when infants start to respond reliably to a few words (e.g. *no*; their own name) and to follow verbal commands ('Say bye-bye'; 'Clap your hands'), as long as they occur embedded within a specific context (Huttenlocher, 1974). By 11 months of age, infants usually have a receptive vocabulary of approximately 10 words, and they typically begin to understand these words across different contexts (Benedict, 1979). By 13 months of age, they understand on average 50 words (Benedict, 1979; Snyder et al., 1981). Soon afterward, they begin to carry out commands such as 'Give mommy a cookie' and 'Show daddy your bottle' that contain relational information between a direct and an indirect object (Greenfield & Smith, 1976; Huttenlocher, 1974).

There is considerable variability around each of these age norms. Thus, while an 'average' 13-month-old infant may comprehend 50 words, it is not unusual for an infant of this age to have a considerably smaller or larger receptive vocabulary (e.g., Snyder et al., 1981, reported a range of 17 to 97 words). However, even with such a spread, infants reach milestones in comprehension far before they pass comparable milestones in production. Throughout the second year, receptive vocabularies are noticeably larger than productive vocabularies, often by a factor of 5 to 10 (Benedict, 1979). This generalization is particularly well-illustrated by a subset of reticent infants who convince others that they understand far more than they say; for example, one of Benedict's subjects understood 182 words, while producing only 10. Interestingly, researchers have yet to find any normally developing infants who say many different words while understanding relatively few (Snyder et al., 1981).

These observations support the widely held contention that comprehension precedes production during the developmental period when infants are acquiring words. This state of affairs makes intuitive sense. It is likely far easier to recognize a word than to generate it on one's own. But it also implies that data crucial to theories of early symbol formation are well hidden from view. To make inroads into covert areas, researchers have coupled methodological acumen with sharply pointed questions about the relation between the reception and the expression of meaning.

One productive line of inquiry has involved the comparison between the types of words found in early receptive and productive vocabularies. For example, Helen Benedict (1979) used both parental reports and observational procedures to compare the first 50 words infants understood with the first 50 words that they produced. She found that both vocabularies contained words from several classes of words. Further, names for things and action words dominated both vocabularies (see also Nelson, 1973). In light of these overriding similarities, slight differences in the two lexicons can provide insight into how meaning is first encoded. For example, Benedict noted that action words were more prevalent in early comprehension, particularly object-related words such as *give* and *kiss* and locative actions such as *come here*. She used this contrast to identify a subtle difference between how infants' spoken and heard words may intertwine with actions:

> Comprehension is an action-dominated mode, in the sense that the child's understanding of words triggers an action response. Although it is less obvious, production is also action-dominated, but here words accompany rather than trigger a response. To give an example, if the experimenter says *throw* to the child, typically the child will get the ball and throw it, thus showing his understanding of the action word. ... At the same time the child says *ball*, a general nominal [or naming word]. In this case, the child does the action and uses his words, in their most general sense, as supplements or adjuncts to his action. (1979, p. 198)

A second strategy is to compare errors across production and comprehension to seek commonalities in the way in which infants construct categories. Although relevant data are rare (Ingram, 1989), it is evident that infants overextend words in comprehension as well as in production (Huttenlocher, 1974; Rescorla, 1980). By discerning the pattern of comprehension overextensions, researchers are gathering crucial evidence about the earliest organization of systems of word meaning. For example, Mervis (Mervis, 1984; Mervis & Canada, 1983) predicted and found an interesting pattern in how infants overextended the three words *kitty, car,* and *ball*. She used a standard probe during which an infant was asked if he saw a particular object (e.g., 'Is there a kitty?') as he looked at an array of four different toys (e.g., a house cat, a tiger, a lion, and a duck). Infants tended to accept the experimenter's label for toys which were good exemplars of an adult's category (*kitty* for the house cat) and when it functioned as and was shaped like this exemplar (the tiger or the lion). However, they did not accept it for toys (the duck) that did not have the attributes of the good exemplar.

A third line of inquiry involves tracking the pattern of word comprehension over time. Sharon Oviatt (1980), for example, designed an experiment in which infants of different ages were provided equal exposure to a previously unknown name for an interesting object (such as a live animal) or for a simple action (such as pressing to activate a toy). After infants heard the word repeatedly for three minutes, their comprehension was probed to see if they would orient to the named object (e.g., *rabbit*) or perform the specified action (*press it*) when the new word – but not when another word or a nonsense word – was heard. Dramatic improvement occurred during the period from 9 to 17 months. Infants 9 to 11 months of age were as interested as others in the materials and naming, but few acted as if they understood the target word during the posttraining probes. In contrast, many 12- to 14-month-olds and most 15- to 17-month-olds were able to do so even after a 15-minute distraction period.

...

A fourth approach to the development of language comprehension explores how infants begin to understand the meaning conveyed by word order. Although infancy ends before word combinations are produced, researchers have long suspected that the precursors of grammar might begin in infancy, hidden in comprehension. But they have puzzled over how to untangle comprehension from contextual supports and from production deficiencies. In everyday situations, it is often difficult to tell for sure if an infant understands word order. Non-linguistic hints often parallel information carried by word order. For example, context rather than syntax may help an infant determine who is doing the scrubbing when someone says, 'Look, Cookie Monster is washing Big Bird.' At other times, infants' motor immaturity hampers them from demonstrating comprehension of a command such as 'Put the dolly on the chair.' To control for both contextual cues and response demands, Hirsh-Pasek and Golinkoff (1991; see also Golinkoff, Hirsh-Pasek, Cauley, & Gordon, 1987) modified the *preferential looking paradigm* [a measure of where the child's gaze rests longest] to test the language comprehension of infants as young as 12 months of age. In their procedure, an infant hears a speaker and sees two videotapes, one that matches and one that mismatches the speaker's message. Hirsh-Pasek and Golinkoff found that 16- to 18-month-old infants are most likely to look at the videotape that correctly depicts a sentence (such as 'Where is Cookie Monster washing Big Bird?') than at an equally plausible scene which reverses the subject and object. Moreover, they found that when a sentence conveys an odd arrangement (e.g., 'She is kissing the keys'), even 14-month-olds will look longer at an image that depicts this arrangement than one that merely contains the elements (such as kissing and keys) in a less unusual arrangement.

In summary, researchers are beginning to access infants' understanding of language during the period when language production is still quite limited. Although the available data are sparse, they establish early language comprehension as an organized process. Further, they suggest that although comprehension may precede production, it may be paced by common cognitive advances.

References for this reading

Benedict, H. (1979) 'Early lexical development: Comprehension and production', *Journal of Child Language*, 6, pp. 183–200.

Golinkoff, R.M., Hirsch-Pasek, K., Cauley, K.M., & Gordon, L. (1987) 'The eyes have it: Lexical and syntactic comprehension in a new paradigm', *Journal of Child Language*, 14, pp. 23–45.

Greenfield, P.M. and Smith, I.H. (1976) *The Structures of Communication in Early Language Development*, New York, Academic Press.

Hirsh-Pasek, K. & Golinkoff, R.M. (1991) 'Language comprehension: A new look at some old themes' in Krasnegor, N.A., Rumbaugh, D.M., Schiefelbusch, R.L. & Struddert-Kennedy, M. (eds.), *Biological and behavioural determinants of language development*, pp. 301–320, Hillsdale, NJ, Erlbaum.

Huttenlocher, J. (1974) 'The origins of language comprehension' in Solso, R.L. (ed.), *Theories in cognitive psychology: The Loyola symposium*, pp. 331–368, Hillsdale, NJ, Erlbaum.

Ingram, D. (1989) *First language acquisition: Method, description and explanation*, Cambridge, England, Cambridge University Press.

Mervis, C.B. (1984) 'Early lexical development: The contributions of mother and child', in Sophian, C. (ed.) *Origins of cognitive skills*, pp. 339–370, Hillsdale, NJ, Erlbaum.

Mervis, C.B. & Canada, K. (1983) 'On the existence of competence errors in early comprehension: A reply to Fremgen & Fay and Chapman & Thomson', *Journal of Child Language*, 10, pp. 431–440.

Nelson, K. (1973) *Structure and strategy in learning to talk, Monographs of the Society for Research in Child Development*, 38 (1–2, Serial No. 149).

Oviatt, S.L. (1980) 'The emerging ability to comprehend language: An experimental approach', *Child Development*, 51, pp. 97–106.

Rescorla, L.A. (1980) 'Overextension in early language development', *Journal of Child Language*, 7, pp. 321–335.

Snyder, L.S., Bates, E. & Bretherton, L. (1981) 'Content and context in early lexical development', *Journal of Child Language*, 8, pp. 565–582.

English in the repertoire

Barbara Mayor

2.1 Introduction

In Chapter 1 the focus was primarily on children growing up in families and communities where only English is spoken. In this chapter the canvas widens to include children learning to speak English alongside other languages, as well as children learning to distinguish between several varieties of English – in other words any child with two or more distinct means of expression.

I begin by looking at children growing up bilingual, who, at the same time as learning to distinguish English from their other language(s), also have to learn when it is appropriate to use one or the other. I go on to consider the extent to which similar challenges may affect a monolingual speaker learning what it means to talk, for example, like a middle-class girl from Scotland or a working-class boy from Australia (i.e. learning to use linguistic means to signal membership of social groups). This is far from simple determinism: I examine how we exercise personal linguistic choices in order to express our individual identities and to achieve personal goals. And throughout the chapter I consider the evidence for when and how these various skills develop.

In our everyday lives we play a variety of social roles, and it is often through spoken language (or silence) that we signal shifts in our social identity or relationship with others. Sometimes we unconsciously converge towards or diverge from the speech patterns of others, either within or beyond our community; at other times we may make a conscious choice to emulate or mimic another person or social group. This chapter explores how, as children and young people, we develop such a **repertoire** of linguistic behaviour.

2.2 Languages for living

ACTIVITY 2.1

Allow 5–10 minutes

Consider the following exchanges and try to identify what is actually happening between the participants. What role do you think the English language – or a particular variety of English – is playing? What effect do you think the speakers are trying to achieve?

Scene 1:
The home of an ethnically Chinese family in Newcastle-upon-Tyne in the north-east of England

MOTHER   *Oy-m-oy faan a? Ah Ying a?*
              (Want some rice?)

DAUGHTER   *[no response]*

MOTHER   *Chaaufaan a. Oy-m-oy?*
              (Fried rice. Want or not?)

DAUGHTER   *[after a 2 second pause]* I'll have some shrimps.

(Li Wei, 1994, p. 86)

Scene 2:
A youth club in an English south Midlands town

I was standing behind the snack bar. Ishfaq [a 15-year-old British boy of Pakistani descent] came into the club soon after it opened and in our first exchange of the evening, he came up to me at the counter and said in a strong Panjabi accent: 'Ben Rampton can I help you?' Though it was me doing the serving, I sustained the joke and asked for 20 Mojos (chews). Then in his ordinary voice he placed an order for 10 Refreshers [sweets].

(Rampton, 1996, p. 166)

Scene 3:
Outside a family home in New Zealand

FATHER   Tea's ready Robbie.
              [Robbie ignores him and carries on skateboarding.]

FATHER   Mr Robert Harris if you do not come in immediately there will be consequences which you will regret.

(Holmes, 1992, p. 47)

Comment

Here are my own conjectures about what may have been happening.

In the first extract it appears that the daughter is resisting the mother's choice of language (Chinese) by responding initially with silence. Her eventual response in English seems to do more than simply indicate a preference for one food over another: she seems to be making a statement about how she relates to her mother and/or her mother's culture.

In the second extract, Ishfaq seems to be consciously mimicking a stereotype of British Asian English to role-play a kind of mock 'colonial' relationship with Ben Rampton (who is a white Englishman). He then reverts to his 'ordinary' voice to re-establish a more equal relationship.

In the final extract the father, having failed to achieve the desired outcome in informal language, opts to address Robbie in a pseudo-legal register, in this case explicitly signalled by a formal term of address 'Mr Robert Harris'. Whether or not this was effective would depend not only on Robbie's understanding of the words uttered, but also on his reading of the double-edged message (i.e. this is only *half* a joke ...).

In all three extracts, of course, it is possible that the participants may have intended something different from, or additional to, what I have construed – it is conceivable, for example, that Robbie's father may have been simply sharing a joke about the speech style of an elderly friend of the family. The complex meanings of any social situation may be lost on a third party, especially one relying solely on a written transcript.

Whether we consider ourselves monolingual in English or bilingual, in our interactions with others most of us have access at any given time to a range of different language varieties to signal our shifting attitudes and identities. Nkonko Kamwangamalu has formulated this as three dilemmas which we face each time we open our mouths:

> Who am I?
> How am I perceived by others?
> How would I want to be perceived?

(adapted from Kamwangamalu, 1992, p. 33)

A key question addressed in this chapter is how and at what age children and young people learn, alongside the more formal aspects of language structure, to negotiate these aspects of their own identity and attitudes towards others through the medium of English and other languages.

'Cooperative conversationalists'

As you have seen in Chapter 1, all babies, whatever the language or languages by which they are surrounded, begin by learning what it is to communicate, and only gradually learn how to use human language to accomplish this. So language acquisition is initially a matter of learning the rules of social behaviour and only later a matter of learning the grammatical rules by which these are realised. Even at the preverbal stage there are many ways in which the discourse patterns differ according to the culture or cultures in which children are being brought up.

Growing up with English

Mine had been an English-speaking upbringing, my father had insisted on it, as that was the language that would 'give us the world'. But here [at the elite Malay College] was the Malay world, and in all its diversity of regional tones ...

English remained, thankfully for me, the medium of our instruction, as it had been throughout our education so far. But soon after I went home for the first term holidays, I overheard my father tell my mother, his voice thick with disgust, 'You hear the boy? He sounds like a Sayong Malay!' (Sayong being a decrepit little village buried amidst banana groves across the river from Kuala Kangsar.)

I think he meant for me to overhear the exchange, rather than address the point directly to me. I think he understood that the damage done to my speech was the result of a young boy's effort to fit in with his peers in an alien environment ...

My niche was, what had seemed such a liability and embarrassment when I first got there, the English language. I became a school debater and a fixture in the College magazine. English, for our generation, was an effortless alternative language, yet there was still considerable respect for those of us most fluent in it. It set a certain seal on the Malay College's quality, that our English debating team could hold its own against those of the nation's other great schools, notwithstanding their more expansive resource of Chinese and Indian youth. For a mere Malay to stand up and strut the oratorical boards, his argument prevailing, his eloquence and arrogance more than match for those of his Worthy Opponents. ... there was some pride in that.

... I held my own, helped my school satisfy its addiction for winning, and was as a result largely forgiven for my cultural deficiencies as a Malay. Rehman (what kind of name is that? 'Raymond'? You sure it's not a spelling mistake?) might not have been able to extricate himself from the slightest literary tangle in Malay, but in *English*, ho, you should have heard him! That guy could *talk*!

(Rashid, 1993, pp. 81, 84–5)

To illustrate the fact that it is often the social routines of language that we learn first, let's look at two contrasting examples. Anthea Fraser Gupta quotes the following typically Singaporean 'checking sequence' between a father and his daughter, aged 2;11. Note the use of the 'pragmatic particles' *meh* and *a* in the questions – an influence of Chinese languages on Singaporean English.

Figure 2.1 Social routines of family life

GIRL Aunty wear red red one, the Aunty wear red shoes.

FATHER Who wear red shoes?

GIRL Aunty.

FATHER Aunty wore red shoes *meh*?

GIRL Red red.

FATHER Red shoes *a*?

GIRL Yes.

(Gupta, 1994, p. 81)

Contrast this with the following exchange between an American mother and her
5-year-old son:

MOTHER How was school today? Did you go to assembly?

SON Yes.

MOTHER Did the preschoolers go to assembly?

SON Yes.

MOTHER Did you stay for the whole assembly or just part of it?

(Berko Gleason, 1973, p. 162)

Both children, in their different ways, are being exposed to what it means to
carry on a conversation. Children are, to quote Evelyn Hatch (1978, p. 384)

'cooperative conversationalists'. And, as we have seen from Chapter 1, language learning normally evolves out of learning how to carry on conversations, rather than the other way round.

In certain contexts it is a matter of learning when *not* to speak as much as when to speak. The children of Trackton (a pseudonym), a poor black community in the USA documented extensively by Shirley Brice Heath, were explicitly taught by adults to be as 'un- cooperative' as possible in conversation with strangers whose purposes in the community were not known (Heath, 1982b, p. 115). I shall be returning to the Trackton study later in the chapter.

Communicative competence

In the 1960s US theoretical linguist Noam Chomsky (1965) drew a distinction between: linguistic **competence** – the knowledge of the language system which speakers of any language possess (arguably in differing degrees), enabling them to distinguish utterances that are grammatical in the language from those that are not; and linguistic **performance** – the frequently ungrammatical and/or imperfectly delivered actual utterances of language in use. This distinction was soon challenged in the early 1970s by applied US linguist, Dell Hymes, on the grounds that performance is itself rule-governed, and that speakers need to acquire distinct skills in performance, such as knowing when to speak, which variety of language to choose, what is the socially appropriate turn of phrase to achieve the desired effect, etc. He termed this **communicative competence**. In other words, as well as learning the sounds and structures of particular languages, children are learning the discourse strategies of their communities.

> [A] normal child acquires knowledge of sentences, not only as grammatical, but also as appropriate. He or she acquires competence as to when to speak, when not, and as to what to talk about with whom, when, where, in what manner. In short, a child becomes able to accomplish a repertoire of speech acts, to take part in speech events, and to evaluate their accomplishment by others.
>
> (Hymes, 1972, p. 277)

In the sections that follow, I look at how even very young children who are learning English alongside another language acquire the communicative competence to use their two languages appropriately. I go on to consider evidence for similar social and stylistic variation among children with only varieties of English at their disposal.

2.3 Bilingualism: a special case?

Many children are brought up in homes where both English and another language are in daily use.

Figure 2.2   Bilingualism in daily use in Singapore and Wales

ACTIVITY 2.2

'Raising our twins bilingually' (Reading A) is by Sylvia Rojas-Drummond and Hugh Drummond, a Mexican British couple who chose to raise their twin sons bilingually in Spanish and English.

Read this now and, as you do so, make notes on the following:

- the ways in which the twins' language use fluctuates over time, especially: possible motivating factors for using English or Spanish at particular points; any indications of *passive* knowledge as well as active skills; and the extent of (and reasons for) language mixing;
- the apparent (or purported) relationship between the twins' languages and other kinds of allegiance, especially: points in the text where a link is assumed between language, culture, nation, etc; and any factors which would seem to challenge the existence of such fixed links;
- any particular kinds of knowledge or skill the twins may have been learning in addition to those usually acquired by monolinguals.

Comment

As the evidence for the first of these points is to be found from a close reading of the article, I don't propose to expand on the detail again here. However, do keep a note of your observations and compare them with some of the evidence I present later in this chapter, to see how far the twins' behaviour is typical or idiosyncratic.

The evidence for the second point is dispersed throughout the article, but note that it is assumed that the twins will be exposed to 'both languages and cultures' in the home and in the school, and the reference to 'mixed-nationality social groups'. In everyday conversation we may (like the authors of the article) use the terms language/culture/nationality in an interchangeable or interconnected way implying, for example, a direct link between bilingualism and biculturalism. In practice, the relationship between these terms is a complex one but there are times when it is valuable to distinguish them. For example, it may well have struck you that – even setting language aside – our legal nationality may not correspond to either our place of birth or our place of residence, let alone anything so nebulous as our 'culture'. Hugh Drummond is British born, but he was entitled to acquire Mexican nationality by virtue of his marriage. He has also spent a considerable time in the USA, as well as in Mexico with its own mixed-cultural heritage. In addition to this, 'British culture' (itself a nebulous concept) has moved on during the years of Hugh's absence. (It is commonly observed that cultures in 'exile' are frequently more conservative than those left behind.) So how much culture does he actually still share with his father or nephews from the south of England? Note also that American teachers have, for at least some of the time, been entrusted with the task of conveying 'British culture' in a notionally 'British' school. How all these issues relate to the English *language* itself is yet another question, which I continue to explore throughout this chapter.

With regard to the third point, I would want to argue that there is very little linguistic knowledge or skill that is *unique* to the bilingual learner. During the course of the chapter I hope to be able to demonstrate that *all* children need to develop in two important aspects:

- They need to recognise their various languages or varieties of language as separate *systems* (of sounds, grammar, meaning, etc) in order to keep them apart as and when necessary.
- They need to learn how to *use* their various languages or varieties of language appropriately, according to who they are talking to and what they're talking about – what Gupta (1994) calls the 'appropriate environments' – in order to achieve particular effects.

Children learning English 'monolingually' (who may in fact command several varieties of their single language) are also learning to make such distinctions and choices among the language varieties available to them. However, bilinguals represent a particularly stark case of the general phenomenon. As Romaine puts it, 'A choice between different forms of one language ... can convey the same kinds of social meanings as a choice between languages ... What distinguishes bilinguals from monolinguals is that bilinguals usually have greater resources ... The skilled monolingual is one who is able to summon the maximum of pragmatic resources within one language' (Romaine, 1995, pp. 170, 173). We also need to remember that bilinguals normally have access to more than one variety within *each* of their languages, increasing their overall repertoire.

'Bilingualism as a first language': acquiring competence in two formal systems

So what are the key differences between the experience of learning English monolingually and that of learning it bilingually or multilingually from birth? What of those who, to quote the memorable phrase of Canadian linguist and educationalist Merril Swain (1972), have 'bilingualism as a first language?' The answer hinges on the relative extent to which the child experiences *language* as an undifferentiated phenomenon, or recognises *languages* as separate systems. To a large extent, this will depend on maturation. The monolingual baby learns how to talk (in the sense of physically articulating sounds) at the same time as learning to distinguish the meaningful sounds of one particular language, and learns to make sense of language per se at the same time as learning the rules of one particular system, in this case something called 'English'. The bilingual baby who acquires two languages simultaneously will be in a similar situation, except that the corpus of incoming data will be broader. Much of the research in this area has concentrated on whether the baby is apparently separating the languages into two distinct systems at all (see, for example, the classic studies reproduced in Hatch, 1978, and the overviews in Romaine, 1995, and Genesee, 2000). In practice, separation of vocabularies and of the sound systems seems to begin earlier than separation of the grammatical systems, but the evidence varies according to the context of acquisition and the languages involved, and this is still an area of ongoing academic research (see, for example, Deuchar and Quay, 1998).

Some researchers have argued that, in the first stages of development, the bilingual or multilingual child has a single semantic (i.e. meaning) system across the two or more languages. For example, Marianne Celce-Murcia (1978, p. 50) quotes her daughter Caroline, aged 2;4, as having an initial preference for the French word *couteau* and the English word *spoon*. She speculates that this was because the alternatives (English *knife* and French *cuiller)* were more demanding to pronounce. Significantly, in those cases where a young bilingual child apparently has a word in *both* languages for a single referent, it tends initially to have a slightly different meaning in each language – in a similar way to so-called synonyms in a single language.

The gradual development of two parallel vocabularies across the bilingual child's two languages goes hand in hand with a growing awareness of the potentially different semantic coverage of terms in the two languages. David Deterding (1984, p. 30) quotes a telling example from his son, Alexander, who was growing up bilingual in Taiwanese Chinese and English. When, at 2;3, Alexander learnt to tell his English *sheep* from his English *goat*, he also learnt that this particular distinction was not relevant in his Chinese (where *yang* may denote 'sheep' or 'goat'). Robbins Burling's son, Stephen, who was growing up bilingual in English and Garo, a language of northern India, also learnt to integrate his knowledge of the world across his two languages: 'When ... at 2;9 he suddenly grasped the meaning of color terms and was able to consistently call a red thing red, he was able to do so in both English and Garo simultaneously' (Burling, 1978, p. 69).

A major task for both the monolingual and the bilingual child consists in learning which contrasts (phonemic, tonal, grammatical, semantic) within a language are significant in making meaning. The bilingual child must additionally learn in what ways these rules can be generalised across the two (or more) languages and, if not, whether the languages differ in any systematic way. Chapter 1 discusses how there are certain patterns in the acquisition of English grammar and phonology that are followed by most children. Because of the different grammatical and phonological structure of different groups of languages, this pattern is not automatically replicated across languages. However, there is evidence (see Burling, 1978) that once a bilingual child has become aware of a particular structure or concept which can be applied to either language (anything from the voiced/voiceless contrast in consonants to the concept of spatial relationship) this will be reflected simultaneously in both languages, regardless of the one through which it was acquired. On the other hand, aspects of language which are specific to only one of the child's languages (such as grammatical gender and verb tense rules, polite terms of address or the significance of tones) will need to be specifically 'tagged' to the language concerned.

Acquiring English as a second or additional language

Children growing up in bilingual homes are, however, vastly outnumbered by another group of English learners. Because of its international status, English is acquired as a second or additional language by many children around the world as part of their encounters with the wider community outside the home. (See Chapter 6 for a fuller discussion.) How does this affect their experience of learning the language? As we have seen in Chapter 1, the various aspects of language develop at a different rate throughout life: in very broad terms, there is a rapid development of the sound system at an early age, overlapping with and followed by a rather slower development of grammatical sensitivity, and a development of meaning and the strategies of discourse which continues throughout life. Depending on the age at which English is encountered, therefore, these different aspects will be more or less established in the child's first language.

Because, when they are learning English as an additional language, even quite young children will have already progressed beyond the 'two-word' stage in their first language (see Chapter 1) and will be capable of retaining brief stretches of speech in their short-term memory, they are often able to articulate accurately whole clusters of words in English. In addition, they have some social experience, so they are usually able to deduce the social meaning of these clusters from the communicative context without necessarily analysing them into their component parts. Examples include: *Come on* and *Please push me* (Yoshida, 1978, p. 96); *Get out of here!* and *Good-bye, see you tomorrow* (Huang and Hatch, 1978, p. 122); *Don't do that!* and *That's not yours* (Hakuta, 1986, p. 126); and *Shaddup your mouth* and *Knock it off* (Fillmore, 1979, p. 211). It has been argued that such **prefabricated chunks** of language (also known as **formulaic speech**), because they are socially embedded and therefore highly memorable, play an important role in motivating the learner. It is only gradually that the internal structure of the units (i.e. the meaning of the individual words) is recognised, and the child begins to manipulate the components to express a personal intention.

It is acknowledged that learners of additional languages run the risk of transferring inappropriate features of the first language into the second. This can vary from an obvious 'foreign' accent to the occasional import of an idiom, and can include pragmatic aspects, such as when to speak, how loud to talk and so on. This phenomenon is sometimes called 'interference'.

However, the notion of 'interference' is not always helpful, since many errors made by young second language learners resemble the developmental stages of first language learning, such as simplification of grammar and over-generalisation of rules. For example, Roar Ravem (1974) studied the acquisition of English *wh-* questions (i.e. questions beginning with *who, what, which, where* or *why*) by his Norwegian-speaking son and daughter over a period of four months in Britain. He found that, like monolingual children, they used structures such as *Where Daddy go?* and *Where Daddy is going?* before they produced the mature form *Where is Daddy going?* According to Ravem, this did not reflect interference from their native Norwegian, which would probably have led to a form such as *Where go Daddy?* Instead they produced *Where Daddy go?* just like first language learners (Dulay and Burt, 1976, p. 69).

Some provisional 'errors' made by second language learners of English do not appear to be strictly attributable either to interference or to developmental processes. Rather, they result from the interaction between the two languages, and the developing bilingual's attempt to integrate the new system with the old. Dulay and Burt (1976) described this as 'process transfer' rather than 'product transfer', in other words the transfer of general *principles* about how language works:

> Children learning English as a second language create somewhat different and more sophisticated rules than those created by first language learners. For example, second language learners probably know a language requires certain frills, such as grammatical morphemes. It is natural, then, that when learning a second language, they should tend to *overuse* or misuse some of these frills, since their past experience tells them that a

language requires frills. This results in error types not typically made by first language learners. For example:

He not eats.

She's dancings.

(Dulay and Burt, 1976, pp. 72–3)

'Error' in second, as in first, language learning, is best regarded as a sign of active learning – evidence that learners are applying their own provisional rule systems as opposed to merely imitating. As learners have access to more linguistic input, their provisional hypotheses will gradually be refined until their language approximates more closely to idiomatic usage. Hakuta quotes a good example of this process from a 5-year-old Japanese girl called Uguisu:

> Uguisu's development in English contained some intriguing examples of transfer from Japanese. Her use of the English word *mistake* is an example. In English, the word is most frequently used as a noun, as in *You made a mistake*. In Japanese, the word is most frequently used as a verb, *machigau*. Uguisu's initial use of *mistake* was as a verb, the way she used the concept in Japanese. She used utterances such as *Oh no, I mistake, Don't give me more because you're mistaking, Because I just mistake it,* gradually changing to the more native-like use, such as *I made a mistake.*

(Hakuta, 1986, p. 114)

Naturally, languages will differ in the extent to which they share common features with English. A large part of the bilingual learner's task consists in developing a sensitivity to what the two language systems have in common and where they differ. On the basis of experience in another language, the child may begin by expecting certain linguistic cues (what Dulay and Burt above call the 'frills') which are absent in English, or vice versa. But this is all part of an active strategy. As Pit Corder said, 'It is one of the strategies of learning to find out just how far down the scale it is going to be necessary to go before starting to build up again' (Corder, 1978, p. 90). Thus, a speaker of, say, Cantonese is going to have to go a great deal further 'down the scale' to find common linguistic rules with English – whether of pronunciation, grammar or vocabulary – than is a speaker of a more closely related language such as, say, Spanish.

In this journey towards idiomatic usage, age is a significant factor, and much will depend on the learner's sense of identity in their first language and their attitude towards English and English speakers. Although there is much individual variation, the evidence points to a greater resistance to forming such new identifications beyond puberty. Thus some older learners, while acquiring communicative competence in English, may nonetheless effectively declare themselves as 'non-native' speakers through their distinctive use of the language.

Codeswitching and language choice

In societies where English functions alongside other languages, there may be an elaborate pattern of appropriateness which either dictates or strongly influences the choice of one or other language in particular contexts outside the home. English, for example, might become the language of literacy and formal education, whereas another language might be used for commercial transactions, and yet another perhaps for popular entertainment, and so on. Thus English and other languages, or particular registers of these, may become polarised to cover different ranges of experience.

Not all situations, however, will be so clear-cut – and the bilingual always has the option of choosing against the norm for special effect. In the company of other bilinguals, moreover, the bilingual speaker has the further option of incorporating features of one language within the other or even of changing language completely within a single utterance, that is, **codeswitching**. Indeed, as Shana Poplack classically demonstrated, codeswitching 'may itself form part of the repertoire of a speech community' (Poplack, 1980, p. 614). In this way even a single speech act can serve to express multiple identities, and thus to signal what Monica Heller (1992, pp. 134–5) has called 'double affiliation'.

Thus, in addition to the complexity of learning to manipulate the systems of two or more languages, the bilingual child is also learning how to use the languages appropriately, how to manipulate all the available linguistic resources in order to achieve the desired effect: choosing the right language for the right occasion, knowing when to mix languages and when to keep them apart, and so on.

In some bilingual families, as in some communities, there are regular patterns of interaction, in which particular languages are used with particular people – for example, one language with the mother and one with the father (as in the Rojas-Drummond family in Reading A) – and children will often challenge their parents for using the 'wrong' language. One of many examples of this comes from Redlinger and Park (1980), who quote the startled reaction of Danny (2;4) to the utterance of a German sentence by his normally English-speaking mother: '*Nicht Vogel! ... Du sag birdie.* ("Not [*Vogel!*] ... You say *birdie*".)' (p. 342). This choice, presumably triggered by the company of a German-speaking researcher, clearly affronted the normal rules of family interaction.

A child may of course manipulate these normal patterns of interaction to achieve personal goals. Harrison and Piette (1980) quote some vivid examples of even very young children demonstrating these skills to good effect:

> Ioan [is] a bilingual Welsh/English boy of 3;3. ... In his extended family Ioan could, in his third year, tell which relatives were bilingual, like himself, and which inserted odd bits of Welsh but lacked fluency. In a transcript of Ioan ... he switches into English on seeing his monolingual English grandmother come into the room where five people had been

talking Welsh. ... Five turns follow in English and are all about his reluctance to go to bed. Then another adult asks in Welsh if he wants to stay, and Ioan replies in Welsh. Subsequently the talk moves to another topic. Ioan remains. At a point when his grandmother is talking, in English of course, with his father, Ioan selects Welsh to tell his mother he does not want to go to bed ... Arguably we have here switchings that are so framed as to help bring about what Ioan wants ... Apparently his bilingualism is a tool for discourse.

(Harrison and Piette, 1980, p. 222)

In other bilingual families and communities, there is greater evidence of *interactional* codeswitching within and between speaker turns (as in Activity 2.1 above). In such contexts, the choice to follow or diverge from the preferred language of other participants within the interaction can be interpreted as part of a pragmatic strategy. In the following example, 8½-year-old Kristof's alternation between Hungarian (represented here in italics; the English translation is given in the right-hand column) and American English seems to mirror his fragile sense of independence from his mother.

K	*Limonádet csinálok*	I'll make a lemonade.
M	*Tudom, hogy inni akarsz, majd én adok.*	I know that you want to have a drink. I'll get you one.
K	*Csinálj limonádét.* I'm gonna get the ingredients. I know how much sugar I want in the lemonade. *[Lifting bottle]* Oh my God. Let me just do it by myself. *[Spilling water]* Ah! Sorry, sorry! *Nagyon nehéz volt ez.* *Bocsánat.*	Make a lemonade. It was too heavy. I'm sorry.

(adapted from Myers-Scotton and Bolonyai, 2001, p. 15)

The researchers comment that:

... switching back to Hungarian has its costs [for Kristof]: he cannot maintain the image of an independent person. But the switch also has its rewards ... the accident happens when he is speaking English [which] symbolises independence from parental control for him. The accident caused him to lose face, and his self-image as an autonomous boy is damaged. By 'returning to the fold' of Hungarian, he can at least gain face by refurbishing his image as a compliant son.

(Myers-Scotton and Bolonyai, 2001, p. 16)

For 17-year-old L, an Arabic-English bilingual boy resident in London, the switch away from his mother(M)'s preferred Arabic (represented here in italics) towards English appears to be more decisive:

L	*ana Daher khallasit dars elyum*	I am going out I've finished studying for today.
M	*shu ´imilit*	What did you do?
L	*´aher SafHat mitl ma ilna*	Ten pages as we agreed.
M	*la´ ´asher SafHat min kil madde*	No, ten pages from each subject.
L	Na na I'm outta here.	

(adapted from Al-Khatib, 2003, p. 418)

Romaine (1995, p. 121) argues that in codeswitched discourse of this kind all linguistic choices can be interpreted as an index of the 'social relations, rights and obligations which exist and are created between participants in a conversation'. As Al-Khatib (2003, p. 418) comments, 'L marks his defiance by a change of code ... at a site of social conflict where the role relations ... are challenged and new roles and relations are projected'.

Erving Goffman (1981) has defined such shifts in personal alignment as changes in 'footing' and the boundaries of the events themselves as 'frames'. These are clearly evident in children's role play, where the children effectively take on the perspectives of imaginary others in imagined situations.

We can see from the examples in the box that young bilinguals tend to associate the English language with particular kinds of practices. English, we may deduce, is something spoken in school, especially by teachers, and is the language of cowboys or possibly people in films more generally, as well as the language of teenage rebellion. The children's other languages seem to be associated with the management of play, with personal relationships, and the home setting. But, even among this small sample of young people, there are differences in the roles played by English. In addition, some of the young people are already familiar with more than one variety of English and aware of different social meanings between varieties.

> **Fancy footwork at play?**
>
> At age 8.11 Mario and Carla [Spanish-American children] were playing cowboys and conversed entirely in English, as cowboys would be expected to do ... Whenever they stepped outside these roles and gave instructions on how the play-acting was to proceed, or to offer protests, they switched to Spanish [see Fantini, 1985, p. 71]. If a child got hurt, he would be comforted by an older child in Spanish, even though an immediately preceding interaction between the children might have been in English [see McClure, 1977, p.93].
>
> (Romaine, 1995, p. 228)
>
> In their play [the ethnically Chinese children] reflect the language patterns of their school: when they pretend to be Malay girls in the class they speak Malay ... When they address the teacher, or play at teacher–child interaction, they speak English. They even make an effort at using Standard English in their imitations of the teacher. They sing a 'goodbye song' in Mandarin.
>
> (Gupta, 1994, p. 169)

2.4 Learning social and stylistic variation within English

As I remarked at the outset, it is not only bilinguals who are able to apply their linguistic repertoire to social acts: monolingual English speakers also have access to a range of different language varieties to signal their shifting attitudes and identities and to achieve particular goals. Again the key question to consider is how and at what stage these skills are acquired by children.

Pioneering research on social and stylistic variation in English was conducted in the 1960s by US sociolinguist William Labov. Not all of Labov's work was with young people, but one influential study among the black male adolescent street gangs in Harlem, New York, focused on the subtle and systematic ways in which an individual's orientation towards the gangs was reflected in the forms of language chosen (Labov, 1972). Labov described the use of language in these circumstances as a 'fine-grained index of membership in the street culture' (Labov, 1972, p. 255). Labov's approach, although subsequently critiqued, was the cornerstone of much later research in the sociolinguistic tradition (for example: Cheshire, 1982; Youssef, 1991), and was influential in the development of sociolinguistics as a discipline.

Labov's original hypothesis had been that young children were not sensitive to social variation in language and did not learn to make stylistic choices themselves until early adolescence. Specifically, he claimed that children pass through predictable stages of linguistic development in the acquisition of Standard English and that it is not until the age of 11 to 12 years that full 'stylistic variation' is achieved, where 'the child begins to learn how to modify his speech in the direction of the prestige standard' in more formal situations, such as reading out loud or an interview with a stranger (Labov, 1964, p. 91). How far do you think this claim can be sustained in the light of the evidence above from young bilingual children, or from your own experience? Leaving aside the question of what variety serves as the 'prestige standard' for a given child in a given situation, we do not have to look far to find counter examples to Labov's claim, where even very young children show themselves sensitive to contextual variation in language.

'Talkin' nice'

Figure 2.3 'Talkin' nice'

In the tradition of Labov, Valerie Youssef (1991) conducted a longitudinal case study of three small children between the ages of 2 and 4 years on the Caribbean island of Trinidad, where the characteristic differences among speakers are 'not outright distinctions in the use of particular forms, but rather differences in proportional usage of those forms' (Youssef, 1991, p. 89). During the course of the study the speech of the three children diverged along predictable social-class lines, with the most middle-class boy, Kareem, using increasingly more Standard English features, and the most working-class boy, Keeshan, using increasingly more Trinidadian English features. This already throws into question one of Labov's original assumptions, namely that increasing awareness of social variation would automatically cause children to orient towards a more standard form of English.

The other significant finding was that all the children were clearly sensitive from the outset to contextual features according to the social context. Thus Janet (the 'middle' child of the three in terms of social class) at the age of 3;9 produced 100 per cent Standard English past tense verb forms in conversation with her mother (who was very particular about the use of Standard English, as the language of 'advancement'), but only 54 per cent with the family helper (a Trinidadian English speaker), 47 per cent with her brother, and 40 per cent when playing with her peers out of her mother's earshot. The middle-class boy, Kareem, from the age of 2;10 'started to attend a preschool in which he learned about what he referred to as "talkin nice" and increasingly acquired Standard English features which he varied stylistically according primarily to addressee' (Youssef, 1991, pp. 94, 90). He was exposed to Standard English stories from an early age, and gradually incorporated the past tense forms into his own narratives, though still with due regard to his addressee. The following (oral) account was produced at the age of 4 (Standard English verb forms are italicised and more Trinidadian forms made bold; we may presume that *comed* is an instance of child language rather than the adult Trinidadian form):

> When we *finished* we comed out. We **dress up** an we **bathe** an we *went* by the Tobago airport and **wait** for the aeroplane ...We *went* by a shop to buy some flying fish to eat ... We *had* to wait long and long.

> (Youssef, 1991, p. 94, original italics, bold added)

Youssef contended that 'Overall [the children's] development reflected the extent and nature of expected usage of the respective markers for the social circumstances in which each lived' (Youssef, 1991, p. 93).

Similar findings emerged from two studies (Romaine, 1975; Reid, 1978) conducted in a very different social context, that of urban Edinburgh in Scotland. Both Romaine and Reid found considerable evidence of both social class and stylistic variation among their young subjects. In the case of Reid's 11-year-old boys, there was also a significant 'school effect'. Moreover, Reid found that most of the boys in the study were already fully aware of the need to switch varieties of language, particularly the boys from the 'posh' school, who used a broader vernacular when interacting with their peers elsewhere. (Throughout this section, words which may not be obvious to speakers of other varieties of English are glossed in brackets.)

KEVIN   ... that's what we're really here [at this school] for ... to talk
               nice and that.

MICHAEL   ... up at X school once, playing basketball ... they started to take
               the micky out of [tease] all of us ... because of the way we speak
               ... [so] you just keep your mouth shut and you don't say much.

IAN   I talk with a bit of a Scottish accent when I'm out in [one of
               the outlying towns] ... I don't really go from ... clean ... straight
               to dirty ... it's just a slight change in the way I talk ... if I talk to
               them with a sort of clean accent ... they'll think ... a bit of a
               bore really ... if you talk with the same accent as they do
               they'll just think ... you're one of us in a way.

                                                          (Reid, 1978, p. 169–70)

The boys were also aware of the pressures exerted on them (by mothers in
particular!) to be more careful about their speech in other people's houses:

KEVIN   ... especially when their mother's wi them ... ken [you know] ...
               they just gie [give] them a wee [small] flick ... to tell them to talk
               nice.

                                                             (Reid, 1978, p. 169)

All of this led Reid to conclude that 'there are features of their speech which
relate in a systematic way to their social status and to the social context in
which their speech is produced' (Reid, 1978, p. 169–70).

ACTIVITY 2.3

Allow about
5 minutes

During the course of one interview, Romaine (1975) elicited some distinctly
different stretches of talk from a 6-year-old Scottish girl. Consider what factors
might be influencing the girl to use such different styles at the two points
reproduced below. With just a transcript to rely on, your conclusions can obviously
only be tentative. (To make the passages more intelligible, the spelling conventions
have been slightly adapted from the original, with the author's permission.)

1   I fall oot [out] the bed. She falls oot the bed and we pull off the covers.
    I fell oot the bed so D says 'Where are you J?' I says, 'I'm doon [down]
    here'. She says 'Come up. Babies dinnae [don't] do that. They should be
    in their co' [cot]' So she gets oot the bed. She falls oot cause she
    bumps her head on the wall and she says, 'Oh, this is a hard bed too'
    so she says, 'Oh, I'm on the fler [floor]'.

2   It's a house, my house that I live in now, cause I fle'ed [flitted, i.e. moved
    house]. The house is still in a mess anyway. It's still got plaster and I've
    no fireplace now, all blocked up. Workin men plastered where they
    used to be, there and there, and they did the same to the fireplace.
    They just knocked it all ou' [out].

                                                    (adapted from Romaine, 1984, p. 100)

Comment

You will probably have noted the higher density of vernacular features in the first extract. My own interpretation is that this represents a humorous narrative in which the little girl is clearly very engaged, and in which she includes stretches of direct speech quoted from another vernacular speaker. Both these factors, as well as the obvious hilarity of the original situation (I can almost hear the giggles!), are such as to trigger her most informal style. The second extract, in contrast, represents a more sober account, possibly triggered by a more formal question from the interviewer, where a more standard style might be expected. It is conceivable also that the girl may be unconsciously echoing whole phrases she has heard uttered by adults about the building work.

Like Reid's schoolboys, Romaine's young subjects were often quite lucid about their language practices. The following extract is taken from an interview with a 10-year-old girl:

INTERVIEWER   Does your Mum ever tell you to speak polite?

CHILD   [If] there's somebody poli' [polite] in. Like see, some people moved en. There's new people in the stair [tenement flats] we've moved up tae [to] and they come in and I'm always sayin 'Doon Shep', cause it's my wee dog, so I say 'doon'. My Mum say 'That's not wha' you say' she says, 'It's "Sit down, Ken"', cause she doesn't like me speakin rough.

INTERVIEWER   Why do you think she doesn't like it?

CHILD   Well, if I speak rough she doesn't like it when other people are in because they think that we're rough ta'ies [tatties, i.e. potatoes] in the stair.

(adapted from Romaine, 1984, p. 126)

Knowing one's place: relative status in the family and beyond

Michael Halliday (1978, p. 1) argued that 'A child creates, first his child tongue, then his mother tongue, in interaction with that little coterie of people who constitute his meaning group'. In other words, the child begins by learning what it is to speak like a child and only gradually experiments with other roles.

The baby's first experience of language is likely to be in dialogue with a caregiver. As described in Chapter 1, adults in many English-speaking cultures tend to use a particular style of language when communicating with babies, usually referred to as child directed speech (CDS) or, more colloquially, 'baby talk'. This has been well summarised by Jean Berko Gleason, who carried out her studies in the USA:

> Briefly we can say they raised the fundamental frequency of their voices, used simple short sentences with concrete nouns, diminutives, and terms of endearment, expanded the children's utterances and in general performed the linguistic operations that constitute baby-talk style. There was a lot of individual variation in the extent to which all of these features might be employed. One mother, for instance, spoke in a normal voice to her husband, a high voice to her 4-year-old, a slightly raised voice to her 8-year-old and when she talked to her baby she fairly squeaked.
>
> (Berko Gleason, 1973, pp. 160–1)

Berko Gleason also documented the extent to which older siblings were able to vary their speech to accommodate the communicative needs of younger siblings.

> [T]here were age differences in the ability to use baby-talk style. The older children were in control of the basic features of baby-talk style – their sentences to the babies were short and repetitive, and uttered in a kind of singing style. In one family I asked an 8-year-old to ask his 2-year-old brother to take a glass to the kitchen. He said:
>
> > 'Here, Joey, take this to the kitchen. Take it to the kitchen.' (Baby talk intonation, high voice).
>
> A little while later, I asked him to ask his 4-year-old brother to take a glass to the kitchen. This time he said:
>
> > 'Hey, Rick, take this to the kitchen, please.' (Normal intonation).
>
> ... The original aim of this study was to see if, indeed, children talk in different ways to different people. The answer is yes; infants are selective about whom they talk to at all. Four-year-olds may whine at their mothers, engage in intricate verbal play with their peers, and reserve their narrative, discursive tales for their grown-up friends. By the time they are 8, children have added to the foregoing some of the politeness routines of formal adult speech, baby-talk style, and the ability to talk to younger children in the language of socialization.
>
> (Berko Gleason, 1973, pp. 163–7)

Some older siblings demonstrate great social sensitivity to the communicative needs of younger brothers and sisters. Here, two Singaporean brothers, aged 7;8 and 4;5 respectively, are attempting to assemble a plastic skeleton. The older boy is aware of the need to use Standard English with the interviewer, but switches to more friendly Singaporean English to address his little brother (note the use of the pragmatic particles *ah* and *lah*).

Figure 2.4   Sensitivity to the communicative needs of others

ELDER BROTHER	*[to adult interviewer]* I don't know whether he knows how to do it. *[3 sec pause]* *[then to younger brother]* A – all this are bones *ah?*
YOUNGER BROTHER	Yah.
ELDER BROTHER	All this are human bones *lah*.

(Gupta, 1994, p. 77)

Sensitivity to relative status in relationships is particularly apparent if we look at children's developing recognition and use of the different ways of asking questions, making requests and issuing commands in English.

Heath, whose research in the poor black US community of Trackton was mentioned earlier, looked particularly at the use of questions among members of the poor black American community she was researching. The ability of the children to mimic the adult style of firing questions at them was impressive. For example:

Mandy, a child 4;1 years of age, was observed playing with a mirror and talking into the mirror. She seemed to run through a sequence of actors, exemplifying ways in which each used questions:

How ya doin, Miss Sally?
Ain't so good, how you?
Got no 'plaints. Ben home?

What's your name, little girl?
You a pretty little girl.
You talk to me.
Where's yo' momma?
You give her this for me, okay?

When Mandy realized she had been overheard, she said 'I like to play talk. Sometimes I be me, sometimes somebody else.' I asked who she was this time; she giggled and said, 'You know Miss Sally, but dat other one Mr Griffin talk.' Mr Griffin was the insurance salesman who came to the community each week to collect on insurance premiums. Mandy had learned that he used questions in ways different from members of her community, and she could imitate his questions. However, in imitation as in reality, she would not answer his questions or give any indication of reception of the messages Mr Griffin hoped to leave with her.

(Heath, 1982b, p. 119)

It would appear that English-speaking children, at least in North America, take some time to develop sensitivity to the full adult repertoire for 'getting people to do things'. Although they understand only too well the force of adult commands, because of their relative lack of social power children are rarely in a position to issue instructions or make direct requests themselves, unless it is to even younger children, and it is easy to get things wrong:

Figure 2.5 'I think I'm somebody big.'

7-YEAR-OLD BOY	*[to 11-year-old girl]* Bring your li'l self here.
BYSTANDER	Who you think you are?
7-YEAR-OLD BOY	I think I'm somebody big.

(adapted from Mitchell-Kernan and Kernan, 1997, p. 204)

In order to choose the appropriate expression for the occasion, a child needs to be aware not only of the range of linguistic forms available to perform social acts such as requesting or demanding, but also have a sense of how likely the addressee is to comply with the request. Even very young children – perhaps because of explicit teaching – seem to be sensitive to the effect of 'please', especially when addressing adults. With or without 'please', however, children addressing adults usually resort to indirect means of getting what they want, such as asking questions or making hints. Shuy (1978, p. 272) relates how 5-year-old Joanna got herself invited to dinner by making three 'statements': about the absence of the family car, the fact that her mother worried if she missed meals, and finally 'You know, I eat almost anything'!

Learning to be an English-speaking girl or boy

At the same time as we are learning what it is to be a child, in most societies we are also learning our increasingly demarcated gender roles and relationships, and these too are reflected in girls' and boys' increasingly differentiated use of language. There is some evidence that, after a brief burst of directness, girls (like adult women) in many English-speaking societies revert to more indirect language. In an article full of vivid case studies, Carol Gilligan (1995) describes how previously bright and mischievous American girls such as 8-year-old Diane (who literally blew a whistle at the dinner table whenever she got interrupted!) and 8-year-old Karen (who walked out of the classroom when her teacher refused to call on her to answer) progressively lose their voices until, near adolescence, they are repeatedly heard to say 'I don't know', when in fact they *do* know. As one girl called Iris put it, 'If I were to say what I was feeling or thinking, no one would want to be with me. My voice would be too loud' (quoted in Gilligan, 1995, p. 207).

Classic studies have found that certain interactional features (e.g. interruptions, direct requests) are associated more with boys and men, whereas others (conversational support features such as *mmh, yeah* and *right*, and indirect requests) are associated more with girls and women. (For a fuller treatment, see Maybin, 2007, pp. 5–42.) The evidence is often striking, but needs to be interpreted with caution: even young people's use of interactional features varies from one context to another as well as depending on what they are trying to achieve as they talk. Marjorie Harness-Goodwin (1990), in a study of black working-class children aged 8–13 years in Philadelphia, found that when playing in single-sex groups, girls' interaction was collaboratively organised.

They made use of indirect request forms that drew in other participants (*Let's ask her, Maybe we can slice them like that*). This was in contrast to boys' use of more direct forms such as *Gimme the pliers*. But the girls were perfectly capable of using direct commands when they needed to, as when one girl told a younger child *Don't put that down! Put that back up! It's supposed to be that way.* Gender-based features of talk, like other aspects of social behaviour, also evolve over time.

Early evidence seemed to confirm that girls – particularly as they became adolescent – would adopt more standard varieties of speech than their male counterparts, when they judged that the occasion demanded it. As one of Reid's 11-year-old Scottish boys observed, 'some girls ... when they talk to their teacher, they talk sort of posh ... and when they talk to their pals ... they just talk normal' (Reid, 1978, p. 169). Interestingly, in an experiment conducted by Edwards (1979), this tendency for girls to talk 'posher' sometimes led to middle-class boys' voices being mistaken for girls' voices and working-class girls' voices being mistaken for boys' voices.

Macaulay (1978), in a study of 10-year-olds, 15-year-olds and adults in Glasgow in Scotland, looked at the interaction between age, sex and social class, and found that the speech of the children diverged according to social class as they got older, with the 10-year-olds of all social classes speaking more like each other than the 15-year-olds. Among the 15-year-old middle-class children, the girls already sounded much more like middle-class women than middle-class boys, and the boys sounded rather more like working-class men than middle-class men. In other words, the girls' class and gender identities appeared to reinforce each other, whereas for the boys there was more of a tension between the two. Of course these findings only represent general tendencies, and individual girls and boys may choose to 'break the mould' in a variety of ways. Arguably, also, some of these social distinctions may have blurred in the intervening decades.

However, the perception of vernacular English as more 'masculine' (i.e. more associated with boys/men than with girls/women) can start at an early age. You may remember from the beginning of this section the case of Keeshan, one of the Trinidadian preschool children studied by Youssef (1991), whose language became 'broader' as the study progressed. One of the factors to which this was attributed was his growing identification with men in his community (*dem fellas* as he called them).

Further evidence of the link between masculinity and the vernacular is available from Australia, where Edina Eisikovits (1989) conducted a study of sex differences in the speech of two groups of working-class inner-city adolescents, from school years 8 and 10 (average age 13;11 and 16;1 respectively). In common with other studies of a similar kind, Eisikovits found more evidence of social conformity among the girls, including a sensitivity to stylistic variation in language use; among the boys she found a tendency towards self-assertion and toughness, reflected in a strong preference for the

vernacular third-person negative *don't* (as in *He don't wanna work so he told
'em down the Dole office he wanted to be an elephant trainer!*) and for
swearing:

> That such prestige value is attached to non-standard forms by the males in
> this study may be seen from the direction of their self-corrections. Unlike
> the older females who self-correct towards standard forms, for example:
>
> D   Our Deputy-Principal was really nice and he sort of let my group, the
>   kids I hang – hung around with, get away with almost anything.
>
> E   An me and Kerry – or should I say, Kerry and I – are the only ones
>   who've done the project.
>
> the older males self-correct in the opposite direction, favouring the non-
> standard over the standard form. For example:
>
> F   I didn't know what I did – what I done.
>
> G   He's my family doctor. I've known im ever since I was a kid. An 'e
>   gave – give it to me an 'e said, 'As long as it's helping you, I'll give it
>   to you' you know.
>
> That such consciousness of external prestige norms is only just developing
> among the older girls is evidenced in the contrary direction among the
> younger girls who self-correct in line with the males, for example:
>
> H   It don't work out anyway – it don't work out no ways.
>
> (Eisikovits, 1989, p. 45)

What we need to remember in the case of Eisikovits's research – indeed any
research which looks at the effect of social variables – is the possibility that
the gender/class/ethnicity of the researcher may itself skew the results in a
particular direction. For example, in this case, the girls, identifying with
Eisikovits's gender, may have consciously or unconsciously accommodated to
her more middle-class speech, whereas the boys may have diverged in an
effort to assert their masculinity.

Acts of identity: learning to express one's *self*?

The picture emerging from this section so far may appear overly deterministic.
Are English-speaking children indeed locked into set paths according to their
social class, ethnicity, gender, etc? Sociolinguistic work has generally
concerned itself with the way in which language variation can be correlated
with social factors of one kind or another, in other words with the *systematic*
social variation of language in use. But, as Robert Le Page and Andrée
Tabouret-Keller have pointed out, this assumes that distinct languages and
fixed membership of social groups can be taken as given. Their influential
book *Acts of Identity* (1985) set out to:

... throw some light upon the ways in which such concepts as 'a language' and 'a group or community' come into being through the acts of identity which people make within themselves and with each other ... in other words, how the individual's idiosyncratic behaviour reflects attitudes towards groups, causes, traditions ...; and how the identity of a group lies within the projections individuals make of the concepts each has about the group.

(Le Page and Tabouret Keller, 1985, p. 2)

The point about 'projections' is a key one: unless we have a keen shared sense of the stereotypical linguistic behaviour of other social groups, we will have no fixed models to converge towards or diverge from. However, Le Page and Tabouret-Keller have drawn attention to the fact that our acts of identity may be constrained by the extent to which:

(i)   we can identify the groups

(ii) we have both adequate access to the groups and ability to analyse their behavioural patterns

(iii) the motivation to join the groups is sufficiently powerful and is either reinforced or reversed by feedback from the groups

(iv) we have the ability to modify our behaviour

(Le Page and Tabouret-Keller, 1985, p. 182)

Whereas children may take some time to achieve the first of these as their circles of interaction gradually increase, they will have a distinct advantage over adults in terms of the last.

Further evidence of individual agency in the expression of identity is apparent in the findings of Arvilla Payne (1980), who was interested in the extent to which young children acquire the accent of their peers rather than that of their parents. Payne conducted a survey of families who had moved from a variety of locations into a middle-class suburb of the US city of Philadelphia; she was looking particularly at the characteristic local pattern of pronunciation of a particular vowel sound. Her general conclusion was that children arriving after the age of 8 stood a far lower chance of sounding like a 'local' than those who arrived before. In other words their linguistic identity by this age had become relatively fixed. However, she found that, whereas a handful of children had been strikingly successful in acquiring the local vowel pattern, and the majority had been somewhat confused about it, one family of five boys originally from New York City (who had moved to Philadelphia at ages ranging from 0–9, and were aged 10–20 at the time of the study) had been strikingly resistant to the pattern. We can only speculate as to why this might have been the case. However, the key point is that the whole family appeared to be exercising not only sensitivity to the social variables themselves but also a degree of personal (or, in this case, collective) choice. In other words, there was nothing predetermined about the outcome.

Trudgill (1986), reviewing a range of evidence from different parts of the English-speaking world, came to the following conclusion:

> Labov ... has argued that, while children younger than eight appear to be certain to accommodate totally, there can be no assurance that, after the age of eight, children will become totally integrated into a new speech community. I would also add that, after the age of 14 one can be fairly sure that they will not. The problem years are eight to 14, with the degree of integration depending on many different social and individual factors.

(Trudgill, 1986, pp. 33–4)

So where does this leave us with regard to Labov's earlier claims, quoted at the beginning of this section? His ideas were obviously useful in identifying key stages in a child's sociolinguistic development, and – along with others – he was correct in identifying puberty as the stage when children's social identity through language becomes more self-conscious. However, his research had been based in relatively stable communities with a single local vernacular against which an individual could progressively measure any encounters with the Standard English of the wider world. Where the original hypothesis fell down was in generalising from the monolingual and (relatively) monodialectal childhood experience. In cases where children are exposed from a young age to more than one variety of language, or where they move between language communities, perception of the different social values attached to each language variety is likely to develop from infancy onwards, in tandem with their developing sensitivity to linguistic forms. Indeed the evidence is that, far from becoming more flexible around puberty, they are likely to become less so, as they become more committed to a particular set of identifications.

2.5 Conclusion

You may find it useful at this point to reconsider the three questions posed by Kamwangamalu:

> Who am I?
> How am I perceived by others?
> How would I want to be perceived?

(adapted from Kamwangamalu, 1992, p. 33)

In this chapter we have already seen how young speakers may:

- unconsciously adopt (i.e. converge towards) the speech of others because they identify with it (e.g. Keeshan from Trinidad with *dem fellas*, or the Rojas-Drummond twins with their cousins from England);

- consciously emulate the speech of those groups they wish to be close to or to impress or to get something out of (e.g. the Scottish girls who talked 'posh', or the Spanish-American children who wanted to comfort each other);
- consciously mimic the speech of others – or more precisely, their stereotypes of others – while at the same time distancing themselves from the stereotype (e.g. Ishfaq in his humorous exchange with Ben Rampton quoted at the start of this chapter or little Mandy's imitations of Mr Griffin).

The last of these may look like an intricate feat to accomplish, but it is something that we do every time we adopt a 'funny voice' in order to get away with saying something ironic or comical or provocative. There are various linguistic and paralinguistic devices, such as intonation, rate of speech or facial expression, which we may use to proclaim that it is not our own 'true' voice and that we are merely acting a part – but there is usually a convenient degree of ambiguity involved! (In his book *Crossing*, Rampton (1995) explores some of these complex phenomena with particular reference to adolescent ethnic identity.)

All of these acts of social 'positioning' may be accomplished in English at a variety of linguistic levels, from sounds (accents or pitch) through vocabulary or grammar to discourse patterns or choice of language itself.

ACTIVITY 2.4

Allow about
20 minutes

You may find it useful, by way of consolidating your work on this chapter, to prepare a matrix similar to the one below, drawing on examples from the chapter as well as on your own experience and observations. To start off the process, I have placed the examples just mentioned in the relevant cells.

	Accent	Vocabulary	Grammar	Discourse patterns	Language choice
Unconscious convergence	Rojas-Drummond twins (Reading A)	Keeshan? (Youssef, 1991)	Keeshan (Youssef, 1991)		
Conscious emulation	Scottish girls? (Reid, 1978)		Scottish girls (Reid, 1978)		Spanish-American children (McClure, 1977)
Conscious mimicry	Ifshaq (Rampton, 1996)			Mandy (Heath, 1982b)	

We have seen that children start to learn the communicative norms of their community even before they learn their first word. From a very early age, whether bilingual or monolingual, they become aware of the social significance of different varieties of language, including different varieties of English, and learn how to vary their own language according to the perceived context and the desired outcomes. However, before bilingual children can manipulate their two languages to express social meanings, they first need to recognise them as two distinct systems: different aspects of the languages appear to 'separate' at different stages in the child's development.

Different identities and social meanings are expressed in some communities via different dialects, in others via different languages, whereas in others codeswitching allows hybrid identities to be expressed and mixed messages to be conveyed. Up to adolescence, children are learning to use these different varieties and mixtures of language to express their identities and achieve their goals, both as members of social groups and as individuals; sometimes these different identities may reinforce each other, sometimes they may be in conflict. Beyond adolescence, young people and adults will almost certainly have become more fixed in their linguistic identities, but will continue to exploit all the resources in their repertoire as they continue to develop more sophisticated discourse strategies.

READING A: Raising our twins bilingually

Sylvia Rojas-Drummond and Hugh Drummond
(The authors both teach at the National Autonomous University in
Mexico City.)

Specially commissioned for Mayor (1996, pp. 71–7).

We are an Anglo-Mexican married couple resident in Mexico City. Sylvia is a
native Mexican who studied English in school and university, then did her
doctorate in the USA and returned to Mexico. Hugh is a native Englishman
who moved to Mexico after completing university in England, then picked up
Spanish as an adult, in social contexts. In addition, he did his doctorate in the
USA. Each speaks the other's language quite fluently, but with some errors of
syntax, vocabulary, pronunciation and so on.

When our twin boys Alan and Ian were born in Mexico City in July 1985, we
established as a central goal that they should learn both languages and be
exposed to both cultures as much as possible. They need spoken and written
Spanish to participate fully as Mexican citizens and members of the
international Spanish-speaking community; likewise, they need spoken and
written English to interact successfully in Britain and the USA and to gain
access to much scientific and technical literature. We expected it to be difficult
to achieve full fluency in both languages, since the boys would presumably
tend to speak only the language that prevails in most contexts (usually
Spanish), and they might even confuse the two languages. We know many
adults from homes with two native languages who failed to learn one of their
parents' languages (and resent the failure). Hence, we adopted an explicit
policy of exposing the boys to both languages and cultures, and of

Figure 1   Ian and Alan aged 6 years

encouraging them to speak English in particular (the 'endangered language' in the Mexican context), while at the same time keeping the two languages separate by context.

At the time of writing, Alan and Ian are 9 years old and they are in the third grade of a bilingual primary school that aims to expose children to both languages and both cultures, in all areas of the curriculum. It is populated mostly by Mexican children but a majority of children have one or two native English-speaking parents. About 60 per cent of class time is with a British or American teacher who speaks English and aims to refer principally to British culture; 40 per cent of class time is with a Mexican teacher who speaks Spanish and refers principally to Mexican culture. In the playground the children speak almost exclusively in Spanish, and most third graders continue to struggle with English, even after several years of exposure (including preschool).

Alan and Ian currently speak Spanish with native-speaker proficiency and accent; they speak English very fluently but with a slight Mexican accent and some errors that are typical of native Spanish speakers. Also, their vocabulary in English is mostly British, but they use some American terms (possibly more than Hugh uses). Their fluency in English has enabled them to act frequently as classroom interpreters. However, they have not always been bilingual: both have together been monolingual Spanish speakers and monolingual English speakers, in dramatic response to their changing social and linguistic circumstances. Furthermore, the boys' willingness and ability to speak each language have fluctuated (in a very coordinated fashion for both) as the family has moved back and forth between Mexico and England.

Although we have lived mostly in Mexico since the twins were born, during the year that the boys were 3;1–4;1 the family lived in Oxford, England, since Hugh and Sylvia were academic visitors on sabbatical. On the basis of these geographical moves, the boys' linguistic development divides naturally into three phrases: infancy in Mexico (0–3;1), the one-year interval in England (3;1–4;1), and five years back in Mexico (4;2–9;2). (See note in the Introduction to this book for the convention used for representing children's ages.)

During their infancy in Mexico, Alan and Ian spoke only Spanish, even though they had considerable exposure to English: Hugh always spoke and read to the boys exclusively in English, whereas Sylvia used Spanish, and they spent nearly as much time with Hugh as with Sylvia. The boys understood English as well as Spanish and they relished English rhymes and fairy tales, but their emerging language production was all Spanish. Hence conversations with their father were habitually bilingual: he spoke English and they spoke Spanish, with excellent mutual understanding. Now and then Hugh would ask the boys to say something in English and they would comply with a few hesitant self-conscious words, then revert promptly to Spanish.

Why did the boys choose Spanish? Probably this was not a result of a greater attachment to Sylvia, since Ian (but not Alan) actually appeared more attached to Hugh during the first two or three years. We suspect the boys' choice was a natural response to differential exposure to the two languages, and an adaptation to their social environment: not only the boys' mother, but their nanny, their Mexican relatives and all strangers spoke Spanish, so English may have represented only about one-third of total input. Thus, during this period all their productive speech was in Spanish, although they could understand English. This monolingual situation changed radically after they turned 3 years of age.

When our family moved to England we spent the first month staying in Hugh's parents' home in London. On the very first day, both boys started uttering phrases and sentences in English! It was as if their capacity for producing English had developed to some degree but in a latent state, and it became manifest when the context called for it. As they had been expecting, English language was all around them, and they responded by speaking more and more English, both to parents and grandparents. Initially they seemed shy, and Ian would mutter softly into his chest, but confidence came very quickly and within a few weeks both boys were speaking English nearly as fluently as they spoke Spanish, and rapidly building their active vocabulary.

Near Oxford, the boys attended a village playgroup and frequently interacted extensively with their English-speaking friends. Now they were living in an environment where their mother and a Spanish au pair were the only people using Spanish; none of the children in their playgroup knew any Spanish.

As the weeks passed, their English increasingly lost its touch of Spanish accent (although never completely), and they even began using English for talking together. The language they speak between them has, over the years, been the best indicator of which language is dominant for them. This rapid orientation towards using English for communication was accompanied by an increasing unwillingness to speak Spanish. Now, even if Sylvia spoke to them in Spanish they would reply in English. Also, when Sylvia took them to the nursery and as they were approaching their friends, they explicitly asked Sylvia not to speak to them in Spanish, since they did not want to appear different from the others. We think that it was the social pressure, as well as their own need to communicate and integrate to this new culture as fast as possible, that brought on the dramatic change from being monolingual in Spanish to being effectively monolingual in English.

This year was to be Alan's and Ian's big opportunity for becoming fluent in English. For this reason, combined with their evident reluctance to speak Spanish, Sylvia spoke to them in English too. Now, only the au pair ever spoke to them in Spanish, and they almost always replied in English. So we decided to stop actively monitoring the development of their Spanish, and assumed, incorrectly, that their skills in producing it were simply dormant. We were therefore astounded when their Uncle Robin unwittingly tested their Spanish production one day by asking them to translate an English sentence – and found that they apparently had none. Just five months into our stay in England, the boys were apparently unable to translate simple sentences from English into Spanish. At first we thought it was translation itself that they couldn't manage. However, over time we became aware that Alan and Ian no longer expressed themselves in their first language, although they clearly could understand when spoken to in Spanish. This was not a cause of alarm; after all, within half a year we would be back in Mexico and immersion in Spanish would soon restore their performance.

In September 1989 the family returned to Mexico. Alan and Ian had just turned 4 years of age and were by then speaking English like ordinary English children of their age and with a British accent. We remember vividly when our Mexican family (including the boys' cousins, uncle and aunts) picked us up at the airport; they all looked astonished when they spoke to Alan and Ian in Spanish (as they had always done), and the children simply declined to reply! During the car journey to our home the children eventually produced a few short phrases in Spanish after being instigated to repeat them, but only with a lot of difficulty and shyness, as well as with a strong 'foreign' accent. Their capacity to produce Spanish had definitely become rusty.

Once back in Mexico, Hugh continued to speak to Alan and Ian in English and they consistently replied in the same language. Sylvia, on the other hand, went back to using Spanish. For a short while after our arrival, although the children showed signs of understanding what Sylvia said, they responded in English. A few weeks later, however, both children used Spanish when spoken to in that language, as they related more to their Mexican family and friends. Impressively, the strong 'foreign' accent they had displayed when speaking Spanish on their arrival only persisted for the first month or so. Then it gradually decayed and within roughly four to five months the children were speaking Spanish fairly fluently, and without a foreign accent.

A few months after returning to Mexico, then, the children showed their first truly bilingual production: consistently, they spoke quite competently in Spanish with their mother, relatives and friends, and English with their father. Interestingly, they continued speaking English together for up to seven months! But then a switch to speaking Spanish together came, very rapidly and dramatically.

Hugh was absent doing fieldwork for a month between March and April 1990 when they first spoke Spanish together. As Sylvia recalls, it was as if the switch happened from one day to the next, sometime in the middle of that month. And since that day they have rarely spoken English together.

When Hugh returned, he was surprised to see that, not only were the children now speaking Spanish together, but they were reluctant to speak in English to him. Within a few weeks, however, and through Hugh's insistence, they became again willing to speak to him in English. From this time onwards, the boys have shown an increasing bilingual capacity, accompanied by a growing consistency for choosing the contexts for speaking either language and automatic switching of codes in mixed-nationality social groups.

Although at present the children are quite fluent in both languages, apparently the two underlying language systems are not kept completely apart. Influences have been evident in both directions throughout the boys' development, and occur at different levels. Some examples are phonetic, as when they have pronounced certain words as they would be pronounced in the other language, or when reading or writing 'phonetically' in English. Others are morphological, such as Ian incorrectly saying *atachadas* in Spanish – drawing on the English root *attach* and adding the Spanish morpheme *adas* to refer to the past participle, feminine gender, or his invention of the Spanish word *superba* – from the English *superb* with the feminine gender morpheme *a* added. Still others have been syntactic, for instance Alan referring to some blue shoes in Spanish as *los azules zapatos* – using the English word order for noun and adjective, or his saying in English *Till when are you coming back?* from the Spanish *Hasta cuando vas a regresar?*

At school, as well as at home, Alan and Ian are gradually becoming literate in both languages too. At the beginning, both children read and wrote English and Spanish 'phonetically' (which is appropriate for Spanish but not for English). This tendency in English has persisted for quite a while, but they are gradually reading and writing better in both languages, and particularly in English, which is the more difficult language to grasp in the written mode given the lack of close correspondence between writing and speech. Gradually, also, the children have come to discriminate when reading in each language and to adapt their strategies accordingly. When this differentiation started to take place, Alan would explicitly ask which language a certain text was in before starting to read, apparently so as to adapt his reading strategy to that language. Today, their reading in both languages comes increasingly naturally and easily. Here again, in general Hugh reads to them and they read to him in English, while with Sylvia these activities are carried out in Spanish.

Figure 2   The Rojas-Drummond family at the time of writing (home video footage)

An interesting example of the boys' capacity for automatic codeswitching happened recently when Alan was reading the book *Charlie and the Chocolate Factory* to Hugh in English in Sylvia's presence. After reading for a while in English, he would turn to Sylvia and narrate or explain to her previous events from the story in Spanish so that she could follow the parts he was reading. Then he would continue to read in English to Hugh, stop to explain again to Sylvia some events in Spanish and return to reading in English to Hugh, oscillating back and forth spontaneously and accurately. Both children show this capacity in various situations, as when speaking in turn to Hugh and Sylvia, naturally, rapidly and accurately switching back and forth between languages.

The children's accents in English seem to us to be essentially British (resembling Hugh's north-east London accent), with some influence from Spanish and American English. However, we recently experienced a striking example of the children's tremendous linguistic adaptability. At Christmas, Hugh's father and two nephews came from England to spend a month with us. Just one week after their arrival, we could see signs of the boys, especially Alan, picking up a stronger southern British accent, as well as a rapid incorporation of new phrases and vocabulary in their productive speech. By the end of the month this influence was more evident still.

Experiences like this give us confidence that the children would be quite capable of adapting linguistically and culturally again if we were to live in England. Indeed, on a recent visit to the USA, they conversed freely and fluently with many Americans. At the same time, however, it reminds us that we must frequently seek out opportunities for them to practise their English and relate to British culture if we want them to continue growing up bilingual and bicultural – a challenge we face for many years to come.

[Postscript: At the age of 19, Alan and Ian, for the first time in their lives, went their separate ways – Ian to higher education in Mexico and Alan to higher education and work experience in Europe.]

3 Learning to read and write in English
Pam Czerniewska

3.1 Introduction

This chapter is about children's early experiences of English as a written language and the first stages of their development as literate language users. Becoming literate, in English or any other language, is not simply a matter of learning how language is represented in writing, it also involves learning how written language is used in the home and community. I begin by showing how children can be involved in the literate world around them long before formal schooling begins. I discuss children's early involvement in literacy as a social activity, along with studies of how they first learn to read and write informally. I end with a discussion of how early literacy experiences relate to children's entry into the education system, and of the issues faced in the formal teaching of reading.

3.2 Emergent literacy

From the beginning of their lives, children act and react to the experiences around them, making sense of the particular functions and forms of literacy in their own communities. Taking part in literate activities does not depend on being able to read and write in the adult sense. Favourite product labels, restaurant signs, notices about missing cats and so on may be recognised long before individual letters are known. Where children are encouraged to experiment with writing even before their marks are intelligible to others, they will often produce 'pretend' shop signs, shopping lists, telephone messages and newspapers (see, for example, Figures 3.1 and 3.2 from my own children).

Children's understanding of 'environmental print' is seen as an important route to literacy (Goodman, 1984). Children develop a network of understanding about literacy, one that helps them discover principles of reading and of writing, and builds on the understandings they have already developed about spoken language. Thus, from an early age, they are seen as actively involved in working out the literacy practices around them.

In an environment of written texts, children will use many strategies to work out what adults are doing with newspapers, books, pens, computers and all the other things associated with literacy and they will attempt to join the adult literate world in different ways, as the following examples demonstrate.

Figure 3.1   A shop   **Figure 3.2**   An invitation to a party (Alexandra aged 3;10)
sign (Christopher, aged 2;10)

A 4-year-old was drawing at his kitchen table when he began saying his
mother's name over and over again. 'You're reading' his mother
exclaimed, realizing that he was reading aloud from a label. Delighted, the
child rushed out of the room. A few minutes later he returned holding a
favourite book and said: 'No, I can't read properly yet'.

(Czerniewska, personal experience)

In an Australian nursery, four-year-old Heidi drew a large detailed picture
of a dog. Down the side she wrote some letters (many from her own
name). Asked by her teacher what her writing said, she replied, 'I don't
know'. 'Well, you wrote it', her teacher replied. 'I know ', said Heidi, 'but
I can't read yet'.

(adapted from Cambourne and Turbill, 1987, p. 12)

Alison, aged 4 years, attending a nursery school in Newcastle-upon-Tyne
(in the north of England), discovered that it was not her turn to join her
favourite 'Soft Play' activity. Several minutes later she went to her teacher
and presented her with a piece of paper saying: 'I can go to Soft Play
because I'm on the list. Look!' [see Figure 3.3].

(National Writing Project, 1989, p. 13)

The children in these examples, although not yet in full-time schooling, have
already had many lessons about literacy. Through their daily interactions at
home and beyond, they are finding out what it means to be a speaker, reader
and writer in the community in which they live, and have already developed
some reader-like and writer-like behaviours. They are beginning to understand
how reading and writing are defined by their community, how literacy affects

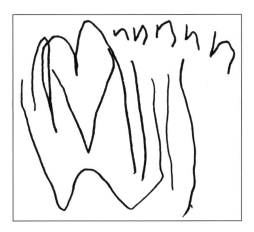

Figure 3.3   Alison's list

people's lives and what it will do for them. The young child's first discoveries of reading and writing have been termed (e.g. in Teale and Sulzby, 1988) **emergent literacy**, an expression that captures how children who live in a literate community are in the process of becoming literate almost from birth in a world of environmental print.

ACTIVITY 3.1

Ongoing, but allow about 20 minutes

If you have access to a young child or children, you might like to try to find out what they think you're doing while you are reading. You'll need to be quite subtle in your questions, although most children enjoy saying how adults behave. You might try sitting reading to yourself and, when this attracts interest, ask the child/children what they thought you were doing.

Gillian Lathey (1992) tried doing the type of investigation described in Activity 3.1 in her attempt to uncover some of the ways in which 3- and 4-year-olds thought about the process of reading. Armed with a pile of children's picture books and her own books, she stationed herself in a London nursery's book corner reading silently. Children's natural curiosity helped her get into conversations such as this:

LATHEY   You know when I'm reading something like this – what do you think – what do you think happens? How do I do it?

BEN   By talking like this: *[he holds the book and runs his finger backwards and forwards along the fly-leaf]* Chatter chatter chatter chatter chatter chatter.

(Lathey, 1992, p. 74)

Ben, like a number of children, associated reading with talking and with running the finger along a line of print. After all, for many children hearing books read aloud will be the most familiar experience. Other children in Ben's class, however, had a more sophisticated understanding of the distinction between oral and silent reading:

OLEUWASEUN	Some people read quietly.
SADE	They – they're reading it in their head they are.
LATHEY	They're reading it in their head are they?
SADE	In the brain. They go dm dm dm dm dm dm dm dm dm …

(Lathey, 1992, p. 75)

Sade's and Oleuwaseun's construction of silent reading must, Lathey argues, have been influenced by the adult models at home (in fact, each one had a parent who was a college student) and by the conversations adults had with them about reading.

The interplay of literacy and daily life

ACTIVITY 3.2

Allow about
10 minutes

A useful way to consider the range of literacy practices in a literate community is to begin by thinking about all the literacy events that happen during the course of a day in your own life. Jot down some of the literacy events that you encountered in the past twenty-four hours.

Comment

The list of literacy activities from the first hour of a day in my life at home in England looked like this:

- checking the calendar for the day's appointments
- helping my child with his reading book
- reading over my older child's homework
- glancing at yesterday's paper
- looking up the TV schedule and setting the video
- completing a coupon on a cereal packet and addressing an envelope for it
- writing a shopping list
- opening and reading letters
- flicking through a mail-order leaflet for books
- signing a birthday card.

Characteristically, in a literate community, a set of literacy-related activities would be familiar and well-rehearsed – some even ritualistic – within a particular home. In this way, it is argued, such literacy practices are learnt by children from an early age. Many of the interactions with print will happen in combination with different types of talk – oral reading of a family letter, or discussion of the day's events, or argument over a cereal packet offer, perhaps – and many will combine both reading and writing. Importantly, most of the activities are not about reading or writing as such, but rather they concern the social organisation of people's lives. Some activities will be compulsory (e.g. completing tax forms), others will be associated with particular family members (e.g. grandpa always does the crossword), and a few may have restricted access (e.g. letters may be written in a language understood by only some family members). Together, the events provide a 'filter through which the social organization of the everyday lives of the families is accomplished' (Taylor, 1983, p. 26). Taylor makes the point that children are not only learning about reading and writing, they are learning a lot about family life and the purposes that reading and writing serve.

Children's early understanding of the nature of literacy activities may be shaky – one child, aged 3 years, thought that all the letters put in the postbox (including those she 'wrote' herself) were for the postman. But these constructions of how things work serve to show how children follow individual paths of literacy development. They are working out, through their interactions with the practices of their community, how reading and writing function – albeit making quite a few mistakes as they go.

A collaborative venture

As with the acquisition of oral language, the child is not alone in the discovery of literacy. As Bruner puts it, children are not on solo flights mastering a set of skills but are involved in a collaborative venture:

> I have come increasingly to recognize that most learning in most settings is a communal activity, a sharing of the culture. It is not just that the child must make his knowledge his own [*sic*], but that he must make it his own in a community of those who share his sense of belonging to a culture. It is this that leads me to emphasize not only discovery and invention, but the importance of negotiating and sharing.

> (Bruner, 1986, p. 127)

Researchers have only recently begun to examine the effect of different cultural settings on how children learn to produce and understand texts. Hall (1987), in his discussion of emergent writing, suggests that parents often fail to notice children's very early writing and that researchers have collected hours of oral language from preschoolers but have not amassed anything like as many examples of emergent literacy. Similarly, while much has been said about the language styles adopted by adults while talking to young children, there is little equivalent data on the forms for introducing children to writing practices.

Each child will acquire a personal history of interactions with different language varieties, different speakers, readers and writers. Given that there will, therefore, be much diversity among communities in which children learn to write and read English, we always need to question the extent to which any findings on children's learning can be generalised from their own to other communities.

Taking different paths to literacy

The paths taken to literacy thus vary from context to context. Different communities will mesh written and spoken language together in different ways for any literacy event, and the types of practices that are encouraged for different members of a community will vary, as will the value placed upon literacy.

Shirley Brice Heath's classic ethnographic study (1982a; 1983) was influential in unearthing differences in English literacy practices among three US subcultures. The contrasts in behaviour identified by Heath among three literate and geographically close communities caused conceptions of preschool literacy to be radically revised. Her focus was on 'any occasion in which a piece of writing is integral to the nature of the participants' interactions and their interpretive processes' (Heath, 1982a, p. 93). Thus, it included events from filling in a form to singing with a hymn book. She observed closely three communities in the US Piedmont Carolinas, which she called Trackton, Roadville and Maintown. All of the communities were English-speaking and all the observed literacy was in English. Her findings showed how, from their culture, children learn different means of using and making sense of print and different ways of relating their knowledge of the world through talk and writing. In her words, communities introduce children to different 'ways of taking' meaning from literacy events.

In Maintown, the middle-class community in her study, the children learnt about literacy in an environment filled with print and with information derived from print. From six months on, these children heard and responded to books and referred to book-related incidents in their interactions. As they got older, Maintown children learnt certain rules about book reading, such as the types of questions that can be asked and the fact that interruptions are allowed. They also learnt ways of talking about texts and began to use the types of language structures more often heard in books than in speech. All this acted as a useful introduction to the practices they later encountered in school.

At first, Maintown seemed to have much in common with Heath's second community, Roadville, a white working-class community whose members had worked for four generations in the textile mills. Here, as in Maintown, books played a central role in children's lives and their rooms were full of alphabet friezes, musical toys and the like. The difference that Heath noted was in the use of books as teaching opportunities – times when children were expected to get things 'right' – rather than as opportunities for stories to be explored. The world of books entered far less into 'real life', and book reading was less interactive between adult and child, especially when a child reached school age.

The third community, Trackton, provided a further set of contrasting uses of language. Trackton had a black working-class community, historically connected with agriculture but more recently (relative to the time of Heath's research) with the textile mills. A Trackton child did not experience the baby paraphernalia of friezes, mobiles and pop-up books. The rich language opportunities came not from books, but from adult talk and oral narratives. A child who experimented with adult reading and writing behaviours was not seen as doing anything of special interest. But the environment was far from lacking literacy and children often arrived at school able to recognise much environmental print. Reading in Trackton was not a private affair, it was highly social, a time for discussion and negotiation of meaning. A letter, a set of instructions or a story might be interpreted, reshaped and reworked through a lot of talk.

The types of contrasts drawn among the different communities reflect the range of interactions possible under a label such as 'reading a book' or 'writing a letter'. Each of the three communities intertwined talk and writing in very different ways. Such evidence brings into question any simple oral–literate division, suggesting rather a set of features that cross-classifies the groups. For example, Maintown and Trackton valued imagination and fictionalisation, while Roadville did not. Direct teaching about language was valued in Maintown and Roadville but not in Trackton. Negotiation over the meaning of a book or letter happened in Trackton and to some extent Maintown, but was not valued in Roadville. Children were seen as needing their own specially designed reading materials in Maintown and Roadville but not in Trackton. When children, with their different experiences of interacting with print, enter school they will find that only some of their literacy practices are valued. For some children, then, school literacy may seem very different from the literacy found in their own homes.

Schieffelin and Cochran-Smith (1984) similarly looked at literacy before schooling in three very diverse cultural settings: a Philadelphia nursery school in the USA where children's parents were literate in English and who placed high value on reading and writing activities; a Kaluli community in Papua New Guinea where some adults learnt to read English at the local mission but where literacy played no part in the home activities and was not seen as important for the children to engage in; and a Sino-Vietnamese refugee family in Philadelphia who were literate in Chinese but whose literacy priorities focused on the functional need to learn English.

Schieffelin and Cochran-Smith found that the concept of literacy has many different meanings and many implications:

- For the Philadelphia nursery children, literacy was a range of activities in which reading and writing were seen (among other things) as important for self-expression, for learning about and telling others about their world, and for social transactions among friends and adults.

- This view of literacy was in sharp contrast with the Kaluli literacy practices, in which literacy was not indigenous but brought in by members of a radically different culture (Christian missionaries teaching from the Bible) who had their own agenda for its use. In Kaluli homes, literacy did not play a significant part nor was it encouraged among children – in fact parents were found to discourage children's interest in books.

- In the third community studied, Schieffelin and Cochran-Smith observed that for the Sino-Vietnamese families in Philadelphia, an English literate tradition is being added to an even older Chinese one. For recently arrived refugees, the acquisition of functional literacy in English was a priority. Their involvement in English literature for personal expression and enjoyment was not evident, and its eventual development was not certain.

The authors conclude that 'being literate' can mean quite different things in different communities. As they put it: 'Clearly, it is crucial that we do not equate the form, function, and meaning of literacy events across cultures, communities, or social groups' (Schieffelin and Cochran-Smith, 1984, p. 22). One consequence of this diversity is that it is difficult to describe the process of becoming literate in English in general terms.

In the chapter so far, I have tried to convey a picture of children, from their earliest years, encountering print with its many functions, forms and purposes. I will now go on to look closely at the writing system that children learning English (sometimes alongside other languages) need to work out.

3.3 Working out the principles of the English writing system

My son Christopher, whose first language is English, came home from school and told me that in Egypt in the old days they wrote in pictures. That was how he was going to read and write, he said, because it would be easy. He proceeded to draw a picture of two birds, plus various other items, including what looked like a child's mug and a fruit pie, accompanied by the words *mag* and *pie* (Figure 3.4). Then he read it aloud to everyone as 'magpie'.

This anecdote – and many similar ones could be provided – illustrates the long and often complicated routes that children take before discovering how the writing around them is organised. They will try out different ideas about writing – testing, through their interactions with adults, what works and what does not. Some hypotheses will be appropriate for the writing system of English, some more appropriate for writing in another language. Often there will be more than one writing system used in their home, and differences in their form and functions will be explored and sorted out. The writing that goes on in the formative preschool years does not consist of unstructured doodles; rather, it provides evidence of children's search for the principles underlying the adult system(s).

Figure 3.4 Christopher's picture writing (aged 5;11)

A child's-eye view of the written word

To find out about the child's search for the key to the writing system, it helps if the world of written texts is seen through a child's eyes. As adults, we may think of the written word as quite distinct from other kinds of symbol systems. Adults learn to filter out much of the print that surrounds them, often ignoring symbols from other languages that they don't understand and unconsciously categorising symbols into different sorts of writing. A walk along a local shopping street will demonstrate the diversity of written symbols from which children can begin to construct the adult writing system. For example, in my local shopping area (north London, England), there are street signs, posters, shop names, notices and leaflets which use alphabetic script predominantly, though they also include some rather arbitrary abbreviations (e.g. George Bros. Ltd), as well as **logograms** (where a symbol stands for a single word), as in the Arabic-based numeral system, various weights and measures and company logos (e.g. 1kg for £1, H for hospital and M for Macdonalds, or the heart used on car stickers to mean 'love'). In addition, there are **pictograms** (where an image denotes a whole phrase or concept), such as road traffic signs, the crossed cutlery symbol for a place to eat, and assorted symbols for men's and women's toilets.

For children, though, the world of written texts is not limited by the adult divisions into 'writing' and 'not-writing'. So, given the many possible ways of representing language, what does the child need to select as 'English'? Mathematical and musical notation, map signs, computer graphics, bar codes, punctuation marks, road signs and so on are there to be worked out by children for their meaning and their place in the adult system. These other notation systems are rarely recognised as part of the literacy learning process. Young English-speaking children often use the words 'number' and 'letter' fairly interchangeably and they need to learn that, in English, whereas the *numeral* '6', say, stands for the whole word 'six', the visually very similar 'b' is a *letter* that has no individual meaning.

Daniel's emergent understanding of number

At 1;11 while playing with two bits of banana Daniel said, seemingly to himself, 'nana bit two'. Shortly afterwards came his birthday and the discovery that '2' was associated with him and could be used to label cards, cakes and even trains (in picture books). He began to say often, on seeing a written '2': 'My two!' It appeared that he did not have an understanding of what two things this 'two' applied to; but Daniel did know he was bigger than a friend, 'Baby Aran' who was, he knew, 'one'.

Daniel had grasped that the 'two' of spoken language can be indicated by a digit. He could not read the word 'two', that is recognise 'two' as conveying the meaning of '2', but seemed to understand that the digit in some way stands apart from the alphabetic system of written language. At this time, while Daniel had considerable cultural knowledge of the concept of 'two' – its significance in his society and ways it can be used – his understanding of it as a mathematical symbol was emergent.

(Gillen, 2003, pp. 18–19)

A child's orthographic experiences will also include many non-English (or, more accurately non-Roman) scripts such as, say, Chinese and Arabic, which might be used in the child's own home or seen displayed on shop fronts and menus. It is clear that what children observe about their community's writing system involves much more than the written script used in one particular community. As Temple et al. observe, 'Children may very well be more aware of the alternatives than adults are, because our long experience with alphabetic writing tends to blind us to the possibility that there may be ways of representing words with symbols that are different from the ways we do it' (Temple et al., 1982, p. 15).

ACTIVITY 3.3

Allow about
10 minutes

To gain an impression of how the world of print can appear to a young child, try to find an example of printing in a language that is unfamiliar to you, or a mixture of English and a language you don't know, and see what you can make of it. For example, you could use information on a food packet, or instructions for assembling or using a piece of equipment.

Comment

You may have found that one or two familiar or recognisable words emerged from the message. If the message was printed in English as well as the other languages, you may have been able to compare them and reach some understanding of the meaning. Perhaps there were familiar symbols associated with the writing, which helped in grasping the meaning.

Examples of English-speaking children's early writing illustrate some of the possibilities that children explore. Numbers, letters, musical notation, non-English symbols and their own invented signs all occur side-by-side in collections of emergent writing. The example in Figure 3.5 was produced shortly after the festival of Hallowe'en (when traditionally the dead are believed to return to earth). The arrangement of ghosts strongly resembles a

Figure 3.5   'Ghost song' with musical notes (Christopher aged 5;1)

pumpkin, a conventional symbol of Hallowe'en. This combination of pictures and symbols occurs frequently in children's early writing and seems to indicate that children are not simply learning to produce a written script but are grappling with the many different iconographic elements of a cultural event.

The example in Figure 3.6 was produced by a monolingual English-speaking child with one bilingual parent. The child had seen Chinese characters at school while learning about the Chinese New Year, and he was adamant about the relationship between his made-up Chinese characters and the English words (written in later by an adult).

Yetta Goodman (1984), whose studies were mainly based in the USA, views the children's writing development as a process of hypothesis making, experimentation and then refinement of hypotheses. After observing the writing of 3- to 6-year-olds in the USA, Harste et al., (1981) commented:

> It is as if, among the 48 children studied, every convention that has been adopted by written language users worldwide was being reinvented and tested by this group of very young language users. Some tried writing right to left, others bottom to top, and a not surprising majority, given the

Figure 3.6 Exploring Chinese symbols

culture they were in, wrote left-to-right, top-to-bottom ... Some used space and distance freely about the page, others drew dots between conceptual units, some drew circles around sets of markings, others wrote in columns to preserve order, while still others spaced their concepts using what we would see as the conventional form for this society ... The symbol system itself proved no less interesting. Children's markings, while having many English language features, ranged from pictorial graphs to symbol-like strings.

(Harste et al., 1981, p. 137; quoted in Bissex, 1984, p. 101)

To summarise the argument so far, children face the task of sorting through the available information about writing in order to work out the principles underlying their home/community writing system. For many children, there will be languages other than English used in the home and local community and these may be written according to different conventions.

Is literacy easier or harder to acquire in English than in other languages?

Downing (1973) and Downing and Leong (1982) asked the question: how does the child's experience of the task of becoming literate vary from one language to another? They looked at fourteen different languages, including English, and identified some major tasks facing the young learner. One critical task is to work out which unit of speech is coded by any particular language. Two principles are usually identified as the basis of the different writing systems: symbols should represent meaning, or symbols should represent sound. More frequently, scripts are a combination of the two. The different writing systems can be categorised into three broad groups:

- logographic systems, where each character represents a morpheme or minimal unit of meaning (Chinese is predominantly logographic, though it also contains some phonetic information);
- syllabic systems, which use symbols to represent syllabic units of sound (Japanese uses a partially syllabic system, though it also includes meaning-based and alphabetic units);
- alphabetic systems, where symbols represent individual phonemes or meaningful units of sound (used by the majority of world languages).

The Chinese concept of the logogram relates closely to the concept of a word, but is not always equivalent, since many words (both in English and in Chinese) are compounds of two or more morphemes. However, a largely logographic language such as Chinese will still need many more characters than an alphabetic system because, in any language, there are many more morphemes than there are speech sounds. It has been thought that this makes the learning task for Chinese children far harder, involving considerable memorisation. The situation is more complicated than this, though, as Chinese characters may also contain information about their pronunciation. As Kenner explains, 'Most characters contain two parts, a semantic radical which gives a clue to the meaning and a phonetic radical which gives a clue to the sound. Each character is made up of a combination of strokes and has a pattern which children learn to recognise' (Kenner, 2004, p. 36).

In contrast with Chinese, Japanese writing uses a partially syllabic system. Again, however, it is more complicated than that statement might suggest, as four different scripts are used: hiragana, katakana, Chinese characters and Roman letters. Downing (1973) points out that initial reading materials use syllabic characters exclusively, and only later will children need to learn the other characters. (Similarly, in alphabetic languages with a very regular orthography, such as Spanish, initial literacy may to some extent be *taught* syllabically). However, like other children around the world, it is likely that Japanese children will have experienced many different writing systems in their home and local environment and will have explored the possible relationships between speech and writing some time before they reach the specially designed readers presented to them in school.

Alphabetic systems present another kind of learning task. In some languages, for example Finnish or Polish, there is a very close relationship between the phonemes and the letters. This means that a fluent reader familiar with alphabetic systems would soon be able to read aloud in Finnish, though unless they knew some Finnish they would not understand what they read.

English writing is more complex, as there are fewer symbols in its alphabet of twenty-six letters than there are sounds in the spoken language, and the standard orthography does not correspond precisely to any given accent of English. As the many jokes about English spelling demonstrate, the combinations of symbols in English often do not bear a direct relationship with the sounds. Some symbols are used to represent more than one sound. For instance, the letter *a* represents different sounds in the words *cat*, *play* and *are*. Children learning to read and write English have to become aware of such inconsistencies. In English, there are many letter combinations which may have to be memorised as though they were logographs (e.g. *knight* and *through*) and others as though they were morpheme or syllable-based (e.g. the ending *-tion*). Also, the English spelling system often contains information about the grammatical relationships between words at the cost of losing phonetic information. For example, the past tense is commonly represented as *-ed* in the spelling, even though its pronunciation varies according to the context: compare, for example, the pronunciation of *-ed* in *wanted*, *laughed* and *called*. The young child learning to read and write English seems to face a more challenging task than, say, the child learning to write Spanish, with its more regular spelling conventions.

Apart from the task of working out how speech is coded in writing. Downing pointed out other aspects of the task which differ among languages. One difference is in the way the temporal order of speech relates to its spatial order. For example, in Hebrew or Arabic, sounds are represented from right to left on the page, while the classical way of writing Chinese was from top to bottom (although in modern practices this is changing). In Japanese, writing can be either vertical or horizontal, while in English it is left to right. Another difference is in the design of the symbols. Arguably, variants on simple shapes are harder to remember than more complex ones; a view supported by the many confusions that learners of English have with the stick-with-loop symbols *p*, *b* and *d*, and with *g* and *q*.

In a similar way to Downing, Barton (1994) asks whether different writing systems have advantages for the young learner: are some easier for the young reader or writer to learn? It seems that logographic systems such as Chinese are easier at first for the reader to learn. Interestingly, a child who begins to read English by recognising whole words by sight (i.e. without analysing their individual letters) is effectively interpreting English as logographic. Systems with a heavy syllabic element such as Japanese appear easier to read than alphabetic systems, and Japanese children are reported to experience fewer reading problems. The advantage of alphabetic and syllabic systems is that once the initial breakthrough happens, any new word can (more or less) be worked out, while the learning of new logographs has to continue for many years.

It is not clear whether there are advantages in the different systems for beginner writers. Learning to write English is problematic because of the vagaries of the spelling system, but children can be very inventive and produce complex messages that are intelligible to the reader. The conclusion seems to be that the English writing system has some differences from other scripts in the advantages and disadvantages that face the learner, but the effects are too complex to assess.

Becoming biliterate

It will already have become apparent that *all* children experience a range of forms and functions of writing, but that children acquiring literacy in bilingual or multilingual communities are faced with greater complexity. Mukul Saxena (1993), for example, described the complex choices available for spoken and written communication among the British Panjabi community in Southall, London. The dominant written language in Britain is of course English with its alphabetic Roman script. However, within the three main British Panjabi cultural groups – Muslims, Hindus and Sikhs – other written languages are also widely found, respectively: Urdu, normally written in Arabic script; Hindi, normally written in Devanagari script; and Panjabi, normally written in Gumurkhi script (though each language can be and sometimes is written in the script of another). Factors such as religion, age, schooling and social roles all affect the language(s) used in both speech and writing, with many people speaking and writing more than one. Literacy events in the home and community will involve a complex interaction of different spoken languages and literacies. In planning a letter, for example, people might discuss the contents in one language and write the letter in another, even switching between languages and scripts within a letter.

When we look at the early writing explorations of such children, it is clear that they are able to develop two or more literacy systems alongside each other with relative ease. As part of their involvement in the National Writing Project (1990), Jacqui Clover and her team, which included bilingual teachers, worked with 5- and 6-year-olds, developing their confidence as writers and their awareness of the functions of writing. The children made books, and worked alongside adults who wrote with them and for them in a number of different scripts. The writing produced by the children showed their considerable knowledge of various writing systems. The text produced by Raki (who was attending an east London primary school where the pupils were nearly all bilingual) includes English, Urdu and Bengali (Figure 3.7). Interestingly, all were written left-to-right; she had not yet adopted Urdu right-to-left orientation.

Figure 3.7   Raki's text (National Writing Project, 1990, p. 40)

Charmian Kenner's study of biliterate children in a nursery class in London (Kenner, 2004) explores in greater depth the complexity of the everyday learning process for the biliterate child, She studied three pairs of children learning to read and write in English in parallel with becoming literate in their own community language, respectively Chinese, Arabic and Spanish.

ACTIVITY 3.4

Now read 'Young children learning different writing systems' by Charmian Kenner (Reading A).

As you read, make a note of any special skills or attributes that the biliterate children seem to be acquiring.

Comment

You may have noted some of the following at various points in the reading:

- biliterate children develop a wider range of 'visual and actional capabilities';
- they learn to 'recognise what counts as important in each script' and to 'identify what really matters when distinguishing one character or letter from another'; in so doing, they build up 'a vocabulary for concepts of shape, angle and size';
- they learn to 'adapt to different contexts' and, in particular, to recognise that their classmates 'might not have the same expertise';
- they develop an interest in 'exploring connections' between their writing systems;
- they can use their different scripts to express a distinctive personal identity.

In this part of the chapter I have tried to describe some aspects of the process in which the young child engages when learning to write in English. In order to do this, it was important to show how English relates to other writing systems and the choices children have to make about what belongs to English writing and what to other languages.

3.4 The transition to school literacy

Makers of meaning

The picture of the child that emerges from most of the studies described so far in this chapter is of a 'maker of meaning'. This is in contrast with models of learning that see the child as a 'receiver of knowledge'. The theories about reading development of the later part of the twentieth century, particularly those emerging from the USA, UK, New Zealand and Australia, showed a marked shift away from reading as a skill to be acquired towards reading as a system of meaning to be discovered by the child. US researchers such as Frank Smith (1978) and Kenneth and Yetta Goodman (Goodman et al., 1978) were influential in the 1970s and 1980s in many English-speaking countries for their then radical views about the role of the child as the central agent in the reading process. Reading happens, they argued, not because children have been fed information about shapes, sounds and words, but because they approach any text with the assumption that it is going to make sense and that they can work out that sense by using everything they know about spoken language when attacking written language. From this perspective, a child who looks at a page that says *The elephant walked out of the gate* and reads *The elephant went out of the zoo* knows an awful lot about language and reading, whereas a child who reads *goat* instead of *gate* in that context may know about initial consonant sounds but is not using their knowledge of language to produce a sensible text.

The 'truth' of convention and the 'truth' of things experienced

As adults we know that 'truth' is a semiotic construct [i.e. a concept with a socially rather than scientifically agreed meaning]; children take a different view. Social truths derive from the exertion of power sustained over time, and individuals meet that truth in the guise of 'convention'. Children do not initially have access to this 'truth', and are instead reliant on the evidence of their senses to tell them the 'truth' about the world. 'Spelling' ... is a very good case in point. Spelling is 'knowing how to write words correctly'; it is very much the 'truth' of convention ... I wish to look briefly at the spellings of a child, where the 'truth' is what the senses perceive, and what his attempt at interpretation tells him as the sense of the world that is spelled [Figure 3.8].

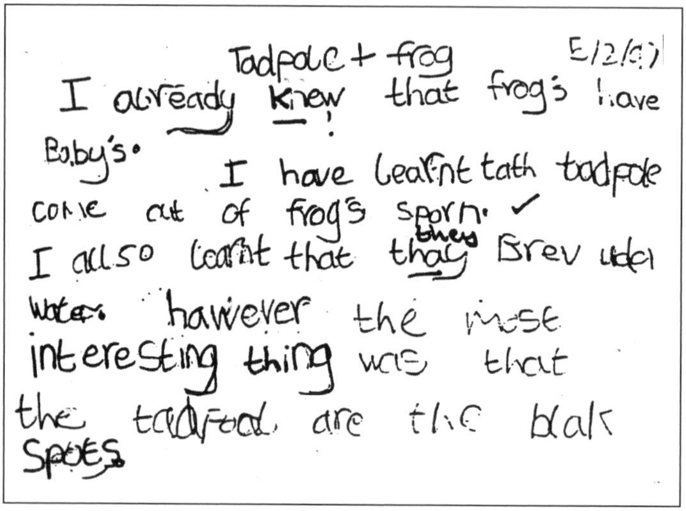

Tadpole + frog   E/2/07

I already knew that frog's have Baby's. I have learnt tath tadpole come out of frog's sporn. ✓
I also loarnt that they Brev uder wotor. hawever the most interesting thing was that the tadpool. are the black Spots

Figure 3.8 Frogs born

Let me focus on two aspects of this example in turn. Take first 'spelling', this time as transcription of sounds into letters. We notice that James spells *their* as *there*, *little* as *littel*, and *nothing* as *nofing*; he also spells *can't* as *con't*, though in this case instead of *spelling* incorrectly, he might just have been 'miswriting' the letter *a* as an *o*. In the case of *nofing*, however, the *f* is definitely what he will hear in his (north) London dialect. And there is nothing at all that would make plausible for him the *th* letter sequence as a means of transcribing what he hears as an *f*. In the case of *littel*, speakers of his dialect insert the 'weak' vowel 'schwa' between the two consonants in these contexts, rather than treating the *l* as a semi-vowel. The spelling of *there* is an instance where he is unaware of the 'truth' of convention, which separates two lexical items which are identical in the sound of speech by a difference in orthography. For most children with no hearing difficulties this is the 'truth' of the evidence of their ears: [they] transcribe the sounds of the speech they hear with razor-sharp accuracy; they are acute analysts of the sounds of speech.

But there are other 'truths' as well: and most strikingly these are the 'truths' of meanings that are made here. The phrase 'frog's spawn' is obviously not known to James, but that does not mean that he does not need to know its 'truth'. In this case he is asked to perform a semantic 'transcription' rather than the phonetic one just exemplified. He takes the route that seems most promising: 'this topic is about the life-cycle of frogs', he seems to say to himself, 'so clearly this phrase is about frogs (being) born'. This too is the 'truth' of evidence – not the evidence of his ears, but the evidence of his rigorous logic.

[A six-year-old girl from a different school in north London] took a different route to the 'truth' of this phrase. She wrote [Figure 3.9] *I have learnt that tadpole come out of frog's sporn*. This is a 'truth' which is in part phonological (and therefore conventional): she knows that in English word-initial consonant clusters such as *sp* (as in *sporn*) are permitted, but that *sb* is not (a problem that James did not have to deal with, as in his 'spelling' he had separated the *s* and the *b* in frog*s* *b*orn). And in part it is a 'truth' which is syntactic: English has many noun phrases such as *X's Y:* – 'my mum's bag', 'the dog's collar', – and this is the 'truth' that leads to her transcription and spelling.

Figure 3.9 Frog's sporn

... In the case of these six-year-olds, perception is already shaped by considerable cultural knowing, though the principle of 'truth to experience' remains.

(Kress, 2003, pp.160–62)

One argument that follows from the emphasis on the child's role in finding meaning from print is that any reading activities that remove the sense of texts, such as meaningless exercises in letter sounds, or the use of reading primers with highly controlled vocabularies, will mystify rather than help the apprentice reader. In consequence, there was a move in the 1980s and 1990s, among many UK and US teachers in particular, towards the use of real books as opposed to specifically designed basic texts. However, the 'real books' approach was itself the cause of considerable controversy, and the pendulum has since swung back towards a more analytical approach to the teaching of initial literacy, including a strong emphasis on 'phonological awareness' (see, for example, Bryant, 1994, and Goswami, 2002, pp. 41–60).

Evidence from more recent research by psychologists Nation and Snowling (2004) has essentially confirmed some value in each view, giving supporting to a hybrid approach which recognises the value of early oral experiences in preparing for literacy.

Beyond phonological skills

It is well accepted that there is more to reading than decoding. Children also need to comprehend what they have to read. While phonological factors provide an essential substrate to decoding, other aspects of oral language, for example vocabulary and listening comprehension, are important for reading comprehension. ...

During development, English-speaking children must learn to read not only regular words with systematic grapheme–phoneme [i.e. symbol to sound] correspondences but also exception words that do not conform to such 'rules'. One way for children to learn to read exception words is by using the context in which these words are written to decipher their meaning and sound. To take an extreme example, ... the pronunciation of [BOW] can only be disambiguated by context (he took a *bow* at the end of the performance/he took a *bow* and arrow from his bag). ... It might be argued that children with good oral skills develop better word recognition systems because they have always used context proficiently in this way. Put simply, their richer vocabulary and syntactic skills have placed them in an excellent position for deciphering words that do not conform to consistent grapheme–phoneme correspondences.

(Nation and Snowling, 2004, pp. 343, 352)

'Top down' vs 'bottom up' models

It is not only among educational professionals that debate has raged about the most effective approaches to the formal teaching of initial literacy. Nation and Snowling's work quoted above is part of a long tradition of psychological research, concerned to understand the cognitive processes involved in reading.

ACTIVITY 3.5

Now read 'Uncovering the key skills of reading' by Roger Beard (Reading B).

As you read, make a note of the various component skills which, according to different researchers, seem to distinguish good readers from poor readers. Are there any recurrent elements identified? Are these complementary or contradictory?

Comment

You may have noted some or all of the following factors as significant in fluent reading:

- cracking the 'letter-sound code' of the writing system (Gough);
- good readers 'perceive whole words as quickly and easily as single letters' (Catell); 'automaticity comes from having read words, not from skipping them' (Adams); 'fluent readers are distinguished by rapid word recognition' (Stanovich); 'the use of contextual cues to help identify a word is usually unnecessary because words are recognized from visual information so quickly' (Oakhill and Garnham);
- 'hypothesis forming about "the meanings that lie ahead"' (Goodman); the identification of 'meaning without, or ahead of, the identification of individual words' (Smith); ,
- 'it is the less skilled readers who rely more heavily on contextual clues to support their reading' (Hurry); 'good readers may be more sensitive to context, and yet less dependent upon it, because information is more easily available to them from other sources' (Stanovich); 'the hall-mark of skilled reading is fast *context-free* word identification combined with a rich *context-dependent* text understanding' (Perfetti); 'fluent readers are distinguished by ... effective comprehension strategies' (Stanovich);
- 'good oral skills ... vocabulary and syntactic skills' (Nation and Snowling, 2004, as quoted earlier in this chapter).

In the light of the above, Stanovich's conclusion that the 'various component subskills of reading can cooperate in a compensatory manner' seems justified, and it seems reasonable to concur with Beard that good readers rely on 'effective use of information from a range of sources'.

3.5 The role of story reading

Wells (1986) studied English preschool and primary school children from a range of social backgrounds in Bristol, England, in the 1970s and 1980s, and drew strong conclusions about the kind of home experiences that prepare children well for the literacy practices of school. He reported that shared story reading was significantly associated with two literacy measures: a 'knowledge of literacy' test at age 5 and a test of reading comprehension two years later. He attributed this (Wells, 1986, pp. 151, 157) to three possible reasons:

- Children become familiar with the characteristic rhythms and structures of written texts that will support their later reading and writing development.
- They extend the range of their experience and discover the 'symbolic potential of language: its power to create possible or imaginary worlds through words'.
- Stories provide an excellent context for collaborative talk with adults.

Dombey (1992) has also drawn attention to the value of shared story reading in the family as an intimate and enjoyable time when new meanings are created through collaborative talk. There is the opportunity of many different meanings developing through the connections made between text and life experiences. 'In this way literacy becomes implicated in the creation of ways of thinking' (Barton, 1994, p. 147).

Most UK primary classrooms indicate the high value that is placed on storytelling. There will often be a book corner with an inviting display of picture books, story sessions during class with all children gathered around the teacher, small group shared reading times with a teacher or volunteer 'listener' and, often, books that can be taken home. The value of stories for the child beginning to read is also emphasised at the time of writing by their important role in the 'Literacy Hour', which the National Curriculum in England and Wales strongly recommends that children in primary schools participate in daily (though the literacy activities undertaken by children and teachers are not confined to stories). The approach has gained considerable support among the teaching profession. But questions need to be raised about some of the underlying assumptions.

Degrees of continuity in literacy practices

It may be assumed from the above that books and their possible worlds are unproblematic. But children can face considerable conflict in the stories that they read, especially if what they read in English does not represent their own community's culture. There is also the risk of assuming that the attitudes to reading found in one community will be the same in another. Reading in the research described above is, without question, seen to be fun and emotionally satisfying. But what happens when reading is defined differently by adults? Solsken (1993), for example, found in her study of children in the USA that not all parents treated reading as fun. For many parents, reading was viewed as 'work' and, furthermore, it was often seen as a female activity. As a result, boys, in particular, were sometimes found to resist reading activities.

A closer look at the assumption that bedtime reading is a 'good thing' for children's later success at school reveals a more complicated relationship between literacy practices at home and at school. The focus on bedtime stories may seem to put an unfair emphasis on a set of social practices peculiar to a specific group. Such a bias may seem to devalue all the other equally important domains of literacy or to ignore the many other uses of literacy, such as those described by Heath (1983) in the communities she studied.

Eve Gregory (1992), who spent two years observing urban multilingual reception classrooms in the UK, concluded that you cannot take one cultural practice and assume that it will remain the same in a new context. Whereas at home the central purpose of story reading is usually to enjoy the story together, at school the focus is on teaching about reading. The teacher will choose books that are enjoyable, but story-time is primarily a means towards a specific curriculum end. As such, a teacher will be aiming to develop the pupils' knowledge and understanding about literacy. Gregory argues, from analysis of her observations, that children come to school with different experiences of shared reading and some may find it hard to work out the teacher's 'ground rules' for story-times – when the teacher is talking about the story and when about their own life experiences; what comments about the story are acceptable and what are not; what kind of reactions to the story they should make. For some children from cultural backgrounds very different from that of the teacher, the 'ground rules' may be particularly problematic.

3.6 Conclusion

What are the main conclusions that can be drawn from this chapter?

First, many young children have a continuous involvement with literacy from their earliest years. Literacy is part of their social world, and many children will experiment with its forms and functions long before they are formally introduced to it in school.

Second, the learner of a written language has to sort out how literacy is used in a particular culture. Learners can take different paths to this understanding, but they will do so by trying to make sense of the written texts they encounter and the literacy events they observe and become involved in. Literacy events are important not only for helping children attend to significant features of written English (such as the relationship between phonological features of the spoken language and its alphabetic writing system, the distinctive styles and rhythms of written language, and the relationship between pictures and texts), but also because they encourage children to perceive the written language as a valuable means of representing and communicating ideas and feelings.

Third, certain early literacy experiences (especially story reading) have been identified as significant for later educational success, but these may impact differentially on children from different cultural backgrounds and may not adequately reflect the full range of literacy activities that children encounter in their everyday lives.

READING A: Young children learning different writing systems

Charmian Kenner
(Charmian Kenner teaches at Goldsmiths, University of London.)

Source: This reading is adapted from Kenner, C. (2004) *Becoming Biliterate: Young Children Learning Different Writing Systems*, Stoke-on-Trent, Trentham Books, pp. 73–89 and 103–8. It draws on research conducted in the context of the ESRC-funded project, 'Signs of Difference', for which the research team consisted of Gunther Kress, Hayat Al-Khatib, Gwen Kwok, Roy Kam and Kuan-Chun Tsai.

Figure 1   Selina's drawing of her mother and sister

Figure 1 shows Selina's drawings of her mother and sister, with the words 'I love my mum' and 'I love my sister' written below in English. Above the picture of her mother Selina [a six-year-old Chinese-English bilingual] has written 'love' in Chinese, whilst above her sister's head she has placed Chinese characters representing the concept of 'Girl Power'.

Here Selina has chosen to combine her writing systems, linking images of two of the people closest to her with ideas holding special significance. Love for her mother is expressed in both Chinese and English. 'Girl Power' is a slogan coined in English by one of Selina's favourite all-female Western pop groups, but Selina uses a translation available in Chinese and links the idea to her ten-year-old sister Susannah.

Selina's representation shows us the world of a six-year-old whose life is lived simultaneously in Chinese and English – a world in which symbols and concepts from two languages co-exist. For Selina, these bilingual links are an important part of her emotional and intellectual development. Yet the institutions of [British] society, including primary schools, tend to separate out the languages in children's lives. Often children are required to use only English at school and other languages are restricted to home and community. The justification usually given is that children will experience confusion if allowed to think and write in more than one language, or that their learning of English will be held back. Our research, however, found a very different story.

The bilingual children in our project were well aware of the differences between their languages and literacies ... But they were also interested in exploring connections between these systems. When writing, they had two sets of resources present in their minds and could draw on either or both of them to make a text. This is the potential creativity and learning power of living in simultaneous worlds. ...

Writing different scripts

... Children becoming biliterate find out that different scripts operate by different rules. Even scripts which look similar have their special attributes. As Brian [a 6-year old Spanish-English bilingual] remarked when comparing English to Spanish, 'They haven't got a N with *this* on top' (referring to the letter 'ñ' as in 'España').

Biliterate children widen their horizons with respect to the making and placing of marks on the page. They have to recognise what counts as important in each script and be able to produce their own version, whether this involves writing from left to right in Arabic and right to left in English, or using Chinese stroke patterns as compared to English 'joined-up writing'. The children in our research project were developing an impressive range of visual and actional capabilities, due to their experience of different scripts. ...

Kress [1997] explains that all modes of representation offer different potentials and limitations. Each writing system uses the visual and actional modes in particular ways. When children produce written symbols they have to pay attention to a number of different facets – the type of stroke to be used, directionality, shape, size, spatial orientation, placement on the page – and these will be culturally specified in the teaching experienced by the child.

From these features, children create their own repertoire of representational resources ... [E]ach child forms particular interpretations of what is important in the act of writing. ... From this they made decisions about how symbols are created and positioned in each writing system. ...

The design of symbols

The precision of Chinese characters

... In [a British] primary school, children are not expected to show [fine] pen control at the age of five. However, this capability is necessary in order to write in Chinese. Children also need to be able to recognise small differences in stroke patterns, to check that they have written each character correctly. Selina [and her] classmates at Chinese school were developing their visual and actional capacities through close attention and continual practice, so that they could produce these complex patterns.

They were helped by their teachers, who would write similar-looking stroke patterns on the board and ask children to spot the difference. Children would volunteer that 'it's too straight' (when the stroke should be curved) or 'it's too far away' (when two strokes should be placed closer together). The teacher would remind them to be precise when writing each stroke, saying for example 'Make sure it's only like a little one – a short line'. As teacher and pupils discussed the stroke pattern together, children built up a vocabulary for concepts of shape, angle and size in both English and Cantonese.

The children themselves were concerned to produce characters which were beautifully written as well as correct. They brought an array of pencils and rubbers to class, sharpening their pencils frequently to produce clearer strokes, and rubbing out over and over again. ...

Key differences in stroke patterns

Ming's family did not put so much emphasis on teaching stroke production, and Ming [another six-year-old Chinese-English bilingual] was less concerned with complete accuracy when teaching his classmates at primary school. However, he showed that he was aware of criteria such as the correct length, angle and balance of strokes when he made comments such as 'Make it even more bigger' or criticised his own writing by saying 'That's too lumpy'. He decided to do a circle round one offending character 'cos that's what my Chinese teacher does when I get it wrong'.

Ming also knew that small variations in stroke pattern could differentiate between two potentially similar characters. When teaching his classmate Roberto to write the character meaning 'six' (Figure 2), Ming suddenly became dissatisfied with his pupil's efforts. He complained that at some points Roberto's writing of the upper vertical stroke was 'too long', and that the lower part of the character was wrong 'because it's next to each other' (the two strokes under the horizontal line were supposed to be further apart). It turned out that these details were indeed significant in differentiating this character from the one meaning 'big' ...

Figure 2   The Chinese characters for (*left*) 'six' and (*right*) 'big'

Joined letter forms in Arabic

Arabic, like English and Spanish, is an alphabetic system, so symbols do not have to be written quite as accurately as in Chinese. Instead of having thousands of characters that are subtly different from one another, alphabetic scripts have a defined set of letters which can be more easily distinguished. Readers usually encounter letters in the context of a word, giving further clues as to what the letter might be.

However, in Arabic a number of concerns still arise for learners about certain details of each letter, because the letters take different forms when they are at the beginning, in the middle or at the end of a word. Children have to know how to produce each shape and how to join it to others. They also need to guard against letters looking too similar to each other when joined.

At Arabic school, teachers helped children to develop their abilities for visual discrimination by writing words on the board and asking which letters they were composed of. They also requested children themselves to write words on the board so that the whole class could decide if the letters had been correctly formed and joined. If children needed help to remember these characteristics and to write the script appropriately, teachers provided support through a join-the-dots model of a word on the board or in exercise books. This was an aid both to perception and action. ...

'You forgot to do that little wiggly line'

Tala [a six-year-old Arabic-English bilingual] decided to teach the word 'mama' (mum) to her friends Tina and Bhumi. Just like her teachers in Arabic school, she provided a join-the-dots version to help her pupils to write the word. She then decided to write over the dots herself, giving them a model to follow (Figure 3). One of the original dots can still be seen in the loop of the first syllable.

Figure 3   Tala's writing of the Arabic word 'mama' (mum). The symbol on the left shows a pronounced 'wiggle'

Writing the word 'mama' in Arabic involves joining the letter 'mim' (for the sound 'm') to the letter 'alif' (for the sound 'a'), twice over. First you have to write the initial form of 'mim', and join it to the middle form of 'alif', making 'ma'. Since 'alif' is one of the 'stubborn' letters which cannot join to the [next letter, which would be on the] left, you then have to leave a gap before starting the next syllable. The second syllable is identical to the first.

When Tina began writing the word, using the model provided, Tala shrieked and grabbed the sheet of paper from her, saying 'Tina, you ain't doing the stick so good – do the circle here and then you do the line'. Tracing the letters with her finger, she emphasised the necessary action for connecting the 'circle' of 'mim' to the 'stick' of 'alif'.

Tina began again, but Tala was still dissatisfied. She said 'you got to do the line, there', tracing the shape with her finger once more, and rubbing out Tina's new version. The 'line' at issue seemed to be the wiggle which follows the loop of 'mim' as it joins to the vertical stroke of 'alif' – this is clearly visible in the left-hand part of Figure 3. This time Tala gave Tina more precise instructions: 'you're doing a circle, right, but you always forget to do the line', while demonstrating writing a circle followed by a pronounced wiggle. Tina understood, and responded by including a wiggle in her next version. Later Tala explained to her other pupil Bhumi, who was trying to write the same word, 'you done it wrong because you forgot to do that little wiggly line'. ...

Just as Selina and Ming focused on specific details of Chinese characters which they considered to alter the meaning, so Tala picked out the 'wiggle' as the key attribute when [distinguishing] two particular letters. This is a complex task for children; out of all the instruction they receive on the act of writing, they have to identify what really matters when distinguishing one letter or character from another. Teachers at Chinese and Arabic school helped children to understand significant details of this kind by emphasising them in discussion. ...

Making your mark

Children also like to develop their own style, particularly when writing their name. Producing a signature is the most personal and self-defining act of writing, and children recognise it as such. This can explain why children's signatures are often unconventional. Brian, for example, wrote his name in a combination of upper- and lower-case letters. It could be assumed that this was because he was still working out the difference between the two types of lettering. However, it also seems that this particular representation of his name became important to Brian, because he continued to use it throughout the year of the research project.

Part of his signature involved the upper-case form of the letter 'N' (see Figure 4). Brian was especially attached to this form of 'N' when writing other words too, probably because he linked it with his name. ...

Figure 4   Brian's drawing of a bear with wings, with the caption 'un oso que vuele' (a bear which flies)

Children often feel strongly about their particular design of a written symbol and are prepared to argue for it. At stake is the issue of social acceptability – does their version fall within the boundaries of conventional meaning? – and also the desire to produce an individual flourish. ...

Embodied knowledges

From their experience of different scripts, the children in the research project were developing different kinds of knowledge in several areas: ways of designing symbols and using the graphic space of the page, and the physical process of writing. The term 'embodied knowledges' can be used to describe this learning, because it simultaneously involves visual, actional and cognitive aspects.

Embodied knowledges are part of understanding how a writing system works. As well as knowing what symbols stand for, children recognise that the visual characteristics of symbols and the actions needed to produce them also hold significance. ... The children realised that their primary school classmates might not have the same expertise in these areas, and sought to give advice. ...

These biliterate children seemed to adapt to different contexts, drawing on their multisemiotic resources in ways they found appropriate. Mainstream educators sometimes think that children will find it hard to switch between ways of writing in different scripts. For example, it is said that children who have learned the precision of writing Chinese will find it difficult to adapt to the relative freedom of the emergent writing they are encouraged to do in [British] schools. However, children like Selina who have grown up with Chinese and English develop capacities from both writing systems, and can use either to their advantage.

Reference for this reading

Kress, G. (1997) *Before Writing: Rethinking the paths to literacy*, London, Routledge.

READING B: Uncovering the key skills of reading

Roger Beard
(Roger Beard is Reader in Literacy Education at the University of Leeds.)

Source: Beard, R. (2003) 'Uncovering the key skills of reading', *Handbook of Early Childhood Literacy,* London, Sage, pp. 199–208.

[This article] attempts to provide an overview of research that has been undertaken to uncover the key skills of reading. It will outline the debates that have been a feature in this area of literacy studies over many years and examine more recent theoretical stances that have tried to reconcile the earlier debates. ...

It needs to be stressed that the article is focused on the key skills of interpreting and comprehending text in printed or electronic media in written English. Similar discussions that are focused on other languages will raise different issues, particularly if the languages are not alphabetic ones like English. ...

There is a huge literature on this topic and the publications that the [article] focuses upon have been selected either because they have been particularly influential or because they are representative of a certain perspective. ...

The language base of literacy

... Some influential linguists (e.g. Crystal, 1976) have shown how the structure of spoken English can be helpfully represented by three strands: pronunciation (sounds and spellings), grammar (syntax and morphology) and meaning (words and discourse). ...

Analysing the strands of language in this way provides a helpful starting point for attempts to uncover the key skills of reading. Taking the three strands in turn, the letter–sound relationships of unfamiliar words have to be decoded; grammatical sequences have to be followed; words have to be recognized;

and the meaning attributed to them has to be understood. Such an analysis seems to imply that successful reading and writing may involve effective use of information from a range of sources. Descriptions of these sources of information have often fallen into one of two groups, often described as 'bottom-up' or 'top-down'. The two groups approach the language base of literacy from different directions. The former gives emphasis to the code that is used in written language to represent the spoken; the latter emphasizes the meaning that is conveyed by the written language. The distinction is clearly made by Jeanne Chall (1983: pp. 28–9). She explains that 'bottom-up' approaches are those that view the reading process as developing from perception of letters, spelling patterns, and words, to sentence and paragraph meaning. 'Top-down' approaches stress the first importance of language and meaning for reading comprehension and also for word recognition. The reader theoretically samples the text in order to confirm and modify initial hypotheses. Each approach will now be briefly discussed in turn before a third approach is considered, one that deals with the interactive nature of reading skills.

Are the key skills 'bottom-up' ones?

One of the best-known bottom-up models of reading has been outlined by Philip Gough (1972). [For a good summary of the technical detail of this, see David Rumelhart (1985).] ...

Gough ... concedes that identifying letters, 'blank, stark, immovable, without form or comeliness', does not come naturally. He stresses that letter recognition has to be accomplished, 'whether by means of alphabet books, blocks, or soup'. However, the fundamental challenge in learning to read, according to Gough, arises in what is commonly referred to as 'decoding', converting characters into phonemes. After discussing the limitations of teaching approaches that use word recognition ('look-and-say') techniques, Gough argues that children should be helped to map the letter–sound code from the start, while assuring them that the code is solvable. Gough stresses that he does not see phonics as a method of teaching children grapheme–phoneme correspondence rules. The rules that children learn are [simply] heuristics for locating words through auditory means. The lexical representations of those words then provide data for the induction of the real character–phoneme rules. Skill in phonics provides children with a valuable means of data collection about the writing system. According to Gough, the reader appears to go from print to meaning as if by magic. But this is an illusion. The reader really plods through the sentence, letter by letter, word by word. Good readers need not guess what the text conveys; poor readers should not. ...

Some criticisms of bottom-up models

In discussing ... bottom-up models, Rumelhart draws attention to several research findings that are difficult to account for ...

First, the perceptions of letters often depend on the surrounding letters. Ambiguous symbols, such as a poorly written *w*, may be interpreted as an *e* and a *v* as in **event**. The reader is saved from this ambiguity if the symbol appears in a sentence like 'Jack and Jill **went** up the hill'.

Secondly, the perception of words depends on the syntactic environment in which we encounter them. Studies of oral reading errors made by children and adults show that over 90% of reading errors are grammatically consistent with the sentence to the point of error (Weber, 1970). ...

Thirdly, the perception of words depends on the semantic environment in which we encounter them. This environment can be seen at work in our perception of homonyms ('*wind* up the clock' versus 'the *wind* was blowing') and also in resolving ambiguities ('They are eating apples' could mean either 'The children are eating apples' or 'The apples may be eaten'). The importance of semantic context in letter identification was noted as early as 1886 by Catell. He found that skilful readers can perceive whole words as quickly and easily as single letters, and whole phrases as quickly and easily as strings of three or four unrelated letters (cited by Adams, 1990: p. 95).

The authors of the most influential bottom-up theories have in time accepted that their original theories have been overtaken by evidence. [For example,] Gough (1985) accepts that predictable texts facilitate word recognition, although he warns that most words are not predictable and so can only be read bottom-up. He accepts that his model did not pay sufficient heed to the problems of understanding text, but believes that it still points in the right direction. ...

Are the key skills 'top-down' ones?

In contrast with the bottom-up models of reading, one of the best known of the top-down models actually includes the word 'guessing'. According to David Crystal (1976) 'psycholinguistics' is the study of language variation in relation to thinking and to other psychological processes within the individual. Kenneth Goodman (1967), however, has given the term a more radical connotation in literacy research. His 'psycholinguistic guessing game' model of reading assumes a close and direct parallel between the learning of spoken and written language. He asserts that learning to read is as natural as learning to speak. He suggests that the basis of fluent reading is not word recognition but hypothesis forming about 'the meanings that lie ahead'. He argues that reading involves the selection of maximally productive cues to confirm or deny these meanings.

In a later paper, Goodman (1985) stresses the tentative information processing that is involved in reading. He argues that reading is meaning seeking, selective and constructive. Inference and prediction are central. Readers use the least amount of available text information necessary in relation to their existing linguistic and conceptual schemata to get to meaning.

Frank Smith's (1971; 1973) model of reading drew heavily on the seminal work of Noam Chomsky (1957). Chomsky had shown how human language acquisition could not be explained by a linear model. Children did not just learn language by imitation or by connecting together various bits of language (e.g. sounds, words or phrases). Using their inherited capacity for language learning (a kind of 'language acquisition device'), children all over the world seemed to learn to speak by a process of hypothesis testing and discovery, through authentic interaction with others. Smith argued that precisely the same kind of argument may be applied to reading. A child is equipped with every skill that he or she needs in order to read and to learn to read. Given adequate and motivating experience with meaningful text, learning to read should be as natural as learning to talk.

As with Goodman's model, there is a strong emphasis on the 'non-visual' information that the reader brings to the text. Reading comprises a process of 'reducing uncertainty' as hypotheses about the structure and meaning of the text are mediated by sentence, word and letter identification if they are needed. Smith argues that readers normally can and do identify meaning without, or ahead of, the identification of individual words. Smith argues that skilful readers do not attend to individual words of text, that skilful readers do not process individual letters and that spelling–sound translations are irrelevant for readers.

Some criticisms of top-down models

As with the bottom-up theories, there have been recurrent criticisms of the top-down ones. Eleanor Gibson and Harry Levin (1975) point out that Goodman's model of reading does not explain how the reader knows when to confirm guesses and where to look to do so. Philip Gough (1981) has consistently challenged how predictable written language is. His studies suggest that, at most, we can only predict one word in four when all the succeeding text is covered. Furthermore, the words that are easiest to predict are often the words that are most easily recognized. When skilled adult readers read a text with content words missing, prediction rates may fall as low as 10% (Gough, 1983; see also Gough and Wren, 1999). ...

One of the most detailed attacks on Smith's theories was made by Marilyn Jager Adams in 1991. Adams acknowledges that Smith's argument was, in some respects, insightful: he was correct in arguing that skilful reading does not proceed on the basis of identifying one letter or word at a time. But extending the ideas about the language acquisition device, the details of which were only speculative, was, according to Adams, an enormous and gratuitous leap. ... Adams feels that Smith is right in warning against an over-concentration on individual words, but wrong to imply that readers should not process them. Skilful readers have learned to process words and spellings very quickly but such automaticity comes from having read words, not from skipping them.

Adams also considers the assertion that skilful readers don't process individual letters. Adams acknowledges that skilful readers do not look or feel as if they are processing individual letters of text as they read, but research has repeatedly shown that they do (McConkie and Zola, 1981; Rayner and Pollatsek, 1989). Individual letters and spelling patterns are processed interdependently as the text is perceived and comprehended, in a process of 'parallel processing' (McClelland and Rumelhart, 1986; Rumelhart and McClelland, 1986). According to Adams, to deny letter identification in reading is like saying that there is no such thing as a grain of sand. Skilled readers can process letters so quickly because of visual knowledge of words. This knowledge is based on their memories of the sequences of letters, which make up words. The more we read, the more this knowledge is reinforced and enriched. ...

On both sides of the Atlantic, ... there is a clear consensus that the most influential top-down theories have also been overtaken by evidence. In three recent independent reviews of research commissioned by central government bodies in the UK, Roger Beard (1999), Jane Hurry (2000) and Colin Harrison (2002) all reach a similar conclusion. Hurry concludes as follows: 'It is now very clear that Goodman and Smith were wrong in thinking that skilled readers pay so little attention to the details of print. Research on the reading process in the 1980s produced clear evidence that skilled readers attend closely to letters and words and in fact that it is the less skilled readers who rely more heavily on contextual clues to support their reading' (2000: p. 9). ...

Are the key skills interactive ones?

One of the most influential publications in support of an 'interactive-compensatory' model of reading was written by Keith Stanovich (1980). Drawing on over 180 sources, Stanovich argues that fluent reading is an interactive process in which information is used from several knowledge sources simultaneously (letter recognition, letter–sound relationships, vocabulary, knowledge of syntax and meaning). Various component subskills of reading can cooperate in a compensatory manner. For example, higher level processes can compensate for deficiencies in lower level processes: the reader with poor word recognition skills may actually be prone to a greater reliance on contextual factors because these provide additional sources of information.

Indeed, in contrast to the top-down theories, Stanovich shows that good readers do not use context cues more than poor readers do ... [W]hat is at issue here is not the presence of contextual knowledge in good readers, but their use of and reliance upon it in normal reading of continuous text (good readers may be more sensitive to context, and yet less dependent upon it, because information is more easily available to them from other sources). Stanovich draws on dozens of studies to show that fluent readers are distinguished by rapid word recognition and effective comprehension strategies.

In the UK a similarly extensive research review has been brought together by Jane Oakhill and Alan Garnham (1988; see also Oakhill, 1993). Like Stanovich, they question top-down theories in the light of the relative speeds of the processes involved. They show how, in fluent reading, the use of contextual cues to help identify a word is usually unnecessary because words are recognized from visual information so quickly.

Perfetti (1995: p. 108) notes that research findings suggest that the role of contextual cues in word recognition and in comprehension is radically different from that assumed by top-down models: 'the hall-mark of skilled reading is fast *context-free* word identification combined with a rich *context-dependent* text understanding' [author's original italics].

Some criticisms of the interactive model

Perhaps not surprisingly, the main criticisms of the interactive-compensatory model have come from the bottom-up and top-down theorists. Gough, for example, is concerned that:

> It is easy to create a model which is 'right'; all you need do is make one interactive or transactional enough such that everything in reading influences everything else. The result will be 'right' because it will be impervious to disprove; it will yield no falsifiable predictions. ...
> (1985: p. 687)

... Nevertheless, the interactive-compensatory model does seem to be generally accepted by many in literacy education as one of the most valid ways of representing the key skills of reading ... (for discussion of some of the implications for policy and practice, see Perfetti, 1995; Stanovich and Stanovich, 1995; Pressley, 1998; [Stanovich, 2000; Harrison, 2002]). ...

Conclusion

[B]ecoming a successful reader involves the development of key skills and involvement in many social processes. These processes help learners, for example, to understand what reading is for and what it does; to develop a positive attitude towards reading; to link the acts of reading and writing; to have access to a range of rich and interesting texts; and to be essentially concerned with making meaning.

Definitions of literacy are changing as new kinds of communication skill evolve and are better understood. [See, for example, the debates surrounding electronic literacy in Reinking, 1998.] This [article] has shown how the study of reading processes has also evolved, leading to a more informed understanding of what goes on when we interact with written language.

References for this reading

Adams, M.J. (1990) *Beginning to Read: Thinking and Learning about Print*. Cambridge, MA: MIT Press.

Adams, M.J. (1991) 'Why not phonics *and* whole language?', in W. Ellis (ed.), *All Language and the Creation of Literacy*. Baltimore, MD: Orton Dyslexia Society. pp. 40–53.

Beard, R. (1999) *The National Literacy Strategy: Review of Research and other Related Evidence*. London: Department for Education and Employment.

Chall, J. (1983) *Learning to Read: the Great Debate*, updated edn. New York: McGraw-Hill.

Chomsky, N. (1957) *Syntactic Structures*. The Hague: Mouton.

Crystal, D. (1976) *Child Language, Linguistics and Learning*. London: Arnold.

Gibson, E.J. and Levin, H. (1975) *The Psychology of Reading*. Cambridge, MA: MIT Press.

Goodman, K.S. (1970/1967) 'Reading: a psycholinguistic guessing game', *Journal of the Reading Specialist*, 4 (1): 11–30.

Goodman, K.S. (1985) 'Unity in reading', in H. Singer and R. B. Ruddell (eds), *Theoretical Models and Processes of Reading*', 3rd edn. Newark, DE: International Reading Association. pp. 813–40.

Gough, P.B. (1972) 'One second of reading', in J.F. Kavanagh and I.G. Mattingly (eds), *Language by Ear and Eye*. Cambridge, MA: MIT Press. pp. 331–58.

Gough, P.B. (1981) 'A comment on Kenneth Goodman', in M.L. Kamil (ed.), *Directions in Reading: Research and Instruction*. Washington, DC: National Reading Conference. pp. 92–5.

Gough, P.B. (1983) 'Context, form, and interaction', in K. Rayner (ed.), *Eye Movements in Reading*. New York: Academic. pp. 203–11.

Gough, P.B. (1985) 'One second of reading: a postscript', in H. Singer and R.B. Ruddell (eds), *Theoretical Models and Processes of Reading*, 3rd edn. Newark, DE: International Reading Asociation. pp. 687–8.

Gough, P.B. and Wren, S. (1999) 'Constructing meaning: the role of decoding', in J. Oakhill and R. Beard (eds), *Reading Development and the Teaching of Reading: a Psychological Perspective*. Oxford: Blackwell.

Harrison, C. (2002) *The National Strategy for English at Key Stage 3: Roots and Research*. London: Department for Education and Skills.

Hurry, J. (2000) *Intervention Strategies to Support Pupils with Difficulties in Literacy during Key Stage 1: Review of Research*. London: Qualifications and Curriculum Authority.

McClelland, J.L. and Rumelhart, D.E. (eds) (1986) *Parallel Distributed Processing, vol 2: Psychological and Biological Models*. Cambridge, MA: MIT Press.

McConkie, G.W. and Zola, D. (1981) 'Language constraints and the functional stimulus in reading', in A.M. Lesgold and C.A. Perfetti (eds), *Interactive Processes in Reading*. Hillsdale, NJ: Erlbaum. pp. 155–75.

Oakhill, J. (1993) 'Developing skilled reading', in R. Beard (ed.), *Teaching Literacy: Balancing Perspectives*. London: Hodder and Stoughton.

Oakhill, J. and Garnham, A. (1988) *Becoming a Skilled Reader*. Oxford: Blackwell.

Perfetti, C. (1995) 'Cognitive research can inform reading education', *Journal of Research in Reading*, 18 (2): 106–15.

Pressley, M. (1998) *Reading Instruction that Works: the Case for Balanced Teaching*. New York: Guilford.

Rayner, K. and Polatsek, A. (1989) *The Psychology of Reading*. Englewood Cliffs, NJ: Prentice Hall.

Reinking, D. (1998) 'Introduction: synthesizing technological transformations in literacy in a post typographic world' in Reinking, D., Mckenna, M.C., Labbo, L.D. and Keiffer, R.D. (eds) *Handbook of Literacy and Technology*. Mahwah, NJ: Erlbaum. pp. xi–xxx.

Rumelhart, D.E. (1985) 'Towards an interactive model of reading', in H. Singer and R.B. Ruddell (eds), *Theoretical Models and Processes of Reading*, 3rd edn. Newark, DE: International Reading Association. pp. 722–50.

Rumelhart, D.E. and McClelland, J.L. (eds) (1986) *Parallel Distributed Processing. vol 1: Foundations*. Cambridge, MA: MIT Press.

Smith, F. (1971) *Understanding Reading*, 3rd edn (1988), 5th edn (1994). New York: Holt, Rinehart and Winston.

Smith, F. (ed.) (1973) *Psycholinguistics and Reading*. New York: Holt, Rinehart and Winston.

Stanovich, K.E. (1980) 'Towards an interactive-compensatory model of individual differences in the development of reading fluency', *Reading Research Quarterly*. 16: 32–71.

Stanovich K.E. and Stanovich, P.J. (1995) 'How research might inform the debate about early reading acquisition', *Journal of Research in Reading*, 18 (2): 87–105.

Stanovich, K.E. (2000) *Progress in Understanding Reading*. New York: Guildford.

Weber, R.M. (1970) 'First graders' use of grammatical context in reading', in H. Levin and J.G. Williams (eds), *Basic Studies in Reading*. New York: Basic.

English as a classroom language

Neil Mercer, with contributions from Douglas Barnes

4.1 Introduction

The three previous chapters show how learning to speak and write in English is in part a matter of learning to 'get things done' through the language, and also of using language to construct social identities. This chapter is about the use of the English language as a medium for education in school, a setting which can have a powerful influence on the intellectual, social and linguistic development of older children. Most of the chapter is about talk in the classroom, but later I also discuss some aspects of written language. Two related themes are important throughout:

- the role of language in the process of teaching and learning
- the relationship between English and other languages in the classroom.

Entering the world of school education sets children certain kinds of language-learning tasks. Imagine a child, any child, starting the first day at a school in which he or she will be taught in English. There are three kinds of learning task which that child may face and which are crucial to educational progress:

1　Pupils have to learn the special ways of using English that apply in school, because they are unfamiliar with educational conventions and the technical language of curriculum subjects.

2　Pupils may have to learn to speak and write in English if they have grown up speaking some other language, or to use Standard English if they have grown up speaking a 'non-standard' variety of English.

3　Pupils have to learn the ways in which written English differs from spoken English and how written texts are constructed.

In reality, the size of the task facing any particular pupil under each of these headings will vary. For instance, a child may come from a relatively academic household where there is regular conversation around books, but where a language other than English is spoken; conversely, a child may be a native English-speaker, but have had relatively little contact with more formal or academic uses of the language. However, the three-part distinction can be helpful for making sense of reality in all its complexity, and it is under these headings that this chapter is organised.

4.2 Language, teaching and learning

It is impossible to consider how English is used for the purpose of teaching and learning in schools without considering how language in general is used for that purpose. Today, schools in most parts of the world have much in common in the ways that they function, and this commonality is reflected in the language of the classroom.

One of the most obvious functions of spoken language in a classroom is for teachers to direct and control learners' activities: they can tell pupils what they are to do, how they are to do it, when to start and when to stop. Teachers also use talk as a way of providing children with certain kinds of information which it would be hard to provide by any other means. They tell pupils stories, read poetry to them, describe objects, events and processes. They also assess their learning through talk, as discussed below. But before we look at some examples of classroom language, let us look more carefully at what education is meant to be about, and at the role of language in it.

The essence of formal education is that one person, a teacher, helps another person, a learner, to learn to do things which the learner would not easily be able to learn without some help. The prime justification for setting up schools is to enable the process of teaching and learning to be carried out effectively. But formal education also has some specific aims. One is that pupils should acquire knowledge about particular subjects – science, arts, humanities and so on – represented by 'the curriculum'. And another aim, very relevant to our interests here, is that pupils should learn to use spoken and written language in 'educated' ways. What counts as 'educated' language use is something that is defined within particular societies, though there may be many common features across societies. Educated speakers of English are able to use the language in ways defined as appropriate within relevant **discourse communities** (i.e. networks of people with shared interests, purposes and ways of using language) when they explain ideas, describe events or processes, and construct arguments. In other words, they are able to use appropriate **registers** and **genres** of English. (I take up these issues again in Section 4.4 below.)

One way of defining a schoolteacher is: someone who guides their pupils into active participation in educated discourses (Mercer, 1995; 2000; Mercer et al., 2004). The process of teaching and learning depends on the creation of shared experience and joint understanding. This is also very relevant to our interest in English as a classroom language. As a teacher and a class engage, day by day, in various activities and interactions, they are gathering a resource of shared experience which they can use as the basis for further activity. This is where the role of language is crucial. Teachers and learners can talk about what they have done, what they are doing and what they will do next; and as they do so the talk can thread together experiences shared over long periods of time. Each day's talk in a classroom forms part of a 'long conversation' (Maybin, 1994a) that may continue throughout the days, months or even years that teachers and pupils spend together in school. As we discuss below, the talk between teachers and pupils is also usually recognisably 'educational' in its form and content.

Figure 4.1   The joint construction of biological knowledge?

Figure 4.2   The joint construction of technological knowledge?

Educational dialogues

Because the process of classroom education depends so heavily on language, one obvious requirement for the success of that process would seem to be that everyone involved has a good understanding of English or whatever language or languages are used in the classroom. In many parts of the world this requirement is not met, and later in the chapter I consider what happens in such situations. However, there are other, less obvious aspects of language use in the classroom which are important and problematic for the process of education. All children, even those whose first language is English, have to learn certain things about how that language is used in school if they are to participate fully in the educational process.

The following sequence was recorded in a secondary school in England where a class of 14-year-olds were engaged in computer-based communication with children in a nearby primary school. In a 'fantasy adventure' setting, the secondary students (in groups of three) were pretending to be a group of characters stranded in time and space. Using email, they told the younger children of their predicaments and asked for help. The younger children replied, and the older children used these replies when developing the adventure. The sequence is one small part of a much longer session in which the English teacher was questioning the various groups about the most recent communications with the younger children and about their future plans. Anne, Emma and Sharon are the girls in one group.

Sequence 1

TEACHER	What about the word 'dimension', because you were going to include that in your message, weren't you?
ANNE	Yeh. Um, there's going to be – if they go in the right room, then they'll find a letter on the floor and that'll spell 'dimension', but if they use the wrong numbers, then they won't get a letter and they won't get the dimension at the end, so they can't use it for the password.
TEACHER	What happens if they do go into the wrong room?
EMMA	Well, there's nothing there at all, like there's no letter on the bottom of the floor.
TEACHER	Oh God! So they've got to get it right, or that's it! *[Everyone laughs]* The adventurers are stuck there for ever ...
STUDENTS	Yeh.
TEACHER	... and Cath can't get back to her own time. What do you mean the letters are in the room? I don't quite follow that.
EMMA	Like on the floor, like a tile or something ...
TEACHER	Oh I see.
EMMA	... And it'll be like in the floor when they make it.
TEACHER	Why did you choose the word 'dimension'?

STUDENTS	Don't know. *[The three students speak together, looking to each other, seeming uncertain.]*
SHARON	I don't know. It just came up, you know. I just said, you know, 'dimension' and everyone agreed.
TEACHER	Right, because it seemed to fit in with, what, ... the fantasy flavour?
SHARON	Yeh, with what we was doing, yeh.
TEACHER	OK. Now, why do they go through the maze rather than go back? I mean what motivation do they have for going through it in the first place?
SHARON	Um, I think it was the king told them that Joe would either be in the maze or would be at the end of the maze, and they didn't go back because of Joe, I think it was. I'm not, I wasn't quite sure about that.
TEACHER	You've really got to sort that out. That's got to be very, very clear.

(Mercer, 1995, pp. 30–1, corrected version)

ACTIVITY 4.1

Allow about
15 minutes

Read through Sequence 1 again and consider:

- Who asks the questions?
- What would you say was the main function of the questions?
- Can you see any recurring patterns in the ways the teacher and the pupils interact?

Comment

You will have seen that all the questions in Sequence 1 were asked by the teacher. This is commonly the case in classrooms. The function of these questions seems to be for the teacher to learn what the pupils have been doing, and so be able to provide both some evaluation of what they have done and further guidance on what they should do next. You may have noticed a pattern in the talk between the teacher and the pupils which embodies these functions. The teacher uses a question to elicit information from one or more pupils. She then evaluates the reply given. There is a structural pattern to the talk: a teacher's question is followed by a pupil response, followed in turn by some teacher feedback or evaluation.

'IRF' exchanges

The structural element of classroom talk discussed in Activity 4.1 was first described by the British linguists Sinclair and Coulthard (1975) and is usually known as an **Initiation-Response-Feedback (IRF)** exchange. (The same phenomenon was observed in the USA by Mehan (1979), who called it an IRE sequence, where the 'E' stands for Evaluation.) So, for Sequence 1:

TEACHER	OK. Now, why do they go through the maze rather than go back? I mean what motivation do they have for going through it in the first place?	**I**
SHARON	Um, I think it was the king told them that Joe would either be in the maze or would be at the end of the maze, and they didn't go back because of Joe, I think it was. I'm not, I wasn't quite sure about that.	**R**
TEACHER	You've really got to sort that out. That's got to be very, very clear.	**F**

IRF exchanges can be thought of as the archetypal form of interaction between a teacher and a pupil – a basic unit of classroom talk as a continuous stretch of language or 'text'. However, such exchanges do not typify the pattern of talk in all classroom activities; other kinds of talk involving different patterns of exchanges (for example, in which students ask questions of teachers, or of other students) may happen too.

We can also see IRF exchanges occurring as slightly more complex, linked structures. So, in the following example, the teacher obtains three 'responses' to her 'initiation', and her second 'feedback' comment also functions as further 'initiations':

TEACHER	Why did you choose the word 'dimension'?	**I**
STUDENTS	Don't know. *[The three students speak together, looking to each other, seeming uncertain.]*	**R**
SHARON	I don't know. It just came up, you know. I just said, you know, 'dimension' and everyone agreed.	**R**
TEACHER	Right, because it seemed to fit in with, what, ... the fantasy flavour?	**F/I**
SHARON	Yeh, with what we was doing, yeh.	**R**
TEACHER	OK. Now, why do they go through the maze rather than go back?	**F/I**

IRFs of the kind illustrated in Sequence 1 have been observed as a common feature in classrooms the world over and, although the original research which established their existence was carried out in the UK and the USA, there is no reason to believe that they are a feature of classroom life peculiar to those countries, or to classrooms in which English is spoken. Recent classroom research in several countries, including Brazil (e.g. Magalhaes, 1994), Botswana (Arthur, 1992), India (Sahni, 1992; see also Reading A below) and Mexico (Rojas-Drummond and Mercer, 2004), has revealed that similar patterns of classroom talk occur more widely.

Teachers' questions

Teachers have sometimes been criticised by educational researchers for relying so much on questions and IRF exchanges. Thus, educational researcher J.J. Dillon (1988) and psychologist David Wood (1992) have both suggested that teachers' questions tend to suppress pupils' contributions to classroom talk, because they are usually designed just to elicit one brief 'right answer'. I recorded an example of a teacher doing this in a British school. It happened quite close to the beginning of the third of a series of lessons, for the class in question, on the geography of South America.

Sequence 2

TEACHER	Argentina, what is the capital of Argentina?
PUPIL 1	Argentina City. *[Some pupils laugh, others say 'Sir, sir' and raise their hands.]*
TEACHER	*[To a pupil who has hand raised]* Brian?
PUPIL 2	Buenos Aires.
TEACHER	Yes, good. Buenos *[writing on board]* Aires.

In this sequence the teacher asked a 'closed' question – one to which he knew the answer and had told the pupils the answer in a previous lesson – and the pupils responded by trying to provide the 'right answer'. When one pupil failed to provide the only possible right answer, the teacher ignored the wrong answer that had been offered (thus providing 'feedback' of a kind) and went on to accept a second 'bid' for an answer from a second pupil. This particular kind of use of IRF exchanges – a teacher asking questions to which he or she knows the answer – is the most common in classrooms.

One obvious danger of a teacher relying heavily and continuously on such traditional, formal question-and-answer reviews is that students have little opportunity to make coherent, independent sense of what they are being taught. They are unlikely to be able to consolidate their understanding unless they have to recall and apply the relevant knowledge without the teacher's elicitations to prompt them. They also have little opportunity to develop and practise their own ways of using language as a tool for thinking with, by using it to reason, argue and explain.

However, if we look back to Sequence 1 we can see that the teacher there is *not* using IRFs in this way. Instead, she is asking questions to find out things that she does not already know: to find out about what the students have done and why they have done it. Notice the very different nature of the content and function of the teacher's and students' responses in Sequence 1, compared with those in Sequence 2. The first teacher's questions are 'open', in that she does not have only one possible correct answer in mind. She is asking pupils to *describe* clearly what they have done, to *account* for it, and is encouraging them to *review* their actions. She has joined a group of pupils in the middle of a sequence of work which they are carrying out by themselves. She is using her enquiries not only to assess her pupils' learning, but also to *guide* their future activity. Through questions such as *Why did you choose the word 'dimension'?* and *Why do they go through the maze rather than go back?*, the teacher is trying to direct the girls' attention to matters requiring more thought and clarification when they return to their work. In this way, she is not only focusing their attention on how effectively they use the English language to communicate with the young children in the primary school, she is also shaping their own awareness and understanding of what they are doing.

Although there are obvious similarities, then, in the *structure* of the talk in Sequences 1 and 2, if we also consider the *content* of the question-and-answer exchanges in the two sequences, and the *context* of the activities and shared experiences in which this took place, we can see quite different educational processes going on. So, while I have some agreement with the essence of Dillon's and Wood's critical analyses of how teachers use questions, I am suggesting that we must beware of equating **language structures** (e.g. utterances containing the interrogative or imperative form of the verb) with **language functions** (e.g. the acts of asking a question, issuing a command or passing a judgement). Particular language structures – in this case IRF exchanges – can be used for more than one purpose and function according to the context in which they are used.

The use of IRF exchanges depends on teachers and pupils being familiar with the conventions of this kind of question-and-answer routine, and being willing to abide by those conventions. On the basis of research in classrooms in the UK and the USA, one would be likely to conclude that most children rapidly become familiar with the IRF structure of most classroom talk and participate in it fairly readily (Willes, 1983; Edwards, 1992). However, look now at another sequence. It was recorded by Ian Malcolm (1982) in an infant classroom in Western Australia, where the children (aged 5–6 years) were all Aboriginal Australians. They have just heard their teacher tell a story in which a kitten is found by a girl and the teacher is trying to get them to talk about it.

Sequence 3

TEACHER   How do we know she liked the kitten?
          How do we know she liked the kitten?
          [No responses from children]
          No, you think about it, now. She got the kitten, I mean she found
          the kitten ... an' then she said to Mum and Dad she wanted to?

CHILD 1   Keep it.

CHILD 2   Keep it.

TEACHER   Keep it. So if she didn't want the kitten she wouldn't've
          kept it, would she? What d'*you* think, Brenda?

BRENDA   *[Silence]*

TEACHER   Well, you listen carefully.

(adapted from Malcolm, 1982, p. 129)

Malcolm offers this extract as one which typifies many of the interactions
he observed in Aboriginal classrooms. He found that Aboriginal children
usually seemed extremely reluctant to engage in IRF sequences. He comments
that:

> As the children failed to perform their appointed roles in the discourse,
> the teacher engaged in an ongoing process of attempted repair or revision
> of her intended pattern. The result was, at first, an increased number of
> teacher speech acts, and later a premature abandonment of this speech
> event by the teacher for another in which the children were prepared to
> participate more readily.

(Malcolm, 1982, p. 129)

Malcolm suggests that the children's reluctance is not a matter of their lacking
fluency in English. He offers instead a cultural explanation: in Aboriginal
society such overt interrogations and demonstrations of understanding would
not be considered polite. As Malcolm comments: 'the Aboriginal community
favored and fostered reticence in speech, which is the very issue which
underlies much of the communicative difficulty of the Aboriginal classroom'
(Malcolm, 1982, p. 131).

Research elsewhere – for example in Hawaii, and among native Americans in
the USA and Mexico (Philips, 1972; Paradise, 1996) – has also shown that
children from some cultural backgrounds find IRF patterns of question-and-
answer alien and discomforting. That same research shows that teachers
usually try to uphold these conventions even in the face of such reluctance or
incomprehension. It is also often observed that schools normally make little
effort to incorporate or exploit the language practices which children have had
the opportunity to develop in their home communities, whether these be
the storytelling of Irish travellers in Britain, the 'rapping' and 'toasting' of

African-Caribbean teenagers (Edwards and Sienkewicz, 1990) or the imaginative story-poems heard among young children in working-class black American communities (Heath, 1983). Researchers have for some years pointed to the gulf which commonly exists for children between their experience of language in school and out of school, in many parts of the English-speaking world (e.g. Edwards, 1976; Heath, 1983; Wells, 1986). But one should perhaps be cautious in drawing the seemingly obvious conclusion that, if teachers made great efforts to incorporate children's out-of-school informal language practices into the life of the classroom, this would necessarily either be welcomed by the children or be successful as a strategy for teaching the curriculum. One of the vital qualities of children's informal language practices is that they belong to the children and are an integral part of life outside the classroom.

I have briefly considered how the cultural language practices of children's communities may affect their participation in classroom dialogue. Of course, language use in the classroom is shaped by cultural traditions; we have seen that the use of IRF exchanges can be related to an influential tradition of formal education. The influence of that and other traditions in classroom language is well illustrated in Reading A.

ACTIVITY 4.2

Read 'One cup of newspaper and one cup of tea' by G.D. Jayalakshmi (Reading A). The author describes her observational research in English-medium classrooms in an Indian secondary school. After reading the piece, consider the following questions:

- What patterns of language use does Jayalakshmi observe in the Bhojpur classrooms?
- To what cultural, traditional influences does Jayalakshmi attribute the style of teaching in Bhojpur?
- Does classroom communication in Bhojpur have any features in common with those described earlier in this chapter?

Comment

You will see that Jayalakshmi suggests that, in the secondary English-medium classrooms she observed, one can see the continuing influence of the traditional Indian styles of instruction and storytelling – styles which depended upon the performance of an effective storyteller (or guru) and a receptive audience (the students or disciples). These traditional methods have served Indian scholars well for generations and, as Jayalakshmi also points out, they have been combined with British influences to generate a distinct and well-established Indian style of classroom communication. Among other features, this style involves the frequent use of rhetorical questions by the teacher, marked by intonation, pauses or gestures, which the students are not expected to answer. Frequent use of such rhetorical questions may be a distinctive feature of Indian pedagogy: their use has not been reported in classrooms in other English-speaking countries. Likewise, students contribute to the generation of a distinctive style of classroom language use by jointly reciting what they learn in conjunction with their teacher. Until the 1960s this kind of classroom language activity used to be common in most English-speaking countries, though it is not so universal today. However, note that Jayalakshmi also observes the frequent use of question-and-answer sessions at the end of lessons, usually organised in terms of IRF exchanges similar to those described earlier.

English across the school curriculum

I want now to turn to a rather different aspect of the language demands made on children in school. As they go through their years of schooling, pupils encounter an increasing number of specialised technical terms. Learning these can be an important part of education: used effectively, the technical vocabularies of science, mathematics, art or any other subject provide clear and economical ways of describing and discussing complex and abstract issues. A shared understanding of musical terminology, for instance – terms such as *octave*, *bar*, *key* and so on – makes it possible for two people to discuss, in the abstract, phenomena which otherwise would have to be concretely demonstrated. The discourse of educated people talking about their specialism is comprehensible only to the initiated. Becoming familiar with the language of a subject is therefore an important requirement for entering the intellectual communities of science, mathematics, literature or whatever.

In any classroom where English is the medium of instruction, an important part of a teacher's job is to help pupils learn and understand the specialised English of curriculum subjects. The use of technical language in the classroom frequently causes much confusion and misunderstanding. Teachers seem often to assume that the meaning of a word will become obvious to pupils as they hear or read it being used, while children are usually reluctant to ask questions about the meanings of words because to do so would reveal their ignorance. Some technical English words may be used only rarely in the wider world, but they may represent ideas which are not difficult for pupils to grasp because they can easily be explained or exemplified (a good example is *alliteration*). Others may be impossible to explain through a concrete set of instances. This applies to many scientific concepts describing properties of matter (such as *density*) and processes (*evolution*, *photosynthesis*, etc.). A consequence may be that many technical words become for children mere jargon, words which they know they are expected to use but which mean very little to them.

Educational research has provided many bizarre and salutary examples of how technical English terms may be misunderstood and most teachers will have their own collections. Two examples I have recorded are those of a 12-year-old who thought that *quandary* meant a four-sided figure and a 16-year-old who, after saying that he had never understood *subtractions*, later commented that he could do *take-aways*. Robert Hull, a British secondary teacher, has noted these kinds of problems among 14-year-old pupils: '"Animals harbour insects" meant they ate them. "The lowest bridge-town" was a slum on a bridge ... Expressions such as "molten iron", "physical feature", "factor", "western leader" were often insuperable obstacles to comprehension' (Hull, 1985, p. xi).

For children who are learning English as a second or additional language, the vocabulary and style of technical English may pose even greater problems. And if teachers themselves are not confident users of technical English, good explanations may not be available. For example, Cleghorn et al. (1989) found that Kenyan teachers who were teaching science through the medium of English were often unable to explain in English the meanings of terms they were using (such as *parasite*). They comment: 'When teachers have to search for English equivalents of what is familiar but often not conceptually the same in the local language, the actual meaning of what is being taught can be altered' (Cleghorn et al., 1989, p. 21).

ACTIVITY 4.3

Allow about 15 minutes

This activity is in two parts:

1   Think back to your own schooldays. (For the purposes of this exercise, it does not matter whether you were educated in English or another language.) Can you remember any terms which you never felt confident about using correctly, or any that you now know that you misunderstood? Do you recall teachers ever exploring the meanings of words in class, or discussing misunderstandings with pupils?

2   Look at the list of words below. All these words are expected to be learnt and understood by children as part of the National Curriculum for science in British primary schools (i.e. by children aged 5–11 years). Try to explain their meaning, as if to a child (or to another adult).

evaporation	habitat
condensation	food chain
insulator	cycle
conductor	precipitation
translucence	Newton (as a unit)
force	capillary

Comment

I asked three adults to do this activity. One had completed secondary and university education in England, and one had done so in Australia. Both were aged about 45. The third (aged 20) was currently studying science at a British university. All three said that they had no recollection of teachers explicitly discussing the meaning of technical terms, or of misunderstandings about them being publicly aired and resolved in class. The science student had little difficulty in telling me the meaning of the set of technical terms from science, listed above; the other two adults had some trouble with *translucence* and *force*. But all three commented on how rarely they had reason to use many (if any) of those words once they had left school.

The problems associated with learning to use specific forms of subject-related English in writing are discussed in more detail later in the chapter.

Pupils without a teacher

In several English-speaking countries, it has become increasingly common to set up activities in which pupils work and talk together without the continual presence of a teacher. There is no doubt that organising students to work on their own in groups or pairs generates quite different patterns of talk from those which typify teacher–pupil interactions (Norman, 1992; Mercer, 1995; Barnes and Todd, 1995).

Sequence 4 is an extract from a discussion by a group of 9-year-old children recorded in an English primary school, on the topic of how they speak in and out of school. The children in this group came from homes in which a variety of languages were spoken, including various Indian languages and US (rather than British) English. Their discussion was set up by their teacher, who provided the children with a set of cards that have questions about language use. We pick up the sequence shortly after one of the children has read out a question from a card: 'Do you change the way you talk depending on where you are?' The children's names are Ghazanfar (G), Abraham (A), Surjit (S) and Melissa (M).

Sequence 4

G   At home I, uh, at home I talk, I talk Gujerati and in school and playground with my best friends Urdu.

A   I change the way in school and in the playground.

S   Me too.

M   In the class you know you talk quieter and everything.

A   Yes.

M   At play you can shout your head off so you can get ... all the energy and that.

G   I can't, people look at me ... *[Laughter]*

A   *[Reading from the card]* If so how do you change the way you talk?

S   I don't know.

A   Well I change the way I talk by being quieter.

M   If so how do you change the way you talk.

A   I change the way at school.

S   I speak politely at school.

A   At home I'm a right chatterbox.

S   Yes.

G   Yes, me too I keep talking ...

S   When I'm angry with my parents I don't speak really politely.

M   When I'm at home talking with my mum ...

A   Yeah.

M   I talk American because I'm used to it. When I'm around American people.

A   *[Inaudible]*

G   What?

A   I thought English was the same as American.

M   It's not.

S   It's not because in American our chips, they call chips French fries ... and ...

M   Biscuits ...

S   And they call crisps chips ...

M   ... and they call biscuits cookies and we call trousers pants ...

G   What do you call pants, trousers? *[Giggles]*

S   And they call petrol ... gas.

G   Why do you call petrol gas?

A   Oh God ...

M   It's just our language Ghazanfar.

S   It's just changed a bit.

(The Open University, 1991, p. C19, corrected version)

ACTIVITY 4.4

Allow about
15 minutes

Having looked at Sequence 4, try to specify any ways in which the talk here is different from the examples of teacher-led talk we looked at earlier in the chapter.

Comment

Even though the children are responding here to questions set them by their teacher, you will no doubt have seen that the nature of their talk is quite different from that of the class discussions led by a teacher. Many of them make quite extended contributions. They expand on each other's comments. They are willing to express uncertainty to each other and to offer each other explanations (as in the later part of the discussion, about US English). In this sequence, talk is being used to share knowledge and construct joint understandings in ways that reflect the fact that the participants all have similar status in the discussion, as learners who can contribute from the wealth of their individual experiences.

Collaborative learning of this kind makes considerable demands upon the students' ability to use language as a way of thinking together. The thinking and the talking in these circumstances become inseparable: language is being used, in an educationally appropriate way, as a *social mode of thinking* (Mercer, 1995). The students have to talk about the task and to collaborate successfully, for they can no longer rely on the teacher to define a line of thought and guide them along it. But even when talking and working without a teacher, students are expected to use language in ways that are educationally appropriate. That is, when a teacher asks pupils to 'discuss' a topic, the teacher is usually expecting something quite specific of them – to provide explicit descriptions, formulate reasons and explanations, and agree on possible solutions to problems. One important part of becoming educated in and through the medium of English is learning how to generate such appropriate 'educated' styles of English discourse, and such discourse depends on more than just the appropriate use of technical terms.

4.3 English-medium education in bilingual and multilingual settings

In this section I consider the use of spoken English in classrooms where the main language of pupils is not English. There are two principal sorts of situation. The first occurs in countries where there is English-medium education, even though the first language of most of the children is not English. The second is where pupils whose first language is not English enter schools in a predominantly English-speaking country. I provide examples from both of these types of situation.

In any situation where English is used as a classroom language but is not the main language of children's home or community, teachers may have the multiple task of teaching:

- the English language
- the educational ground rules for using it in the classrooms
- any specific subject content.

Jo Arthur (1992) has carried out observational research on teaching and learning in primary school classrooms in Botswana. As in the Indian secondary school studied by Jayalakshmi (see Reading A), English was used as the medium of education, but it was not the main language of the pupils' local community. Arthur observed that when teachers were teaching mathematics, they commonly used question-and-answer sessions as opportunities for schooling children in the use of appropriate 'classroom English' as well as maths. For example, one primary teacher commonly insisted that pupils reply to questions 'in full sentences', as shown below.

Sequence 5

TEACHER	how many parts are left here? [first pupil's name]
FIRST PUPIL	seven parts
TEACHER	answer fully. how many parts are there?
PUPIL	there are … there are seven parts
TEACHER	how many parts are left? sit down my boy. you have tried. yes. [second pupil's name]
SECOND PUPIL	we left with seven parts
TEACHER	we are left with seven parts. say that [second pupil's name]
SECOND PUPIL	we are left with seven parts
TEACHER	good boy. we are left with seven parts

(Arthur, 1992, pp. 6–7)

You can see that this sequence is made up of a linked series of IRF/IRE exchanges. For example:

how many parts are left here?	**I**
seven parts	**R**
answer fully	**F/E**

The pupils therefore needed to understand that their teacher was using these exchanges not only to evaluate their mathematical understanding, but also to test their fluency in spoken English and their ability to conform to a 'ground rule' that she enforced in her classroom – 'answer in full sentences'. Arthur comments that, for pupils in this kind of situation, the demands of classroom communication are complicated because their teacher is attempting to get them to focus on both the medium (English) and the message (maths). Arthur says that such dual focus is common in Botswana classrooms, as the following sequence from another lesson shows.

Sequence 6

TEACHER	in which continent is your country? in which continent is your country? give an answer
FIRST PUPIL	in Africa is my country
TEACHER	he says in Africa is my country. who could frame her [*sic*] sentence? in Africa is my country
SECOND PUPIL	Africa is my continent
TEACHER	my question was. in which continent is your country?
THIRD PUPIL	its continent is in Africa
TEACHER	it is in the continent of Africa. Everybody
ALL PUPILS	it is in the continent of Africa

(Arthur, 1992, p. 13)

Figure 4.3 English in a bilingual setting

Bilingual codeswitching in the classroom

In circumstances where English is being used as a classroom language but where the pupils' first language is not English, a teacher may **codeswitch** to the first language if problems of comprehension arise. (For a fuller treatment of codeswitching, see Chapter 2.)

Sometimes the first language may be used only for asides, for control purposes or to make personal comments. However, when codeswitching amounts to the teacher translating the curriculum content being taught, its use as an explanatory teaching strategy is somewhat controversial. On the one hand, there are those who argue that it is a sensible, common-sense response by a teacher to the specific kind of teaching and learning situation. Thus, in studying its use in English-medium classrooms in China, Lin (1988) explains a teacher's use of translation as follows: 'The teacher was anxious that her students might not understand the point clearly; she therefore sought to ensure thorough comprehension through presenting the message again in Cantonese which is the students' dominant language' (Lin, 1988, p. 78).

It seems, however, that teachers often use codeswitching in more complex ways than simply translating content directly into another language. On observing classrooms in Hong Kong, Johnson and Lee (1987) noticed that the switching strategy most commonly employed by teachers had a three-part structure, as follows:

1   'key statement' of topic in English

2   expansion, clarification or explanation in Cantonese

3   restatement in English.

Johnson and Lee found that teachers commonly did not provide simple translations of the initial English statement, but rather gave some information in Cantonese which would help pupils to make more sense of the statement when it was restated in stage 3. The implication here is that such teachers are pursuing the familiar task of guiding pupils' understanding of curriculum content through language, but using special bilingual techniques to do so.

An interesting study of codeswitching in bilingual classrooms in Malta was carried out by Antoinette Camilleri (1994). She showed that codeswitching was used as a teaching technique in a variety of ways. Look, for example, at these two extracts from the talk of a teacher in a secondary school lesson about the production and use of wool, based on a textbook written in English. The teacher begins by reading part of the text. (A translation of talk in Maltese is given in the right-hand column.)

Sequence 7

England Australia New Zealand and Argentina are the best producers of wool *dawk l-aktar li ghandhom* farms *li jrabbu n-naghag ghas-suf* O.K. England *tghiduli minn licma post* England *ghandhom* Scotland *maghrufin tant ghall*-wool *u gersijict taghhom* O.K.

they have the largest number of farms and the largest number of sheep for wool O.K. England where in England we really mean Scotland they are very well-known for their woollen products

(adapted from Camilleri, 1994)

Sequence 8

wool *issa* it does not crease but it has to be washed with care *issa din importanti ma ghidtilkomx illi jekk ikolli nara xaghra jew sufa wahda* under the microscope *ghandha qisha hafna scales tal. huta issa jekk ma nahslux sewwa dawk l-iscales jitghaqqdu ġo xulxin uindahhal ġersi daqshekk ġol*-washing machine *u nohorgu daqshekk ghax jixxrinkjali u jitghaqqad kollu*

now this is important didn't I tell you that if I had a look at a single hair or fibre

it has many scales which if not washed properly get entangled and I put a jersey this size into the washing machine and it comes out this size because it shrinks and gets entangled

(adapted from Camilleri, 1994)

Camilleri notes that the first extract shows the teacher using the switch from English to Maltese to amplify the point being made, rather than simply repeating it in translation. In the second extract, she explains the English statement in Maltese, again avoiding direct translation. Camilleri comments that the lesson is therefore a particular kind of literacy event, in which there are two parallel discourses – the written one in English, the spoken one in Maltese.

Studies of codeswitching in classrooms have revealed a variety of patterns of bilingual use (Martin-Jones, 1995). For example, Zentella (1981, pp. 109–31) observed and recorded events in two bilingual classes in New York schools, one first-grade class (in which the children were about 6 years old) and the other sixth-grade (in which the average age would be about 12). The pupils and teachers were all native Spanish speakers, of Puerto Rican origin, but the official medium for classroom education was English. One of the focuses of Zentella's analysis of teacher–pupil interactions was IRF sequences. Both

Spanish and English were actually used by teachers and pupils in the classes, and Zentella was able to show that there were three recurring patterns of language switching in IRF sequences, which seemed to represent the use of certain 'ground rules' governing language choice. These are summarised in Table 4.1.

Table 4.1

	Rules governing language choice	Teacher initiation	Student reply	Teacher feedback
1	Teacher and student: 'follow the leader'	English Spanish	English Spanish	English Spanish
2	Teacher: 'follow the child'	English Spanish	Spanish English	Spanish English
3	Teacher: 'include the child's choice and yours'	English Spanish	Spanish English	both languages both languages

(adapted from Zentella, 1981, p. 119)

We can see that distinctive patterns of language use emerge in bilingual classrooms, overlaying the familiar patterns of teacher-led IRF exchanges. The extent to which features such as codeswitching between English and other languages occur in any particular classroom will depend on a whole range of factors including:

- the degree of fluency in English that members of a particular class have achieved
- the bilingual competence of teachers
- the specific teaching goals of teachers
- the attitudes of both children and teachers to the other languages involved.

Language policy and practice

The behaviour of teachers and pupils regarding the use of English and other languages in class is likely to reflect official educational policy on language use in school. Educational policy on the use of other languages in English-medium classrooms has always varied from country to country. Policy and practice in schools are often influenced by ideas about the supposed cognitive and social effects on children of growing up bilingual.

Policies are also liable to change. The enforcement of a strict policy of prohibiting the use of a mother tongue in school was well documented in nineteenth-century Wales, where any children heard speaking Welsh on the school premises were reprimanded and made to wear round their necks a rope called the 'Welsh knot' to show they were in disgrace. By the late 1980s, however, both Welsh and English had become officially recognised as classroom languages in Wales. Some countries, such as Canada and various states in India, have longstanding policies of recognising English alongside other languages in schools. In the USA, there have recently been strong 'English first' campaigns to establish English constitutionally as the only official language for use in schools and public life, and equally strong opposition from speakers of other languages, particularly Spanish. This brings us to a related issue: the choice of English, as opposed to other languages, as a classroom language.

The choice of English as a classroom language

You might not be surprised that English should be the choice of classroom language in situations where it is the sole official language of a country or state, or where it is spoken by the vast majority of people. Yet English has been chosen as the medium of education in many countries where those conditions do not apply. One example is India where, as described in Reading A, many pupils receive their education in English even though it is not their first language. In officially bilingual countries such as Canada, choices have to be made at the level of state and city about whether French or English (the two official national languages) should be used as the main language in class. In such countries, educational policy may be framed to allow parents some degree of choice of classroom language for their children. Thus in Wales, the balance of Welsh- and English-medium schools is officially monitored and is supposed to be adjusted to suit demand.

Sometimes there is no real 'choice' about whether or not to use English or another language as a medium for education, because English is already the dominant language in a community. If a policy choice does have to be made about whether English or a community language should be used as the classroom medium in a country's schools, the decision may be a matter of political controversy. In many parts of the world, however, there has been a growing sense of local ownership of world languages, such as English, so that they are not seen as representing specific sets of values. (These issues are explored further in Chapters 5–7.)

Standard English as a classroom language

So far in this section we have been considering the situation of pupils whose first language is not English. But what of the many – perhaps the majority of – children who speak another *dialect* of English outside school? It is a fairly common expectation that pupils should use Standard English vocabulary and grammar for the formal business of the classroom – that is, when replying to teachers' questions, or making oral reports or formal presentations to an audience. In public examinations, marks may be lost if pupils express themselves in regional 'non-standard' varieties. As the great majority even of native speakers of English use regional varieties of English – which are by definition non-standard – in their out-of-school lives, this kind of learning is faced by the majority of pupils entering English-medium classrooms.

An insistence on the use of the official, standard variety of English in the schools of an English-speaking country may seem unsurprising, easy to justify and, at first consideration, uncontroversial. But this may become a heated and complex political issue, as has certainly been the case for many years in the UK. The more vociferous advocates of a policy which insists on the use of Standard English as a classroom language in the UK have sometimes argued that the issue is not simply one of a choice between which variety or dialect of English is most appropriately used in the classroom, but one of maintaining standards of *correctness* of English in school. People on the other side of this debate may adopt a variety of positions, but most share a concern about the effects that an official devaluation of the regional Englishes of local communities may have on the self-esteem of pupils who are members of those communities. Related to policy and practice about the use of Standard English as a classroom language is the issue of whether or not pupils should be expressly taught *about* Standard English and other varieties as part of the school curriculum. (These issues are more fully explored in the next chapter.)

4.4 From talking to writing in English: discourses and genres

Figure 4.4   Learning to use English in 'educated ways'

So far, I have concentrated on the use of spoken English as a medium for classroom education, and given little attention to writing. Just as one of the tasks facing all pupils being educated in English is that of learning certain educational **ground rules** or conventions for using spoken English in the classroom, educational success also depends on pupils learning to use the conventions which are used by educated writers.

An important task for students learning to use English in 'educated' ways is that of understanding and using the distinctive register of written English (Halliday, 1985). As Maybin (1994b) explains, 'Written genres tend to be more condensed and abstract, frequently involving the use of nominal forms, for example "the *failure* of the crusades", "the *precipitation* of the solid", "the *betrayal* of Macbeth"' (Maybin, 1994b, p. 156).

They also need to recognise and use the genres typically associated with different areas of the curriculum. For example, they have to appreciate that bubbles in water will be described very differently in a poem and in a report of a scientific experiment.

> Our culture also requires that pupils learn to use genres which are differently structured depending on the purposes and audiences for their writing. For example, they need to be able to reproduce procedures, descriptions, reports, explanations, arguments and various kinds of narratives. These all have distinctive overall structures (for instance, a simple narrative structure involves an initial orientation, a complication, a resolution and a coda), and particular kinds of grammatical uses and vocabulary.
>
> (Maybin, 1994b, p. 192)

However, research has shown that these 'ground rules' are rarely taught explicitly by teachers. Instead, students are expected to infer them from what the teacher says and does, and from whatever feedback the teacher provides on the students' work (Sheeran and Barnes, 1991).

Two approaches to the teaching of school-based writing that have been influential in recent decades have been characterised as 'process writing' and the 'genre approach'. **Process writing**, developed in the USA and Australia, concentrated on the processes engaged in by students as writers in order to produce their written work. Graves (1983) suggested that the student should go through distinct stages of drafting, conferencing, revising and editing before publishing to the class or a wider audience, for example in a class magazine. The student retains ownership of the writing, by choosing the topic and developing a personal voice. The teacher's role is that of a supportive adviser, checking progress through 'conferences' with the student on aspects of the writing. This method has led to criticisms that students often restrict themselves to a limited range of topics and social attitudes, and do not receive clear guidance on the styles and structures expected in different areas of writing and regarded as appropriate to different academic subjects.

A group of Australian language researchers (Halliday and Martin, 1993; Martin et al., 1987) devised an alternative approach to the study and teaching of writing in the classroom, based on the work of linguist Michael Halliday and now generally known as the **genre approach**. One of the aims of this approach has been to focus the attention of teachers and students on how written texts in English are expected to vary according to their nature and function. Maybin (1994b) explains:

> The genre approach developed from the work of Michael Halliday and draws heavily on his theory of functional linguistics. Halliday argues that we have developed very specific ways of using language in relation to how certain things are accomplished within our culture, and that different contexts and language purposes are associated with different registers, or genres of language. Genres encode knowledge and relationships in particular ways through the use of different language structures. Learning about a particular subject discipline, therefore, involves also learning about specific ways of using language. We expect pupils to write in a number of different specific ways in school, and we assess them according to how well they manage to reproduce these different genres ... Proponents of the genre approach argue that making the genres explicit and showing how to write them will enable pupils to understand more fully how knowledge is constructed in different academic disciplines. It will also empower pupils to deal with the various written genres used in the adult world.
>
> (Maybin, 1994b, p. 186)

The founders of the genre approach argued that earlier influential approaches to teaching writing tended to leave the 'ground rules' of writing implicit, and so unclear to students. Denying pupils access to the genre, they argued, means denying access to the subject.

The strength of the genre approach is that it offers teachers and students an analysis of how English or any other language is used in specific social contexts, and attempts to make explicit the 'ground rules' for producing socially appropriate ways of writing. The essence of most criticisms of the genre approach is that:

- It tends to encourage the teaching of narrowly defined models for specific kinds of texts, when 'educated' writing involves the development of a much more flexible and creative ability.
- It tends to support an uncritical view of how established, powerful groups in a society use English (or any other language).
- Learning 'powerful' ways of using a language does not necessarily gain the user access to power.

The usual classroom practice today is to draw from both approaches, rather than adopting one to the exclusion of the other, as both can be helpful in developing students' written skills.

When we look at the use of English in different countries and cultures, it also becomes apparent that genres may vary among countries or cultures. That is, the conventional expectations among teachers about what a 'story' or a 'scientific report' is differ in, say, India, Australia and the UK. When children enter an English-medium classroom, having grown up speaking another language and having had their education in a country with very different cultural traditions, it may be difficult for both teachers and children to distinguish between the first two 'learning tasks', namely acquiring a basic fluency in English and learning the conventions of particular genres of English which are used in school. This variation can become a problem for pupils who move from one country to another, and it can be difficult for a teacher to tell whether a new pupil who appears to be having difficulties with the language demands of education is struggling with general aspects of using English, or is having difficulties with grasping the 'local' ground rules for using language in the classroom.

This kind of difficulty arises in relation to written as well as spoken English, and is effectively illustrated by the research of Alex Moore (1995), who studied the progress of children of migrant families, with English as an additional language, entering secondary schools in the UK. Moore observed teaching and learning over several months in several classes in two schools. One of his case studies concerns the progress of Mashud, a boy of fifteen from the Sylheti region of Bangladesh, who had been in the UK for a year since leaving his native country (where he had been educated in Bengali). Moore focuses on Mashud's classroom education in writing English. Mashud had quite a few problems with 'surface features' of English such as handwriting, spelling and grammatical structures, but was an enthusiastic writer. However, both Moore and Mashud's teacher (Ms Montgomery) noticed that:

> his work had a particular idiosyncrasy in that whenever he was set creative writing – or even discursive writing – assignments, he produced heavily formulaic fairy-story-style moral tales which were apparently – according to information volunteered by other Sylheti pupils in the class – translations of stories he had learned in his native tongue.

> (Moore, 1995, p. 362)

Despite being a willing pupil, Mashud seemed unable to transcend this traditional style of genre and write in the genres that his teachers knew would be required of him in the British education system and in wider society. Further consideration led Moore and Ms Montgomery to some hypotheses about why this was so:

> It has to be said that neither Ms Montgomery nor I knew enough about Bangladeshi or Sylheti story-telling traditions to be able to expound with any degree of confidence on the cause of Mashud's particular way of going about things. The key to our future pedagogy, however, ... lay in Ms Montgomery's very wise recognition that 'there *could be* the most enormous gap between what Mashud has been brought up to value in narratives and what we're telling him he should be valuing'.

> (Moore, 1995, pp. 365–6)

This insight into Mashud's difficulties with genres of writing was supported by a more careful analysis of his texts, which had a linear, additive, chronological structure, associated with oral rather than literate cultural traditions (Ong, 1982). This led to Moore and the teacher designing activities for Mashud: 'If we responded appropriately, Mashud would, we hoped, learn something of what was valued in expressive writing in his new school, and how that was different from – though no better than – what he may have learned to value at school in Bangladesh' (Moore, 1995, p. 368).

This approach apparently proved successful, as during the remaining period of Moore's research Mashud showed clear progress in coming to understand and cope with the demands of writing in the genres of English required in the British school system.

4.5 Conclusion

Classrooms generate some typical patterns of language use, patterns which reflect the nature of teaching and learning as a social, communicative process which takes place in the distinctive institutional settings of school. I have described some common features of classroom language, such as the IRF exchanges which take place between teachers and pupils. These common features reflect, at least to some extent, the common functions of schools the world over. I have argued, however, that we must be careful not to assume that particular language structures can be used for only one communicative, or educational, purpose.

According to their out-of-school experience, pupils may find the genres or discourses of a classroom more or less intelligible and/or acceptable. But I have argued that every pupil who is being educated in English is expected to learn to use English in special ways, which means following the ground rules of language use in the classroom, taking up the specialised vocabularies of curriculum subjects and becoming able to present ideas within the constraints of the accepted genres or discourses of spoken and written language.

Where teachers and pupils are using English as a second or additional language, other distinctive patterns of language use in the classroom also emerge. Teachers and pupils may 'codeswitch' between languages in class, and the content of the talk may reveal teachers' concern with the learning of English as well as the learning of the curriculum subject being taught through English. When considering bilingual and multilingual settings, I have also suggested that it is often hard to separate the language demands that classroom education makes on pupils from its cultural demands.

All the indications are that the worldwide use of English as a classroom language is likely to increase during the twenty-first century. Given the key role that language plays in the process of classroom education, it is likely that policy decisions regarding the choice of English or another language as the medium of education will continue to be controversial.

READING A: One cup of newspaper and one cup of tea

G.D. Jayalakshmi
(Jayalakhshmi is a freelance film maker.)

Specially commissioned for Mercer and Barnes (1996, pp. 142–8). (Revised by the book editors.)

In 1987, I spent two months observing the way English is taught to 16-year-old students in Central School, Bhojpur, in the state of Bihar in India. Although education in India is mainly a state responsibility (India is a union of twenty-four states), the central government in Delhi runs a number of schools throughout the country called Kendriya Vidyalaya or Central Schools. These schools are primarily meant for the children of employees who work in transferable central government jobs, and so the curriculum in all Central Schools is the same. Because central government employees come from different parts of the country, the children in these schools, and indeed in any one class, speak different languages at home, and almost none of them has English as a mother tongue. However, English was the medium of instruction for the pupils I was observing and most of them had studied it for ten years.

The most striking aspect of these lessons was the fundamental similarity, despite superficial differences, in the teaching styles of Dr Keval and his colleague, Mr Sridhar. It could be described as a hybrid of traditional Indian teaching styles and a nineteenth-century Victorian British style transported to India with the introduction of English as a medium of instruction (Jayalakshmi, 1993, Chapter 8).

The classroom arrangement

The teacher stood in front of the classroom with the students sitting in rows on either side. In India today, as in Britain a generation or two ago, this is the normal arrangement of classrooms. It serves to give the teacher a dominant role and it sets up what Adams and Biddle (1970) call a 'central communication system', where there is basically a single speaker (the teacher most of the time) and everybody else listens.

To an Indian, the roots of such an arrangement lie at least as strongly in two Indian traditions – Harikatha and Gurukula – as they do in Western systems of education. In a Harikatha (literally, 'the tale of the gods'), the storyteller either stands or sits in front of an audience which is seated on either side, with a central aisle separating the men from the women, much as in the school. This arrangement is eminently suitable for the transmission of legends and stories – the storyteller's central position ensures that the audience can see clearly and its attention is unwaveringly held by the performance of the storytelling.

Such an arrangement, and indeed an attitude of reverence towards the storyteller or teacher because they are seen as knowledgeable, can also be traced back to the Indian system of teaching known as Gurukula. Drawings and etchings which have survived from as early as 5000 BC show the 'guru' or teacher sitting on a raised platform under a tree with his students sitting in rows in front of him, acknowledging his authority and the learning under his tutelage. The Gurukula system, too, depended on an oral transmission mode where the teacher explicated texts to his students and these were then learnt by rote. Although the students in Bhojpur did not have to memorise their lessons, the education system seems to be similar – it implicitly recognises the teachers' superior knowledge and points to their importance, centrality and authority. The teacher is seen as a repository of knowledge, whose task is to transmit this to less knowledgeable students.

The structure of the lessons

The lessons I observed in Bhojpur all took the form of the reading and explication of chapters from a textbook, and followed the same pattern whether the subject matter was a poem, a short story or an informative piece of non-fiction. The data in the analysis that follows come from lessons conducted by Dr Keval on a chapter about Paul Julius Reuter, the founder of Reuters News Agency.

The lessons consisted of the teacher introducing an idea, reading a paragraph, explaining it and then moving on to the next paragraph until the whole text had been covered. Sometimes the teacher asked questions at the end of his explanations before he went on to read the next paragraph. This seems to have been in order to check students' understanding of his teaching. For the same reason, there was almost always a question–answer session when the entire chapter had been completed, before the teacher moved on to the next chapter.

The storyteller in the Harikatha tradition appears to follow an almost exactly similar pattern, lacking only those genuine questions that require an answer from the listeners. During Harikathas the storyteller recites a passage from a holy text, explicates it, and then moves on to the next passage until the entire tale is told. The teacher's talk in the classroom was similar to this ritualised form of storytelling, not only in having a similar pattern but also because this pattern was rigid and highly predictable. As in any ritual, it exists irrespective of the individual presiding priest: all players in the ritual know what is expected of them and perform accordingly. So, on occasions when Mr Sridhar took over from Dr Keval, there was no ambiguity in the situation. The students and Mr Sridhar knew exactly how to behave and the class was undisturbed by a change of teacher. In Western schools, by contrast, when one teacher takes over from another, for however short a time, the class has to make many more adjustments to the different ways of working introduced by the new teacher.

How do people know whether the Harikatha storyteller is good or not? Similarly, how do students rate the performance of the teacher? It seems to me that the criteria for both these 'performances' are similar. In Harikathas, after the basic text is recited, the storyteller draws upon his own experiences to embellish his tale, often departing completely from the text in order to recount other tales more immediately relevant to modern times. Finally, the storyteller returns to the text to recite the next few lines. A good storyteller is one who shows off his knowledge and wisdom as he explicates the text. It is the ability to move from the specific to the general and return to the specific that is much admired.

Similarly, in Bhojpur my interviews with students suggest that a teacher is judged according to his performance when he explains a paragraph. If he can use the paragraph as a springboard to elaborate his thoughts (even if there is only a tenuous link with what he has just read), then he is considered to be a good teacher. Within this framework, the task of the teacher is to bring his own personal understanding and wisdom to his explanations. This is what gives the class an individuality and flavour and makes one teacher's class better than another's. In this context the students found Dr Keval lively and entertaining and hence a better teacher than Mr Sridhar, whom they considered boring and pedestrian.

Teaching style

The following extract shows one complete flight of fancy by Dr Keval, from the point of take-off from the chapter to the point of landing again. Here, he is elaborating on the statement that Reuter found book-selling a boring profession and sought excitement by turning to the idea of developing a news service. (Note that a question mark in parenthesis indicates that the previous words are spoken with a rising intonation and are followed by a slight pause. A comma also indicates a slight pause.)

DR KEVAL	A book-seller is here and, a circus lady is there. A girl or a boy working in circus. Who is having excitement in his profession?
DR KEVAL AND STUDENTS	A circus girl.
DR KEVAL	[Continues] Or a circus boy. Once I was watching, just a, circus. And I simultaneously started making a poem. Because I was seeing (?) an exciting profession. In book-selling there is no excitement, OK? Just reading and taking books. There is no excitement. There is no excitement in taking a food which is without salt. But there is excitement in

taking what (?) chicken. Well spiced, nicely spiced. Understand? So, people should have excitement in their profession. There are people who wish, who desire, who crave for excitement in their profession. And this very excitement is what (?) a life force, force of life, that, and that is an energy, a wonderful energy that scientists may well research about. So, Reuter didn't find excitement in book-selling. *[Reads]* And he sold off his book-selling ...

(Lesson 1, 6 July 1987)

Like the Harikatha storyteller, Dr Keval takes examples of everyday life – watching a circus, eating chicken – to convey a sense of what excitement might mean. His use of near-synonyms (such as *There are people who wish, who desire, who crave for excitement*) also serves to build his image as a knowledgeable person. The ability to use several slightly different terms to convey the same sense has always been considered a mark of wisdom in India.

Another important respect in which Dr Keval impresses his erudition upon his students is in his use of Sanskrit proverbs which few, if any, of the students will understand. Sanskrit is a classical language and is no longer spoken; nevertheless, it is used to express 'great truths'. This is because it is the language of religion (Hinduism) and the language in which wisdom has been passed down through the ages. Dr Keval uses Sanskrit in his lessons for two reasons – first, to impress pupils with his wisdom; and second, because he believes that his function is to instruct students not just in language but also, more generally, in life. For example, when he explains the way in which John Griffiths helped Reuter secure his first client, he explains that Griffiths is clever because of the company he keeps.

DR KEVAL   सत्संगे गुणा दोषाः।

('Good company produces bad qualities.') [*sic*]

You might have come across this very saying in Sanskrit.

सत्संगे गुणा दोषाः।

[He repeats the saying.]

There I mean, we cultivate qualities by virtue of what (?) company. If we are in good company, we'll cultivate good things, good habits. If we are in bad company we'll be cultivating bad habits. So this will be our attempt to be in good company. Always have control over yourself. Try your best always for keeping good company.

(Lesson 1, 6 July 1987)

This is a particularly illuminating example, because Dr Keval's quote in Sanskrit is actually wrong. He undoubtedly meant to say:

('Good company never produces bad qualities.')

Dr Keval may in reality not understand Sanskrit much more than the students do. He may have learnt the adage by rote, and now recalls it imperfectly. Nevertheless, he uses the misquotation to advantage, as the students appear impressed by his erudition.

In a subsequent interview, Dr Keval explained to me that he explicitly sees his job in the English classroom not just as teaching the language, but also as inculcating moral and ethical values in his students. In this, he seems to be heir to two of the traditions mentioned earlier. First, there is the Harikatha tradition, with declamation in an ethical vein, exhorting listeners to be morally and spiritually upright, much like Dr Keval's lectures. Second, and working concurrently with the first tradition, is the British tradition of teaching English. Dr Keval would have had no difficulty in transferring these Harikatha ideas and values to the English lessons because the inculcation of morality has been a central part of English teaching in India since it first began in the nineteenth century. ... It is therefore not surprising that the teaching of English carries some of that burden even today.

Given the almost absolute authority of the teacher in the class, he cannot be seen to be either wrong or ignorant. How do the teachers in Bhojpur actually convey the sense of authority to their students, and maintain their control over the class? And how do they organise the pacing of their lessons and the dissemination of knowledge? One technique that I observed both teachers employing was the use of rhetorical questions. Often they set up questions and, in answering them, provided explanations:

DR KEVAL   As a cup of tea is essential, more than that is (?) a newspaper. Why? That is hot enough. Your father is very much curious, very serious, very serious for reading the newspaper. What for? Have you asked your father? Your father will tell you the importance of news service. This news service is very important for persons who are interested in political events. The news service is very important for business people who are interested in business news.

(Lesson 1, 6 July 1987)

In the above example, in the first sentence, Dr Keval uses a rising intonation with a short pause as a rhetorical device to provide information. He also uses straightforward rhetorical questions, such as, *Why?*, *What for?*, *Have you asked your father?*, to explain that newspapers carry the latest news from several different fields and would be of interest to a very diverse audience.

A problem with such rhetorical questions is that the same format is used to check students' understanding, or at least attention, as in the following example a little later:

DR KEVAL	Your father, and after a few years, you yourself, would like two cups hot. One cup of newspaper and one cup of (?)
DR KEVAL AND STUDENTS TOGETHER	Tea.

(Lesson 2, 6 July 1987)

The question then is: how do students know when to answer a question and when to keep quiet, allowing the teacher to provide an explanation? On looking at the transcript as a whole, one's first impression is that students do not answer or interrupt the teacher when he is in the middle of an explanation, but as his explanations draw to a close the students respond to the teacher's questions, indicating to him that they have understood what he has to say. How do students in the classroom know that the teacher is in the midst of an explanation rather than coming to the end of it? I would suggest that they do not so much *know* that the explanation is complete or incomplete as help to *make* it complete or incomplete. What seems to happen is that, by keeping quiet, they force the teacher to go on and continue explaining until they feel satisfied. They show their understanding and satisfaction finally by responding positively to the question that the teacher puts to them or by completing a sentence along with him. The status of an explanation as complete or incomplete, then, is not something that exists independently of the students' perceptions of it; it is created by negotiation and shared understanding between the teacher and the pupils about what sort of explanation is satisfactory and what is not. Of course, if the teacher feels that he is in the midst of an explanation, he has the option of simply ignoring students' responses to his rhetorical questions. Thus, although the use of questions and how they are answered is negotiated between the teacher and students, more power lies with the teacher. The students do have some power, however, in that if they do not reply to the questions the teacher puts to them, he is forced to continue explaining till they have understood what he has to say.

Student participation

By answering the teacher's questions simultaneously with him, students demonstrate that they have entered the same frame of reference as the teacher. In so doing, they provide him with verbal clues that indicate they have been paying attention and have understood his explanations. Their choral responses are again not unlike the responses of the Harikatha listeners. In Harikathas too, the audience participates either by repeating the last words of the storyteller before the storyteller moves on to the next section, or more formally, by chanting God's name (Hare Rama or Hare Krishna) at the end of an explanation. Along with the Harikatha tradition is the tradition of choral chants used in catechism, in Sunday schools and in primary schools all over India. This chanting itself has its roots in the introduction of Western education, where typically children were made to chant 'Our Father which art in Heaven' and 'God Save the King' in school assembly every morning. It seems to me that the choral response in Bhojpur is a vestige of this strong acculturation which takes place when students are very young.

Within such a formal context, the students do not seem to have freedom to initiate talk that may lead to interesting discussions. Almost all the student-initiated talk consisted of requests for the meaning of words and generally followed the pattern *Sir, what is the meaning of ...*, asked either in English or in Hindi. Maybe the students know this is the only sort of question that will elicit a response from the teacher. Besides, such questions sit comfortably in a transmission mode of teaching where the purpose is to impart information.

Thus, it appears that given the highly structured and controlled nature of classroom discourse, there is almost no opportunity for students to speak. The only way they can talk is by whispering asides to each other. This, however, is not part of the official discourse and is much frowned upon. It may be that both the students and teachers in Bhojpur realise that there is not much sense in the classroom practices as they stand, but compulsively abide by institutional norms for their own sake, thereby turning classroom procedures into a ritual.

References for this reading

Adams, R. and Biddle, B. (1970) *Realities of Teaching: Explorations with Video Tape,* New York, Holt, Rinehart & Winston.

Jayalakshmi, G.D. (1993) 'Video in the English curriculum of an Indian secondary school', PhD thesis, Milton Keynes, The Open University.

English in the curriculum

Frank Monaghan, with contributions from Barbara Mayor

5.1 Introduction

Why should English be taught in schools to children who already speak English? What is it for? What should children study in English lessons? These may seem surprising questions, but the subject has only been widely taught – even in UK schools – since the late nineteenth century, and ever since those comparatively recent beginnings the teaching of English has been a controversial subject, both within education and in the wider world. The roots of these debates are gnarled and far-reaching.

This chapter identifies major trends in the subject's history in the UK and other parts of the English-speaking world. I will describe some key policy initiatives, pedagogical approaches and methods of assessment that have impacted on English teaching for much of the past century. We will look at a particular example of an 'official' English curriculum, the National Curriculum for English in England and Wales (DFEWO, 1995; QCA, 2006) and at similar examples from other parts of the English-speaking world. The chapter also addresses issues such as standards, definitions of literacy and the place of spoken English in the curriculum, and will identify some possible future trends in the subject.

ACTIVITY 5.1

Allow about 20 minutes

Let us begin with your experiences of English as a school subject. (This activity assumes you studied English at school but, if this is not the case, note down your experiences of studying another language.)

Make a list of the sorts of activities you did. What kinds of writing did you do? Did you read non-fiction as well as fiction? Did you learn poems by heart? What kind of speaking was involved? Were you taught listening skills? What do you think was the purpose of what you learnt and how have you used the knowledge and skills you developed? If you can, compare your experiences with those of one or two people older and younger than yourself.

Comment

Did you find your own experiences differed from those of the other people you consulted or were they broadly similar? When thinking about the sorts of things you learnt, did you find that they have proved useful or irrelevant? Did your work in English emphasise creativity and personal development, or did it emphasise learning rules and 'standards'? Any differences you noted will probably be reflected in the rest of this chapter and should help you make sense of those differences as well as the chapter itself.

5.2 The scope of the English curriculum

Mass education in the UK began with *The Elementary Education Act* of 1870, which provided basic education for children up to the age of ten, and this provision was made compulsory in 1880. English gradually became established as a school subject but it was initially limited in scope to a very basic form of literacy. Dobson provides a rather dismal picture of the teaching of reading and writing that children experienced at the time:

> Children at school in mid-Victorian times were usually taught the letters of the alphabet first, then two-letter words, and went on successively to five- and six- letter words. Some never got past the first stage. ... children were prepared for the HMI's [school inspector's] examination in reading by concentrating on a single book. Some teachers got their pupils to learn it by heart, and occasionally an HMI found a pupil reciting a passage for him with the book held upside down. Inspectors retaliated by requiring pupils to read from the text backwards.
>
> (Dobson, 1984, pp. 43–4)

The twentieth century saw English become fully established in UK schools and its scope expanded far beyond a concern with 'the basics' to include a focus on literature, spoken English, and the personal growth of students. This widening of the English curriculum has led to intense debate about the relative importance of the various components and these controversies have been reflected in both government policy and classroom practice.

Approaches to the teaching of literacy

In the UK during the eighteenth century, as far back as the Industrial Revolution, there were those who saw literacy for the masses as at best a necessary evil to ensure a moderately literate workforce, and at worst – with a nervous glance to the still recent French Revolution and American Declaration of Independence – as a threat to the established social order. Others – with an envious eye on those same events – saw mass literacy as a means of bringing about a new social order based on freedom and equality. This tension between a utilitarian and a libertarian notion of literacy is still current and continues to shape the debate about the purpose of English throughout the English-speaking world.

ACTIVITY 5.2

Allow about
10 minutes

Before reading further, pause to consider how you would define literacy. What is it that pupils need to be able to do to count as literate? Should the English curriculum be about more than 'just' literacy?

In the Middle Ages, to be literate meant simply to know Latin. In the eighteenth century it was often interpreted as being able to read but not necessarily write, as this was considered an unsuitable skill for the mass of people. Today, many people would expect literacy education to include reading not just books and other print media but also electronic text, which is organised in different and possibly more demanding ways due to its use of hyperlinks, allowing the reader to jump between pages and websites at the click of a mouse. Others see a crucial literacy demand in the computer age to be multimodality – the combined use of words and images and perhaps sound in a single text – and argue that we should be teaching children to 'read' visual and oral as well as written texts. The word literacy is thus used to describe very different sets of practices, from 'basic' skills in reading and writing to '**multiple literacies**' – a diverse range of competences, including text literacy, media literacy, information literacy, computer literacy, visual literacy, multicultural literacy, emotional literacy and more. This is not to suggest that these are all discrete forms; there is obviously enormous overlap among them.

We also need to consider not just the mechanics but the social context in which literacy is practised. Brian Street, one of the key figures in the study of 'new literacies', argues that we need to see language and literacy not just as skills that can be acquired but as complex and constantly shifting practices that are deeply embedded in diverse social contexts. For example, the literacy that occurs in religious settings is not the same as that of a supermarket or a university. Street argues (1997, p. 47) that this requires those who design the curriculum, teach it and evaluate it to take account of 'the variation in meanings and uses that students bring from their home backgrounds to formal learning contexts'.

Australia's language and literacy policy (DEET, 1991; see also Australian Education Council, 1994) provides a broad definition of literacy:

> Literacy is the ability to read and use written information and to write appropriately, in a range of contexts. It is used to develop knowledge and understanding, to achieve personal growth and to function effectively in our society. Literacy also includes the recognition of numbers and basic mathematical signs and symbols within text.

> Literacy involves the integration of speaking, listening, and critical thinking with reading and writing. Effective literacy is intrinsically purposeful,

flexible and dynamic and continues to develop throughout an individual's lifetime.

(DEET, 1991, p. 9)

Luke and Freebody (1999) have developed what they term the 'Four Resources Model' which describes what a literate person needs to be able to do:

- *Break the code of texts* [from spelling conventions to text structures]
- *Participate in the meanings of text* [recognising their social origins]
- *Use texts functionally* [recognising the roles they perform]
- *Critically analyse and transform texts* [recognising that they are never neutral and influence how people view the world]

(Luke and Freebody, 1999)

As you read this chapter, you will recognise the roots of these literacy 'resources' and see how some have been more emphasised than others at various times and places. You will also recognise them in the discussion of models of English that now follows.

Models of English as a school subject

The diagram below is adapted from work done by sociologist Stephen Ball and colleagues (Ball et al., 1990, p. 76):

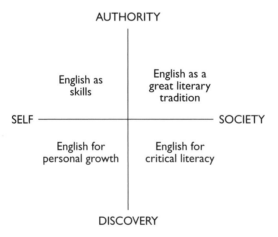

Figure 5.1 Models of English

The vertical axis shows the sources of power, whether *top-down* from AUTHORITY (a coercive power relation exerted through 'official' direction and prescription) or *bottom-up* from DISCOVERY (a democratic power relation developed through individuals' active participation). The horizontal axis shows the relationship between SELF (individual needs) and SOCIETY (collective needs or practices).

English as skills is assigned to the top left quadrant because it represents a model of English in which the prime aim is to equip individuals for their future roles (e.g. as citizens or employees), and this need is imposed by the state through an official curriculum. The emphasis has traditionally been on standards and correctness.

English as a great literary tradition is assigned to the top right quadrant because it represents a model in which an elite imposes a canon of great literature. The emphasis is on exposing students to culturally significant texts that embody society's highest values.

English for personal growth is assigned to the bottom left quadrant because it emphasises personal growth, brought about through individual creativity. The emphasis is on providing students with experiences that relate to them and help develop their own values.

English for critical literacy is assigned to the bottom right quadrant because it represents a model of English in which the socially constructed nature of the subject is revealed through engaging in debate about texts. The emphasis is on exposing the ideological values that reside in all texts, so that they can be critiqued and challenged.

This model is an abstraction and is presented here only to help you think about the subject in a structured way as you work through this chapter. It is highly unlikely that you would be able to walk into a real classroom in a real school and identify the practice you see there using just one of the four labels above; most classrooms would probably reflect all four aspects in differing admixtures. There is evidence (e.g. Cox, 1995; Goodwyn and Findlay, 1999; Marshall, 2000) that most English teachers tend towards a blend of the 'literary tradition' and 'personal growth' models. The 'skills' model may also be becoming increasingly important since the introduction of official frameworks for the teaching of English in the UK, along with assessment systems that carry high teacher accountability. 'Critical literacy' in its pure form is a rare sight in schools but its proponents have raised awareness that all texts reflect and embody social values. You will recognise echoes of the four headings from Ball et al.'s model throughout the rest of the chapter.

5.3 Official policies and assessment practices

English for social cohesion

One of the first UK government reports on the teaching of English, the Newbolt Report (HMSO, 1921), identified its role as providing: 'first, systematic training in the sounded speech of standard English, to secure correct pronunciation and clear articulation: second, systematic training in the use of standard English, to secure clearness and correctness both in oral expression and in writing: third, training in reading' (HMSO, 1921, section 13, p. 19).

This concern with 'the sounded speech of standard English' has echoed down the years and been of enormous significance. It was the belief of the Newbolt Report's authors that if everyone were to use Standard English it would unify the nation and help heal the social divisions that emerged in the First World War, and so avoid the unrest that had led to revolution in Russia. This is an interesting example of how the English curriculum has been seen as a potential solution to social problems. Although recognising the 'intimate associations' of non-standard varieties of English, the Newbolt Report saw it as the duty of teachers 'to fight against the powerful influence of evil habits of speech contracted in home and street ... because inability to speak standard English is in practice a serious handicap' (HMSO, 1921, sections 60 and 69, pp. 59 and 67). The moral and medical metaphors used here have resurfaced at various points, as Standard English has become confused with other types of standards, as in the words of Norman Tebbit, a UK Conservative Government minister in the 1980s, who said in a BBC radio interview:

> ... if you allow standards to slip to the stage where good English is no better than bad English, where people can turn up filthy and nobody takes any notice of them at school – just as well as turning up clean – all those things tend to cause people to have no standards at all, and once you lose your standards then there's no imperative to stay out of crime.

> (quoted in Marshall, 1997, p. 111)

In 2002 the UK Labour Government's then Home Secretary David Blunkett introduced plans requiring migrants seeking permanent residence in the UK to pass an English language test. In an article entitled 'Integration with diversity', he argued for the development of a shared, community-based identity, as opposed to either assimilation to a monoculture or a form of multiculturalism that privileges difference over cohesion. He urged newly settled Britons to speak English at home with their children as 'it helps overcome the schizophrenia that bedevils generational relationships' (Blunkett, 2004, p. 7). (Note the echoes of the medical metaphor we saw in the Newbolt Report.) Blunkett's comments sparked a controversy, with accusations of racism, showing how the role of language in social cohesion is as sensitive an issue today in terms of ethnicity as it was previously in terms of social class.

Official curriculum statements are about more than just graded statements on reading, writing, speaking and listening. They also tend to contain broad statements of purpose that tell us something about how the subject is viewed at the official level. In Victoria, Australia, for example, there is an explicit requirement that at least one of the texts studied by students must be written by an Australian or set in Australia. Again, we see the linking of the English curriculum with questions of national identity.

In the UK the National Curriculum applies only to England and Wales. Wales has separate arrangements for its Welsh-medium schools (in which English is introduced at a later stage). There is also a requirement, akin to that in Victoria, for a 'Welsh dimension' in the English curriculum, with students required to study 'works by Welsh authors writing in English and those works that have a Welsh setting or a special relevance to Wales' (ACCAC, 2000).

In Scotland, schools work to the '5–14 Guidelines' produced by working parties of professionals closely linked to schools. The guidelines for English in Scotland have many similarities with those of England but there is also a greater acknowledgement of the cultural and linguistic diversity in the country, which recognises that many students are bilingual and growing up in a world marked by increasing diversity and interdependence.

In the Northern Ireland Curriculum (introduced in 1989 and last revised in 1996) there is a commitment from primary level to a programme on mutual understanding and cultural heritage that develops both self-respect and respect for others as a means of improving relations between people with different cultural traditions: 'It involves helping pupils to appreciate the shared and distinct characteristics of cultural traditions within Northern Ireland and further afield, to respect and value other cultures and to appreciate the interdependence of people within society' (CCEA, 2004, p. 5).

In Australia a similar broader dimension is emphasised. For example, the State of Victoria combined curriculum statement for English/English as a Second Language (ESL) begins:

> Effective participation in Australian society depends on an ability to understand the various uses of the English language and to employ them effectively for a range of purposes ...

> Students have different social and cultural backgrounds. This study is designed to recognise and value this diversity and to foster self-esteem in all students by enabling them to use the English language confidently.

> (Victorian CAA, 1999, p.7)

It is interesting to note how present the notion of 'society' is in the curriculum for English, in a way that is less evident in other subjects. It can also be seen in the emphasis placed on the role of English in terms of employability prospects after leaving school. Similar sentiments are to be found in the forewords and content of the other curriculum frameworks discussed above, despite their geographical separation and cultural differences.

Standards of literacy

The teaching of reading has a long and controversial history. In terms of the English curriculum it is sufficient to say that the debate largely falls along a particular fault line – how to reconcile a conception of reading as a *bottom-up* process, involving the learning of discrete skills (such as sound–letter correspondences) with a view of it as a *top-down* process, involving the whole person, drawing on their knowledge of the world and texts to predict and check meaning as they read. (For a fuller discussion, see Chapter 3, Reading B.)

Concerns about UK reading standards in the mid 1970s underpinned the setting up of a Committee of Inquiry which led to the Bullock Report of 1975. The report took the view that it was impossible to judge whether literacy standards had fallen or risen since the Second World War because the pre-war tests had not been standardised and so no meaningful comparison could be made. The authors also took the view that, 'there is no one method, medium, approach, device, or philosophy that holds the key to the process of learning to read' (HMSO, 1975, p. xxxii). This flexible approach was reflected in the practice of teachers who generally used a blend of methods to teach their students.

The arrival of a new UK Labour Government saw the introduction in 1998 of the *National Literacy Strategy* (see Ofsted, 2003), which sought to impose a highly prescriptive model of literacy instruction on primary school teachers. This involved the introduction of a daily 'Literacy Hour' in which teachers were advised on how many minutes they should be spending on particular types of activity (see Figure 5.2). There was even some discussion as to whether the subject should change its name from 'English' to 'Literacy'.

This was followed by the *Framework for Teaching English: Years 7, 8 and 9* (DfES, 2001), an equally detailed document that set out a lengthy list of objectives and identified a default teaching approach that was reinforced through training and inspection. Andrew Goodwyn (2003), in a paper entitled 'We teach English not Literacy', reports on his survey of senior English teachers and their responses to the introduction of the Framework in which he found that teachers objected to the way the Strategy forced them to focus on extracts from texts rather than whole books. He describes their fear that, in losing sight of the integrity of the text, students would not be able to make a 'whole' response to it. This serves to undermine one of the central aims of English, as seen by the teachers in his study, which is to enable students to develop a deep and personal relationship with books. These teachers drew a distinction between *literacy* as an educational entitlement and social good and *Literacy* as a reductive practice that damaged the 'proper' relationship between reader and text.

Nonetheless, there can be no doubt that the UK government largely succeeded in imposing its model on teachers, and national test results showed continued improvements in the scores of 7-, 11- and 14-year-olds (Ofsted, 2005). However, a study by Hilton (2001) argues that the tests for 11-year-olds

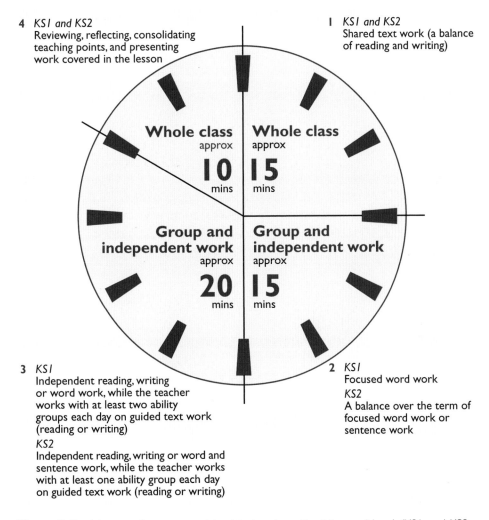

4 *KS1 and KS2*
Reviewing, reflecting, consolidating teaching points, and presenting work covered in the lesson

1 *KS1 and KS2*
Shared text work (a balance of reading and writing)

Whole class
approx
10
mins

Whole class
approx
15
mins

Group and independent work
approx
20
mins

Group and independent work
approx
15
mins

3 *KS1*
Independent reading, writing or word work, while the teacher works with at least two ability groups each day on guided text work (reading or writing)
KS2
Independent reading, writing or word and sentence work, while the teacher works with at least one ability group each day on guided text work (reading or writing)

2 *KS1*
Focused word work
KS2
A balance over the term of focused word work or sentence work

Figure 5.2 How teachers were advised to break up the 'Literacy Hour'. (KS1 and KS2 refer to the Key Stages in the curriculum: KS1 covers the years up to age 7 and KS2 the years up to age 11.)

got easier due to an increase in the number of literal information-retrieval questions and a decrease in the number of questions requiring higher-order inferential reading skills. It has also been argued (e.g. Hunter-Grundin, 1997) that the government relies too heavily on its own test results to support its claim that literacy standards are rising. The argument is that teachers 'teach to the test', focusing their work narrowly on those aspects of English that will be tested and so the results give only a partial impression of students' abilities.

The complexity of the situation is reflected in two studies published in 2003. The *Progress in International Reading and Literacy Study* (PIRLS) is a survey of children's reading taken in thirty-five countries every five years. The 2001 survey (Mullis et al., 2003) showed that students in England compared very well to other countries, being placed third and well ahead of the other

English-speaking countries (New Zealand, Scotland, the USA). However, a follow-up survey conducted by the National Foundation for Educational Research (NFER) showed that children's enjoyment of reading books in England has been in decline since 1998, with the percentage of 11-year-olds who said they liked to read stories falling from 71 per cent to 65 per cent. When analysed by gender, the statistics are even more striking: the figure for girls dropped from 85 per cent to 75 per cent and for boys from 70 per cent to 55 per cent (Twist et al., 2003). The contradictions in the statistics may reflect the ongoing tensions between views of literacy as a means and as an end in itself.

Much of the impetus behind official 'literacy' initiatives comes from the desire of governments to use education as a means of meeting perceived needs of employers for an increasingly literate workforce. The boxed extract, 'Is this OK 4 U?', from the UK newspaper *The Guardian* is typical of many similar stories that have appeared over the decades in English-speaking countries.

Is this OK 4 U?

When Education Secretary Ruth Kelly declared in the Commons recently that she wanted every young person to have a sound grounding in English and Maths after leaving school or college, it seemed her words were aimed at calming disquieting grumbles in the world of business. It was unacceptable, she said, that a large proportion of pupils were weak in the basics of reading, writing and arithmetic. To reverse the trend, pupils would have to pass functional tests in both literacy and numeracy, such as writing a letter or working out family budgets.

Kelly's suggestions appeared to answer the calls of organisations such as the Confederation of British Industry (CBI), which maintains that 50% of employers are unhappy with their employees' basic literacy and numeracy skills ...'.

(Craik, 2005)

This is often presented in the media and by politicians as indicating a decline in standards of literacy skills. There is a continuing debate as to whether standards have actually declined, risen or remained stubbornly unaltered over decades, but what have undeniably changed are the literacy demands that exist in society. It follows that literacy standards will never be 'satisfactory' because once schools meet a current definition of literacy there will be developments outside school that necessitate new skills being added to the repertoire.

The teaching and assessment of writing

Figure 5.3 Writing in school

Since the late 1980s, the English curriculum in UK schools has moved towards a more language-oriented curriculum, reflected in the fact that it is now possible for students to take separate Advanced Level English examinations (usually at age 18) in Language and in Literature. There have been separate examinations in English language and literature at the General Certificate of Secondary Education level (usually taken at age 16) throughout, but at the classroom level they have typically been taught together with the literature at the core of the curriculum and providing the basis for the language teaching. Now this balance has shifted with a requirement for students to recognise and reproduce a wide range of text types, as the extract, 'Writing to inform, explain or describe' (see Figure 5.4), from a specimen examination paper shows (AQA, 2004).

The extract, 'Communication and Organisation' (Figure 5.5), is from the mark scheme for Question 5, 'Describe a place that is special to you', indicating the criteria for the student to receive a Grade C, which is regarded as a reasonable pass (being the fourth highest of 9 grades).

Question 5 appears to seek a very personal response ('describe a place that is *special* to you') but the assessment criteria are largely applicable to more impersonal texts and require the student to produce particular features and effects such as latinate words and parallel constructions in order to gain particular grades. Critics might argue that English is being reduced to the mere reproduction of a set of predetermined features at the expense of genuine self-expression.

There are at least two compelling reasons why English has to be assessed using standard criteria. The first is that the test is testing what the students have been taught, and so it is fair to mark the work accordingly. Second, even

WRITING TO INFORM, EXPLAIN OR DESCRIBE

Answer **one** question from this Section.

You are advised to spend about 45 minutes on this Section.

Remember:

- spend 5 minutes planning and sequencing your material
- try to write at least one side in your answer book
- spend 5 minutes checking:
  - your paragraphing
  - your punctuation
  - your spelling.

EITHER

3 Write an **information** leaflet on an area you know well. You could include information on places to visit and things to do there. ...

(27 marks)

OR

4 Write a letter applying for a part-time job you would like. **Explain** why you would like the job and why you are the right person for it. ...

(27 marks)

OR

5 **Describe** a place that is special to you. ...

(27 marks)

OR

6 **Describe** a person who is important in your life and explain his or her importance to you. ...

(27 marks)

Figure 5.4 Extract from a specimen examination paper for GCSE English Specification A (AQA, 2004, p. 3)

Communication and Organisation	
Skills descriptors	**Content descriptors**
• clear identification with purpose and audience; begins to sustain reader's response	• more evidence of selection of detail for interest and sequencing of description
	• description likely to cover a range of aspects e.g. atmosphere
	• paragraphs are competently linked by content and language
	• control of parallel structure, shaping, links, modifiers will be competent where used
• evidence of structure with usually coherent paragraphs and clear selection of vocabulary for effect	• discursive markers are becoming more integrated and are used to enhance the organisation of the description
	• generally effectively chosen words

Sentence Structures, Punctuation and Spelling	
Skills descriptors	**Content descriptors**
• uses sentence forms for effect	• constructions linked securely to discourse markers; may use parallel constructions, syntactical lists, adjectives, adverbs, minor sentences, for effect
• generally secure in spelling	• generally secure spelling of irregular, latinate, complex words
• generally secure in punctuation which clarifies meaning and purpose	• generally accurate in sentence demarcation, use of commas, question marks etc.

Figure 5.5 Extract from a mark scheme for GCSE English Specification A (AQA, 2006, p. 19)

test items that seem to ask for a personal response must have particular criteria against which they are assessed, otherwise the students would be subject to the whim of individual markers and it would be impossible to compare and order the performance of candidates, which is one of the key purposes of testing.

ACTIVITY 5.3

Allow about
15 minutes

Now look at the writing task below taken from the California High School Exit Examination (CAHSEE) practice test of 2005. How does it compare with the previous UK test paper in terms of the way the question is put and the level of difficulty?

Writing Task

Some students at your school expressed an interest in making the school more attractive by getting rid of the trash on the school grounds.

Write a persuasive essay for your school paper in which you convince the readers of the importance of getting rid of the trash and making the school more attractive. Convince your readers through the use of specific reasons and examples.

Checklist for your writing

The following checklist will help you to do your best work. Make sure you:

- Read the description of the task carefully.
- Organize your writing with a strong introduction, body and conclusion.
- State your position, support it with specific examples, and address the reader's concerns.
- Use words that are appropriate for your audience and purpose.
- Vary your sentences to make your writing interesting to read.
- Check for mistakes in grammar, spelling, punctuation, capitalization, and sentence formation.

(CAHSEE, 2005, p. 117)

Comment

You probably found the tasks almost interchangeable. (Other questions require students to compose a variety of text types, just as in the previous example). Not surprisingly, an examination of the curriculum framework for California also reveals large areas of overlap with that for England and Wales.

In Australia, as in the USA, each of the states and territories has control over its own curriculum, although there have been moves towards harmonising these to some extent through the publication of national documents such as *A Statement on English for Australian Schools* (Australian Education Council, 1994) and an agreement in 1997 to allow national testing at particular points. Here again, the international similarities are striking. For example, the combined curriculum statement for English/ESL at school-leaving level from the State of Victoria Curriculum and Assessment Authority includes the notes quoted here on 'The craft of writing' (see box).

The craft of writing

This area of study focuses on the achievement of competence and confidence in writing for different purposes and audiences and in a variety of forms.

The area of study will include:
- the likely expectations of particular audiences;
- features of texts intended to influence or persuade specific intended audiences;
- effective techniques for engaging readers and maximising the effect of selected information;
- characteristics of sound argument, logical sequencing of information, and appropriate ways of presenting supporting evidence;
- features of mature writing, such as the use of symbolism and extended metaphors;
- the tools of punctuation, syntactic structures, spelling, word choice and paragraphing and other organising structures to meet the demands of complex and abstract subject matter;
- technical and general vocabulary appropriate to selected information and contexts;
- techniques of editing and revision to establish and strengthen a personal voice.

(Victorian CAA, 1999, pp. 28–9)

On the one hand, the similarities among these documents may not be surprising, as all three are dealing with the same language, English, and so it might be expected that they would have broadly similar ideas on what constitutes effective writing. On the other hand, it might also suggest a 'globalisation' of the English curriculum akin to the homogenisation in the commercial world. Just as high streets and shopping centres in the developed world all look remarkably similar, so too do their curriculum and examination systems.

ACTIVITY 5.4

Now read 'Conceptions of English in New Zealand and Australia' by Urszula Clark (Reading A).

As you read, make a note of:
1 any specific factors that needed to be addressed in the New Zealand or Australian contexts
2 elements of the New Zealand and Australian curricula that are common to other English curricula you have examined.

Comment

1   You probably noted the recognition of the Maori language and culture in New Zealand, and the need to address the social disadvantage of the Aboriginal and migrant populations in Australia.

2   You may have noted some or all of the following: the definition of a national variety of English for social cohesion; respect for cultural diversity; language for personal development and self-expression; critical literacy; oracy; and teaching *about* language (often referred to as **metalinguistic knowledge**).

5.4 English as a 'civilising agent'

The great literary tradition

Figure 5.6   Developing a taste for literature?

How does this heavy emphasis on skills relate to the teaching of literature? In the Newbolt Report of 1921, the teaching of English literature was held to be central to education as it embodied the best thoughts of the best minds. The authors believed in the healing power of literature and asserted the need for every individual to experience its curative qualities: 'we claim that no personality can be complete, can see life steadily and see it whole, without that unifying influence, that purifying of the emotions, which art and literature can alone bestow. ... the bulk of our people, of whatever class, are unconsciously living starved existences' (HMSO, 1921, section 237, p. 257).

This belief in literature as a civilising agent arguably has its roots in the work of Romantic poets such as Shelley, who in his essay *A Defence of Poetry* argued that: 'The great instrument of moral good is the imagination .... Poetry enlarges the circumference of the imagination by replenishing it with thought of ever new delight ... Poetry strengthens the faculty which is the organ of the moral nature of man, in the same manner as exercise strengthens a limb' (Shelley, 2006 [1821]).

This view was most notably endorsed in the nineteenth century by educational reformers such as Matthew Arnold, himself an acclaimed poet, and in the twentieth century by the critic and Cambridge academic F.R. Leavis. It suggests a belief in the mission of English as a subject to transform children's lives by exposing them to works of art that will inculcate high moral values and an aesthetic sensibility in order to protect them from the deadening force of the mass culture of the industrial age. In an influential series of essays entitled *Education & the University*, written in the heat of the Second World War (and first published in 1943), Leavis describes the social and cultural disintegration that he sees all around him, leaving society at the mercy of propagandists. He sets out his belief in the redemptive powers of education in general and literature in particular:

> I am concerned in these pages with liberal education at the university level ... representing a wisdom older than modern civilisation and having an authority that should check and control the blind drive onward of material and mechanical development, with its human consequences ... [W]hatever else may be necessary, there must in any case be, to meet the present crisis of civilisation, a liberal education that doesn't start with a doctrinal frame, and is not directed at inculcating one ... [W]e have a reason for making a scheme of liberal education centre in the study of English literature.

> (Leavis, 1948, pp. 16, 20, 17)

Leavis believed that only a small, cultured minority were equipped to fully understand literature and that it was their role to uphold the moral and cultural values embodied in the very best of it, known as the **literary canon**. In the view of his followers, in schools English was the only subject that could develop truly cultured citizens. George Phelps, for example, argued that English should replace Classics (i.e. the study of Latin and Greek language and culture) as the key subject around which all other studies should be built:

> By the continual training in taste and imaginative insight [through the study of English] ... the pupil is trained to grapple intelligently and imaginatively with contemporary problems ... And this training may well fulfil the part played by the Classics in the Middle Ages, restoring a measure of cultural unity and retrieving for the English-speaking peoples that 'unified sensibility' which has been dissipated among the distractions of the Machine Age.

> (Phelps, 1949, p. 162)

Phelps here is describing the sort of curriculum that only an elite of school students might enjoy. The Leavisite approach as a whole was widely criticised on these grounds.

> Leavisite élitism ruled out of discussion whole areas of popular culture and radical art. It has been criticised for elevating writing produced by and about a particular Anglo-Saxon class and gender, so that the 'universal meanings' it embodies are only universal for those who define the world from that perspective. ... Critics have complained that people from cultures outside Britain are represented in the Leavisite canonical texts (if at all) as alien and inferior, women are represented as the objects of male desire and defined in their relation to men, and the working classes are depicted as pitiful or quaint. The existence of this canon as a whole may be experienced as a form of oppression, and a denial of everyday personal experience.
>
> (Maybin, 2000, pp. 186–7)

However, Leavisites also believed in the moral power of English for the less academically gifted. G.B. Talbot (1940, p. 82), for example, made a case for the importance of English in the technical school, arguing that 'the "good workman" must be the "good man"', with English playing an essential role in his development. While the English curriculum Talbot describes for such students might appear somewhat utilitarian – focusing, for example, on descriptions of 'a refrigerating machine' or 'The Making of a Small Yacht' (p. 83) – he also puts forward a case for what would later be described as 'language across the curriculum': the development of English through other subjects.

English for personal growth

By the time of the Newsom Report (HMSO, 1963) on the education of pupils aged 13–16 of average or less than average ability, spoken English was regarded as essential: 'Inability to speak fluently is a worse handicap than inability to read or write. ... Any definition of literacy for [pupils] must include an improved command of spoken English' (HMSO, 1963, para 467, p. 153). This report also regarded it as the overriding aim of English to develop the 'social competence' of the pupil (para 467, p. 153). Literature was to play a central role in this: the report argued that 'All pupils, including those of very limited attainments, need the civilising experience of contact with great literature' (para 473, p. 155). There was also a shift towards a concern with the personal development of the individual as the English classroom could 'allow adolescents to write out of themselves what they are not always prepared or able to talk about' (para 484, p. 159).

John Dixon's *Growth Through English* (first published in 1967) set the agenda for much of the following twenty-five years, and the model of English teaching it embodied continues to exert a powerful hold over many teachers' conceptions of their subject. Dixon argues that, 'In ordering and composing situations that in some way symbolize life as we know it, we bring order and composure to our inner selves' (Dixon, 1975, p. 13). This marks a clear contrast with previous aspirations for English to impose 'order and composure' on society through the adoption of the values contained in the established literary canon. In a time increasingly marked by diversity and mass migrations of people from developing countries to (often) English-speaking countries throughout the world, the literary canon (consisting mainly of works by white, middle-class and now dead men) was seen as increasingly irrelevant and inappropriate as teachers sought to find new ways to connect with and inspire students from diverse cultures and backgrounds. English, was seen as enabling students to get in touch with the higher values, which were regarded as inherent in the individual rather than in canonical texts. The Newbolt Report's concern to shift working-class children away from their 'evil habits' (HMSO, 1921, p. 59) was replaced by an attempt to acknowledge and respect every child's heritage. As the Bullock Report famously put it: 'No child should be expected to cast off the language and culture of the home as he crosses the school threshold, nor to live and act as though school and home represent two separate and different cultures which have to be kept firmly apart' (HMSO, 1975, p. 286).

Douglas Barnes, in his 1976 book *From Communication to Curriculum*, describes classic features of the 'personal growth' tradition – the use of group oral work to enable students to make sense of a text with their peers, an emphasis on the authenticity and validity of their direct and personal response rather than reliance on any learnt 'techniques', an insistence on relevance, and an implied conviction that the purpose of English is to move the students on in their personal development.

This model also valued the use of other media such as television and film, as teachers looked for stimuli with which their students would be familiar and would find 'relevant'. Equally, there was a focus on the spoken word, as attention shifted from the sovereignty of the written text and the discovery of others' knowledge towards the child's own creation of knowledge through language, as exemplified in Douglas Barnes et al.'s influential 1969 book *Language, the Learner and the School*.

Spoken English

In the UK, students' performance in spoken English or **oracy** has been assessed since at least the mid 1960s, with the introduction of the Certificate of Secondary Education (CSE) for students of lower academic attainment, which involved giving a short talk on a topic and answering questions on it. In 1986 the General Certificate of Secondary Education (GCSE) was introduced, which – unlike the examinations it replaced – was taken by students of all abilities. It involved students being assessed across a range of speech genres (interview, debate, group discussion, presentation); that is to say, there was an awareness of genres and audience. In 1987, the UK's School Curriculum Development Council set up the *National Oracy Project* with the aim of promoting and enhancing the role of talk across the curriculum. This involved projects across the whole country and at every level from ages 5 to 16. While this led to ground-breaking research and innovative practice, as evidenced in the publication *Thinking Voices* (Norman, 1992), it was in the absence of a comprehensive and serviceable model that teachers could usefully apply in their classrooms – especially one that could take account of the twin trajectories of personal and academic discourses which, for many children, led them in very separate directions.

The work of Professor Ronald Carter has moved the teaching of oracy on considerably. His analysis (see QCA, 2004), based on the study of large collections (or 'corpora') of spoken texts totalling over 400 million words, has helped to identify the distinctive features of spoken English. The study of the **grammar of speech** as part of the English Curriculum is important, Carter argues, because it is intrinsically interesting and because we need to redress the imbalance that privileges written language. It is important to demonstrate to students how talk is systematically organised; to examine its creative use in everyday situations; to help develop the spoken language of all pupils, but especially those learning English as an additional language – not only in terms of improving their fluency but also their understanding of how interpersonal relationships are mediated through talk in English; and to explore the contrasts and continuities between spoken and written language – why some things work in spoken language that would not do so if written down, and vice versa.

However, such work is far from widespread in schools. Where speaking and listening are taking place, it is the teacher who is generally talking and the students listening, as a national review of English teaching 2000–05 states:

> Too little attention has been given to teaching the full National Curriculum programme of study for speaking and listening and the range of contexts provided for speaking and listening remains too limited. Emphasis on developing effective direct teaching approaches has led, at best, to good whole class discussion but, in too many classes, discussion is dominated by the teacher and pupils have only limited opportunities for productive speaking and listening.

(Ofsted, 2005, p. 1)

English for critical literacy

The **critical literacy** model of English acknowledges its political nature and problematises the distinction between 'schooling' and 'education'. It should be pointed out that this model has not been taken up in its purest form to any large extent by teachers in schools. Nonetheless, it has had influence as a theory and some aspects of it have found their way into classroom practice.

Critical literacy begins with the premise that no text is ever ideologically neutral and that readers and writers are inevitably influenced by factors such as their beliefs, gender, power relations and purposes (Lankshear and Knobel, 2003). This affects every level of the text from the choice of vocabulary to the grammatical patterning, as seen in the use of vivid adjectives in advertising, the use of the passive voice to disguise who is responsible for an action, or the use of the inclusive *we* when trying to influence decisions.

The starting point in this model is that all texts (whether visual, spoken or written) are produced in order to influence the viewer, listener or reader. As a result, there is no reason to privilege literary texts in the English curriculum, as children need to understand how they and others are being positioned by a wide range of texts: the school rules displayed on a notice-board, the packaging on food marketed specifically at them, trailers for films, etc. The model implies commitment to students' direct participation and intervention in society through such actions as researching issues, writing letters to authorities, or creating alternative versions of texts. The purpose of English teaching is to enable students to engage critically with the meanings and positionings of texts rather than to simply have them imposed upon them. As writers, students gain power by being able to compose a range of genres that they can deploy in pursuit of their own purposes, irrespective of whether these are personal or political.

To some extent, the UK *National Literacy Strategy* (Ofsted, 2003) has sought to 'colonise' aspects of the critical literacy tradition with its appropriation of a genre-based approach to the teaching of writing. As we saw in the example taken from the GCSE English examination paper, students are expected to be able to write in a number of **genres** (such as 'report', recount', 'argument' etc.). Though unacknowledged in the documentation, the Strategy draws heavily on the work of Australian-based linguists such as Michael Halliday and Jim Martin (see also Reading A). Martin argues for the explicit teaching of how texts are constructed because success in education is measured by performance in writing which, according to him, was not being taught in schools. This had the effect of disadvantaging working-class, migrant and Aboriginal children whose homes do not provide them with models of writing, whereas, '[b]right, middle-class children learn by osmosis what has to be learned' (Martin, 1985, p. 61).

There are, of course, dangers in assuming that the mere teaching of the genres is of itself empowering. Simply being able to reproduce a powerful text type does not make the writer powerful or mean that the text will carry any weight outside its place of production. There is, as Gunther Kress, currently Professor at the London University Institute of Education, points out, also the risk that the individual becomes an unreflective user of formulaic texts, with the result that the genre and its meaning 'will come to dominate the individual just when the individual feels that he [*sic*] has come to a command of the genre ... Is that what we want?' (Kress, 1994, p. 126).

Kress goes on to argue that students should be equipped with social and cultural knowledge of text production and with the linguistic resources to both analyse and produce powerful texts themselves. The focus is not on the re-production of a given text type, but on the production of meaning to suit the well-informed writer's needs. In Kress's view, it is this competence that will lead to the development of innovatory personal and cultural dispositions that will be needed in the future.

5.5 English teaching: a contested area

Figure 5.7   English teaching: a contested area

As we have seen, the defence of cultural standards has often been intimately linked with the teaching of English. Throughout the late 1970s and 1980s, *The Centre for Policy Studies* (a 'think tank' established by Conservative politicians Margaret Thatcher and Sir Keith Joseph) issued a number of pamphlets on education, including *English our English*, written by John Marenbon, which took a bleak view of prevailing standards in schools:

> When children leave English schools today, few are able to speak and write English correctly; even fewer have a familiarity with the literary heritage of the language. It is not hard to see why. Among those who theorize about English teaching there has developed a new orthodoxy,

which regards it as a conceptual error to speak of 'correct' English and which rejects the idea of a literary heritage.

(Marenbon, 1987, p. 5)

Marenbon went on to identify seven 'tenets' of this 'new orthodoxy':
- English is not just a subject;
- English teaching should be child-centred;
- It is as important to teach the spoken language as the written language;
- Assessment should not concentrate on the pupil's errors;
- Grammar is descriptive not prescriptive;
- No language or dialect is inherently superior to any other;
- Language-use should be judged by its appropriateness.

(Marenbon, 1987, p. 8)

Marenbon (1987, Chapter 5) addresses each point in turn and poses a counter-argument. Whilst he acknowledges that it is important for children to develop emotionally, learn tolerance and think critically, he argues that this can only be achieved through specific and rigorous studies during which children are taught to speak and write Standard English correctly and begin to learn about the language's literary heritage.

ACTIVITY 5.5

Allow about 30 minutes

To what extent do you agree with the approaches represented by the seven statements above? To what extent do you agree with Marenbon that they are responsible for falling standards? Go through each of them in turn and consider what evidence you could bring to bear from this chapter and/or your own experience.

Comment

This activity is primarily designed as an opportunity for you to reflect on the issues, and I am not proposing to provide a formal commentary on each of the statements. What follows is a comment on just one of them – the teaching of spoken English.

Marenbon accepts the importance of spoken language, but argues that:

> ... whereas writing and reading are skills that require specific instruction, children learn to speak and listen just by being present at these activities
>
> ...
>
> The fashionable emphasis on 'oracy' is in part a product of the tendency to regard English, not as a subject, but as an opportunity to acquire a haphazard collection of virtues (maturity, tolerance and so on) ...

(Marenbon, 1987, p.19)

Marenbon's assertion that 'children learn to speak and listen just by being present at these activities' is true at a simplistic level, but does not take account of the very different forms of listening and speaking that take place in schools and the workplace as compared with at home at a caregiver's knee. I would argue that these more public ways of speaking and listening also need to be taught.

English in the future?

ACTIVITY 5.6

Allow at least
10 minutes

As you approach the end of this overview of the English curriculum, pause for a moment and note down the elements of your own ideal English curriculum, along with your justification for each.

At the end of the last century, Gunter Kress was invited by the National Association of Teachers of English (NATE) to look forward to the next millennium and produced *Writing the Future* (Kress, 1995) in response. He asked himself what English was then and what it was likely to continue to be. His conclusions were:

1   English is a carrier of definitions of culture.

2   English is a carrier of definitions of its society.

3   English, the language, is at the moment still the major medium of communication in this society, and the English curriculum must be cognisant of that.

4   The subject English is the only site in the curriculum where all the modes and media of public communication can be debated, analysed, and taught – there is nowhere else.

5   English is the site of development of the individual in a moral, ethical, public social sense.

(Kress, 1995, p. 30)

This neatly brings together the various aspects of Ball et al.'s four models discussed earlier (see Section 5.2) into a coherent whole. In particular, Kress's third statement points to an aspect that has been the driver of much of the change in our understanding of the subject over the last half-century: our conception of the position of the English language in society. Kress here is considering the increasingly multilingual nature of the UK, the position of English as a global lingua franca and the implications of that for the subject English, not least in the choice of literary texts to reflect and address what must inevitably be a more complex representation of cultural heritage.

A further area for future change is being brought about by the rapid pace of developments in digital technology, which means that our understandings of reading and writing have already had to shift, as electronic literacy adds new layers of complexity, bringing with it new conventions of use which appear to be blurring the distinctions between written and spoken grammar. Interactive whiteboards and hand-held computers make it possible to download a vast array of resources from all over the globe and for teachers and students to model texts, share drafts and respond to others' work almost instantly.

A thread that runs through all the major English-speaking countries is that of cultural and linguistic diversity, and it is not surprising that English has become a locus of tension as those societies come to terms with whether they want to pursue an assimilationist agenda, in which English is the agent that melts all the other elements together, or a pluri-cultural agenda, in which English is seen as one of a number of threads that makes up the linguistic tapestry of a country. As Cameron and Bourne point out, 'An authoritarian state frequently uses the 'national language' as a point of unity and social cohesion, and analogously, finds linguistic diversity threatening, a force to be contained or even eliminated' (Cameron and Bourne, 1988, p. 151).

A good example of such tensions is South Africa, where language and education are inextricably entwined as the nation seeks to create a new identity for itself in a post-apartheid world.

ACTIVITY 5.7

Now read 'English in the curriculum in South Africa' by Kathleen Heugh (Reading B).

- Many people would argue that acquiring English is the solution to the educational and economic problems of developing countries. Heugh presents a different view. What are the key difficulties that she identifies in terms of students and teachers?
- Heugh argues that the need of the non-English-speaking majority in South Africa to have education in their own first language has to be addressed. What might be the implications of this for other English-speaking countries with diverse populations?

Comment

It is not surprising that, given the historical and political changes the country has undergone, Heugh presents a complex view of the position of English in South Africa. English tends to be seen as 'the solution' (given the success of the 'Royal Education' programme and outstanding figures such as Nelson Mandela and Walter Sisulu), but it can in fact be regarded as 'the problem', as students have insufficient exposure to the language in order to study through it and teachers commonly lack skills themselves.

In terms of relating Heugh's account of English in South Africa to the situation of English in English-dominant countries (such as the UK and Australia), it is necessary to consider the increasing linguistic diversity of populations. In the UK, for example, some 10 per cent of school students have English as an additional language (and the numbers are increasing). In London, the figure is closer to 30 per cent, and in some states in the USA the Spanish-speaking population outnumbers the monolingual English population. This raises important questions about how English might need to provide an inclusive curriculum for all students. You might also like to consider what implications this could have for, for example, the kinds of literature that are taught. It may be that we need to reconceptualise the subject English as 'Language and Literature' or even 'Languages and Literatures', thus breaking any residual implied connection with a single language or national culture.

5.6 Conclusion

In this chapter I have attempted to provide an overview of the major forces and trends in educational and governmental thinking that have shaped the English curriculum both in the UK and in other parts of the English-speaking world. I ended with some speculations about the future directions of the subject in the context of increasing cultural diversity and technological developments.

In 2005, the UK Qualifications and Curriculum Authority (QCA) launched *English 21*, a national consultation programme on how the English curriculum should look in 2015. How radical a departure or conservative a return that future holds remains to be seen. Given the evidence of the previous century or more, one might safely assume that English is likely to remain as contested as it has been at every other point in time and place.

READING A: Conceptions of English in New Zealand and Australia

Urszula Clark
(Urszula Clark is Principal Lecturer in English, University of Wolverhampton.)

Specially commissioned for this book.

Introduction

By the end of the twentieth century, each major English-speaking country in the world had introduced and formalised a national, formal curriculum for English. Although the cultural, political, and socio-economic circumstances of each country or nation combine in unique ways to form specific societies, when it came to curriculum reform, each looked to the subject of English not only as a means of attaining levels of literacy demanded by an increasingly technological world, but also as a means of redefining national and cultural identity through a common language and its literature. In both New Zealand and Australia, this trend highlighted the nature of the relationship between concepts of national identity and three distinct types of communities – the descendants of settlers dating from British colonial times, indigenous peoples, and those of more recent immigrants.

Formalising a curriculum for a national language *inevitably* raises uncomfortable questions about the relationship between language and ethnicity, gender and social class. In the case of New Zealand and Australia, the introduction of a national curriculum for English came to be concerned not so much with cultural restoration as cultural reappraisal. There was an expectation or pressure for the subject to recognise, absorb, formalise and reproduce national variations of the Standard English language. Other new trends, such as postcolonial and feminist influences upon the subject, have more commonly been absorbed within the requirements for teaching literature, where traditional concepts of 'English literature' have evolved into 'literature in English'.

Rewriting New Zealand English

In New Zealand throughout the 1990s (as elsewhere), the needs of minority groups began to be acknowledged in all areas of public life, including education. In the case of the New Zealand curriculum statement, the need to respect cultural difference is given voice but remains confined to the margins in most policy areas, apart from the linguistic, where it is given prominence.

When the new regulatory framework for all curriculum subjects was introduced during the 1980s, ministers had already approved the establishment of an English Syllabus Committee to undertake the task of developing national syllabus guidelines for the upper secondary level. In the event, the writing of this syllabus became the site of tensions between liberalist, social democratic principles and the resurgence of the New Right, in ways which mirror the struggles over the national curriculum for English in England and Wales. As ever, one major area of contention was over the issue of social integration, and the nature of the future relationship between New Zealand English language and culture and Maori language and culture.

The New Zealand Ministry of Education first published its *English in the New Zealand Curriculum* in 1994, and in a manner customary with such statements written in terms of learning outcomes, set out what children should achieve throughout their schooling. In its section called, 'Characteristics of learning and teaching in English', the first paragraph reaffirms the integral part language plays in the development of personal identity: 'There is a close link between the ability to control the different functions of language and learners' own personal, social, intellectual, and imaginative development. The ways in which learners view the world are moulded by their language development' (see The Online Learning Centre, 2006). The English curriculum document firmly contextualises this development, first within New Zealand itself and second in a global context, while at the same time still retaining its colonial roots:

> Language development and study in New Zealand must be in the context of our own linguistic situation. Attention should be given to the distinctive New Zealand varieties of English and to New Zealand's own literature, while English programmes will continue to draw widely on the rich international and historical resources and achievement of the English language and of literatures in English.

(The Online Learning Centre, 2006)

Statements and profiles: an Australian context

By the 1980s Australia had joined most Western countries in restructuring publicly funded schools to make them more responsive to the needs of the economy. Another important factor of such reform was concern about the failure of schools to provide adequately for all sectors of its population, not least its indigenous Aboriginal population and Asian immigrants.

For some educationists an officially endorsed curriculum and system of assessment can be considered as an instrument of social justice if it can be made to address discrimination against certain social groups in ways in which progressive, constructivist practices had failed to do.

One feature which the Australian curriculum endorsed has come to be called *critical literacy*: that and the teaching practices associated with it places social conscience at the heart of educational practice. Critical literacy is thus distinguished by the beliefs about society and language which underpin the choice of texts and approaches used to teach them. These approaches lead to the questioning of the social and cultural values contained within the texts themselves.

Writing an Australian English statement

The *Statement on English for Australian Schools* (Australian Education Council, 1994) is divided into two strands, text and language, with the study of language rooted in the context of the study of texts. It identifies six main aims: three in the area of language, and three in the area of literature.

The introduction states categorically that: 'Australian English is the national variety of English in Australia, distinguished from other national varieties, such as British and American English, chiefly by pronunciation and vocabulary' (Australian Education Council, 1994). Thus, the linguistic structures and features of grammar remain those associated with Standard English and apply mainly to writing. Its distinctiveness is recognised more in speech, through accent and vocabulary. This national variety is further subdivided into two categories: that of Standard Australian English used in schools, and all other usage, named here as 'colloquial varieties'. The tension between 'knowledge of the ways in which textual interpretation and understanding may vary according to cultural, social, and personal differences, and the capacity to develop reasoned arguments about interpretation and meaning', on the one hand, and learning a standard variety of English on the grounds of extension of repertoire, on the other, is resolved by acknowledging the common language for what it is (Australian Education Council, 1994). Students may discuss cultural, social and personal differences, and argue about interpretation and meaning of what it means to be Australian, but they do so through a common language – Australian English. Thus, although critical literacy is a part of the curriculum statement so, too, is the reproduction of a national variety of English which becomes an acknowledged part of its pedagogy.

Nevertheless, a formalised, explicit curriculum gives the disadvantaged (of whatever race, creed or colour) the information that the advantaged have generally always had. Making the teaching of English explicit has, in Australia, drawn upon the theories of systemic functional grammar, derived from the work of the linguist Michael Halliday and subsequently developed by other Australian linguists concerned with language and education, such as Frances Christie and Jim Martin.

Functional grammar differs from traditional grammar in many respects. Fundamentally, where traditional grammar is concerned with classification of words and their ordering within a sentence, functional grammar emphasises how language is structured in use and how particular meanings are realised. Consequently, it is concerned with the language of texts rather than the analysis of sentences. It is also based on actual discourse rather than self-fulfilling examples and can account for nuances of meaning. Since much of the business of English has been concerned with textual interpretation, particularly at secondary level and beyond, functional grammar – more so than any other – lends itself as a method of studying and interpreting texts.

Conclusion

Within the curriculum documents for English in New Zealand and Australia, an important part of what counts as having succeeded in teaching English is an ability to reproduce the norms associated with written Standard English and increasingly, spoken Standard English. What all of them share is a reinstatement of explicit teaching about language, particularly its grammar, as an important aspect of its reproduction. The teaching of grammar has become an integral part of the writing process, rather than as decontextualised exercises. At the same time, the terminology and concepts of functional grammar have been adapted to form a pedagogic hybrid grammar made up of both traditional and functional grammars.

In New Zealand and Australia, the writing of national curriculum statements allowed for redefinitions of national identity in ways that turned an imported, colonial national language and literature into ones more definably recognisable and distinctive as New Zealand English language and literature, and Australian English language and literature. However, critical linguists would be quick to point out that this singling out of one language as a national language, however inclusive it may purport to be, implies a position of dominance between it and different languages and cultures, and a hierarchy of use which of itself perpetuates social inequality.

References for this reading

Australian Education Council (1994) *A Statement on English for Australian Schools: A Joint Project of the States, Territories and Commonwealth of Australia*, Carlton, Victoria, Australia, Curriculum Corporation.

The Online Learning Centre (2006) 'Characteristics of learning and teaching in English', *English in the New Zealand Curriculum*, http://www.tki.org.nz/r/language/curriculum/characteristics_e.php (Accessed 15 September 2006)

READING B: English in the curriculum in South Africa

Kathleen Heugh
(Kathleen Heugh is Head of the Language and Literacies Studies Unit,
Assessment Technology and Education Evaluation Programme, Human
Sciences Research Council, Cape Town, South Africa.)

Specially commissioned for this book.

English and other colonial languages in the African context

The situation of English in the education systems of former British colonies in sub-Saharan Africa is becoming increasingly contested and yet also increasingly difficult to dislocate from postcolonial practices. For at least two decades, marked by the decision of Kenyan author, Ngũgĩ wa Thiong'o, to write in Kikuyu rather than in English, a chorus of scholarly voices have drawn attention to the 'invisibilisation' of African languages. The use of former colonial languages by the postcolonial elites for high-status functions has been underserving the majority of citizens in African countries, particularly in education. Scholars from across the continent have grappled with the linguistic conundrum in which African societies find themselves.

By the late nineteenth century, European powers were engaged in what was known as the 'Scramble for Africa' as they sought to colonise ever more of the continent. In 1884–85 they held a conference in Berlin (attended also by the USA) to formalise the partition of Africa, agreeing that they could not just plant their flag, but also had to administer the territories they claimed. This ushered in the process whereby European languages were to become inextricably woven into the apparatus of power and marks the point at which the position of indigenous languages in high-status functions and education began to weaken. The colonial languages which displaced African languages for the purposes of rule, education and a new economy designed to serve Europe were, and continue to be, effectively accessible to only a small percentage of people. Power remains, therefore, in the hands of the few.

The history of language and education across sub-Saharan Africa after the Berlin Conference resulted in divergent language education policies offered by the colonial administrations. The French, Spanish and Portuguese administrations favoured an assimilationist stance, whereby limited education in the European language only would be provided for a very small elite group of African men who would become acculturated into the respective colonial system. The British and German administrations favoured a weak form of segregation, and this resulted in education which employed African languages for much of primary education.

Figure 1 European spheres of influence in sub-Saharan Africa towards the end of the nineteenth century. (Note that borders were subject to ongoing disputes between the mid 1870s and the outbreak of the First World War in 1914, and that European influences were at different levels of formality in different territories.)

Various missionary groups provided schooling for African children in the former British and German colonies from the late nineteenth century. African languages tended to be used for four to six years of primary school and this practice was followed by a transition to English-medium education for the remainder of school. It needs to be mentioned that the numbers of students passing through the school system and exiting at the end of secondary school were very small. Nevertheless, missionary education was successful. Students who proceeded to the end of secondary school achieved high levels of proficiency in English and were able to continue to higher education. Since this education was available, in reality, only to a small percentage of students, it tended in Southern Africa to be available to the children, usually male, of the various royal families, hence it became known as 'Royal Education'. In South Africa, over time, the term 'Royal Education' became synonymous with education in English at secondary school and also a very high level of proficiency in English. Oliver Tambo, Albert Ntuli, Walter Sisulu and Nelson

Mandela, all high-profile political leaders in South Africa, experienced this kind of education in the first half of the twentieth century. Such high-profile people, together with their educational, social and political success, have become symbolic of that to which ordinary people aspire. English is imagined as the necessary ingredient of educational, and hence other, success. What has been difficult to accept is that 'Royal Education' worked well because the missionary teachers were highly trained, provided excellent language models for English, the classes were small, and the students came from the socio-economic elite of the time.

African territories began to achieve independence from the late 1950s, only seventy years after the partition. Five decades on, one might have imagined that the influence of colonial occupation would have dwindled and the process of the re-Africanisation of systems would be well underway. In the case of language use, the grip of the former colonial languages over formal education, politics and the economies of Africa remains steadfast. In the 'Anglophone' countries (where in reality only 10–20 per cent of people are functionally proficient in English), there has been a tendency after independence to trim down the number of years of education in the African languages and to introduce a more rapid transition to the so-called 'international language of wider communication' (or ILWC), in this case English. The difficulty with such programmes is that they do not yield positive educational results. In the former British colonies, exchanging late-transition for early-transition programmes is a significant setback. The simple matter is that children cannot and do not learn very much if they do not understand the language through which they are being taught. This is particularly so in African countries where the ILWC is seldom heard or used beyond the larger cities and centres of political power.

English and Afrikaans in South Africa prior to 1994

South Africa's history sets the country apart from most African countries. The British colonial period, particularly after the Anglo-Boer war of 1899–1901, left an indelible print on the linguistic ecology of the country. An aggressive pursuit of an Anglicisation policy prior to the establishment of a Union of South Africa in 1909–10, resulted in a focused linguistic reaction from the Dutch-speaking community. It spawned Afrikaner nationalism and identity and a determination to develop Afrikaans as a high-status language distinct from Dutch, and equal in functional use with English.

Political changes in South Africa brought about National Party rule in 1948, and the introduction of formal apartheid, with its segregationist principles having their logical extension in language education policy. The principle of mother-tongue education for all would serve to keep linguistic communities apart. In the case of Afrikaans- and English-speaking children, this translated into separate schools, with mother-tongue medium education to the exit point of secondary school, plus the teaching of the other official language as a subject. A school-leaving certificate required students to demonstrate a fairly competent level of Afrikaans-English bilingualism. Until 1975, African children were to have eight years of mother-tongue education, followed by a switch in secondary school to joint Afrikaans- and English-medium (half the subjects in one and half in the other language). In such ways, the hegemonic threat of English could be curtailed: English and Afrikaans were accorded equal and parallel official status.

Despite the ideological unacceptability of apartheid, a dispassionate analysis of educational achievement during the forty years of apartheid (Bantu) education prior to 1975 shows positive results. The school-leaving pass rate at the end of the 12th year improved from 43.5 per cent in 1955 to 83.7 per cent in 1976. Although the policy insisted on the change in medium of instruction to *both* Afrikaans and English, it was in reality to English-only until 1975. Not only did the school leaving pass rate improve, but the pass rate in English as a subject increased to 78 per cent by 1978.

During the mid 1970s the antipathy and resistance towards Afrikaans was symbolic of resistance to the political ideology of apartheid. The requirement to learn Afrikaans, and to demonstrate a bilingual competence for employment in the civil service, irked many speakers of English and produced low-level resistance. However the compulsory use of Afrikaans as a partial medium of secondary education for African children produced an explosive reaction in 1976, when students led a rebellion in Soweto. The fall-out of this rebellion was that mother-tongue education for African children was reduced to four years, followed by a switch to English-medium. It was believed English would guarantee access to international knowledge and communication and would advance the possibility of deliverance from apartheid.

Within a few years, however, it became noticeable that academic performance dropped dramatically during the fifth year of school, shortly after the earlier switch to English. The Human Sciences Research Council was tasked to investigate the implications of the switch to English-medium education and discovered that teachers responsible for students from Grades 5–8, having been trained to teach in the mother tongue, were not sufficiently competent in English. Exposure to English in the first four grades could result in an estimated 800 lexical items, whereas the fifth-grade curriculum required a lexicon of 7000 words (Macdonald, 1990). The gap was simply too large and neither the children nor the teachers could cope. With large class sizes, poor resources and poorly prepared teachers who do not have a strong proficiency in English, there is thus little chance of success with too early a switch to English-medium education.

English in post-1994 South Africa

It should not be surprising that almost all of the negotiations which led to the transfer of power in 1994 from National Party rule to a government of national unity, dominated by the African National Congress (ANC), were conducted in English. However, the ANC's own internal position, based on the principle of equality and rights, in combination with the National Party's insistence that the official status of Afrikaans should not be reduced, resulted in a compromise solution. The 1996 Constitution commits the country to eleven official languages. Thus, on paper, Afrikaans and English now enjoy equal status with nine African languages.

Figure 2   Postcard from Robben Island

Naturally, education was one of the sites of specific attention in regard to new legislation and policy change. A new language in education policy was negotiated and accepted in 1997 in which the principle of 'additive' bilingual or multilingual education is foregrounded. This means that every child should have access to mother-tongue education throughout, plus good access to the learning of at least one, preferably two, other South African language(s).

The new language education policy in South Africa, therefore, looks promising. As is the case in almost every other African country, however, policy and implementation do not go hand-in-hand. The language education policy, initially included in a new curriculum in 1997, has been thoroughly undermined in the Revised National Curriculum Statement (DOE, 2002). For the 75 per cent of learners who are speakers of African languages, what is presented as additive bilingual education is effectively three years of mother-tongue education, followed by an inevitable switch to English-medium. The target is thus English-only, not mother-tongue-plus-English.

A study conducted by Horne (2001) showed that, whereas 51 per cent of the Grade 12 school-leavers who applied in 1990 for admission to *technikons* (higher education institutions offering mainly vocational programmes) had adequate (Grade 8 or above) English as a Second Language literacy levels, this had declined to 18 per cent in 2000. According to another study quoted by Horne, only 2 per cent of African language-speaking students who applied to a formerly mainly 'white' metropolitan university in 2000 had ESL literacy levels expected of Grade 12 school-leavers.

A scrutiny of the latest version of the curriculum documentation (DOE, 2002) adds to the disquiet. The Languages Learning Area (curriculum) Statement provides for the teaching and learning of all official languages at three levels: Home Language (L1), First Additional Language (L2) and Second Additional Language (L3). The first matter of concern is that there are differentiated assessment standards required of students who will take the L2 as a language only and those who will also use it as a medium of instruction. Those who take it as a language only (i.e. those whose home language is English or Afrikaans) are expected to develop a smaller lexicon than those who will use it as a medium of learning and teaching (i.e. those whose home language is an African language). At first sight, this may appear logical. However, when viewed through the South African prism of a constitutional commitment to equality and elimination of discrimination, this departs from principle. L1 speakers of English and Afrikaans will continue to have L1-medium education to the end of Grade 12, and take their L2 as a subject only. Thus their assessment standards for the L2 are lower, less onerous and therefore more favourable in terms of final achievement than are those for L1 speakers of African languages. The latter are further burdened by having to switch medium of instruction. Discrimination and inequality continue.

A second level of analysis reveals further problems. Again, using the size of the lexicon as the marker, a comparison between the curriculum requirements for African students during apartheid and the curriculum requirements in post-apartheid South Africa, is confounding. Apartheid education was popularly believed to offer African children a cognitively impoverished curriculum. However, according to Macdonald (1990), its curriculum required a lexicon of 7000 words in English for African children at Grade 5 level. The new post-apartheid curriculum suggests that a student who will learn through the medium of their L2 requires only a lexicon of up to 4500 words in Grade 5 (DOE, 2002, p.81). There are three possible explanations for the discrepancy between the old apartheid curriculum and the new, apparently transformative, curriculum:

- The new curriculum experts may have underestimated the concept base which students require.

- The L2 requirements reflect more realistically what one might expect of a student who is learning a second language as a subject. If this is the case, then it confirms that a student at this stage is not ready to use the L2 as a medium of instruction, since the lexicon requirements of the whole curriculum are greater.

- The new curriculum is offering a curriculum in which the concept base, and hence the cognitive challenge, has been reduced by 40–50 per cent when compared with the earlier apartheid curriculum.

Whichever the reason, the bottom line is that English cannot and does not offer L2 speakers, especially African students, access to the extent of the curriculum which is available to L1 speakers of English.

The final point of inequity is in relation to the use of continuous assessment and the building up of portfolios of work during the first nine years of school. In an attempt to reduce inequalities, educational policy change favoured 'low-stakes' assessment, in which continuous assessment counts for 75 per cent and examinations for 25 per cent by the end of Grade 9. Wealthier parents provide computers and internet access with acres of relevant information in English, easily downloadable and plagiarised. Most African parents do not have such luxuries available to them, and thus the gap between the wealthier and poorer students has widened. What is common, across all language groups, is that the expectation of school students to demonstrate increasing levels of academic literacy as they proceed through the school system is diminishing. It is diminished in poorly resourced classrooms because teachers now resort to the endless gapped exercise worksheet option. It is diminished in well-resourced settings, where students patch chunks of unfiltered electronic text into their assignments. In each case, there are fewer expectations for students to construct their own well-argued debates or analyses. The results are evident in the findings of poor literacy achievement in general and studies such as that of Horne (2001).

At this point, the position of and reliance on English is an entirely vexed one. In a country where the proportion of L1 speakers of English has shrunk to 8.2 per cent, where 13.3 per cent are L1 speakers of Afrikaans and 78 per cent have an African language as their L1, English does not promise to deliver successful education to the majority of children and other learners in the system. A public perception, often advanced by a few English-speaking academics and the new political elite, is that English is *the* lingua franca, or preferred language people use in their neighbourhoods. The reality is that there is no single lingua franca in South Africa: Zulu, Xhosa, Afrikaans, English and Tswana operate as lingua francas in different contexts and different parts of the country. Usually there are two or three lingua francas which co-exist in any particular geographical region.

Yet there is no doubt that the learning of English is highly desirable. Just as an international language of wider communication is a prized ingredient of education across Africa, there are no short-cut solutions to high levels of proficiency in this language. What is required, I would argue, is a minimum of 6–8 years of mother-tongue education, during which time English is taught by a competent and well-trained teacher of the language. Thereafter, the use of a dual-medium model, whereby the L1 is retained for part of the teaching and learning day, and where English is introduced for up to 50 per cent of the school day, could work, as long as the system is adequately resourced. An English-mainly system, however, even if it were better resourced, cannot deliver successful results.

Despite the new political elite's intention of introducing democratic systems and acceptance of diversity, the internal apparatus of the state is propelled toward increasing control and intolerance of difference, including linguistic plurality. More than a decade after the latest change in power in South Africa, despite constitutional and legislative provision for eleven official languages, the official use of the nine African languages has shown little change, and the use of Afrikaans which had previously enjoyed equal status with English, has declined considerably. The position of English as the linguistic lever of power, on the other hand, has never been stronger, while access to the language has become ever more elusive for those outside the socio-economic elite.

References for this reading

DOE (2002) *Revised National Curriculum Statement Grades R-9 (Schools) Policy, Languages, English – First Additional Language*, Pretoria, Department of Education.

Horne, T. (2001) 'Education and language transferees', *Education Africa Forum Fifth Edition: Delivering Africa's Education Renaissance in South Africa*, pp. 40–45, Pinegowrie, Education Africa.

Macdonald, C. (1990) *Crossing the Threshold into Standard Three: Main Report of the Threshold Project*, Pretoria, Human Sciences Research Council.

English for speakers of other languages
Jill Bourne

6.1 Introduction

This chapter looks at the teaching of English to speakers of other languages. This is not a marginal issue. The vast majority of English users across the world have learnt English as an additional language, and much of this learning has taken place at least partly within the formal confines of an English language classroom. Where is English taught to speakers of other languages? How is English presented to such learners? Who learns English, and why? What does it mean to be a second language learner of English? It may be that you learnt English yourself as an additional language, or that you have taught English – in which case you will have a great deal of personal experience to bring to bear on these questions.

Teaching English to speakers of other languages may at first seem to be a more basic activity than teaching English to those who already speak it as a first language. It might seem common sense that it is simply a question of teaching the *system* – the words, sounds, grammar, pronunciation, and conventions of using the English language, as codified in grammar books, dictionaries and textbooks – to those who have not before had access to this system.

With language, however, things are never that simple. First, few people come to English classes without some experience of English. The global spread of English has been powerful. It has left its mark not only in terms of the use of English for a variety of functions in many different societies, but also in its influence on other languages themselves, just as other languages have left their mark on English through this contact.

What this means is that it has become less and less easy to assume either a total lack of experience of English on the part of learners or that learning English will be a neutral, academic experience for them. Policies concerned with language in education seem to recognise this implicitly, often being ambivalent and contradictory. For example, Prodromou (1990) describes how, when there were strong moves to introduce English into primary schools in Greece, there were simultaneous moves to ban English shop names. Baldauf (1990) describes how in Samoa there was a desire to develop English language skills for 'progress' but at the same time a fear of losing traditional languages and cultures, resulting in policies having a positive approach to English but being implemented in ways that were not effective.

Furthermore, a positive national policy towards teaching a language does not necessarily mean that an *individual* is equally positive about learning that language. Learners' attitudes towards English may be ambivalent. There may be material rewards and hence motivation for learning English, but learners may also have an emotional resistance where they feel, consciously or unconsciously, that the learning of the language is being imposed on them, or that they are excluded from a worthwhile role within an English-speaking society. English language learners have to balance costs against benefits.

I follow up these issues later in the chapter, but first I want to look more closely at some of the contexts in which English is being taught and learnt around the world.

6.2 Where is English taught and learnt?

English as a foreign language

English as a foreign language (EFL) is the term traditionally used to describe the sort of English taught in a context in which the dominant language is other than English, and there is little English used in the environment, other than for international communication. Examples of such contexts include Japan, Saudi Arabia and Germany.

Two important trends can be discerned globally. First, within the school system there is a general move towards more English classes for young learners at primary level (from 5 to 11 years). According to a report produced by David Graddol for the British Council, 'Improving national proficiency in English now forms a key part of the educational strategy in most countries' (Graddol, 2006, p. 70), including an estimated 176.7 million children studying English in Chinese schools alone (Graddol, 2006, p. 95). In countries where this is not yet encouraged within the state school system, there is a growing demand for private English classes for children, with many wealthy parents clearly willing to pay to ensure that their children get ahead on the ladder to social success in which they see English as a factor.

A second trend is the shift away from a focus on the language alone and towards combining language teaching with curriculum content, what is called in the USA **language and content teaching**, or in Europe **content and language integrated learning (CLIL)**. In Germany, for example, a small but growing number of schools are setting up 'bilingual sections', which start by offering extra lessons in English and then introduce the teaching of an increasing number of subjects through the medium of English as the child progresses up the school. Similar developments have taken place in the former east European countries, most notably the Czech Republic and Hungary, where there has been a huge investment in the development of English teaching to replace Russian as a first foreign language, supported by both the USA and the UK. In south-east Asia, Brunei has responded to concern over standards of attainment at university level, where much of the reading is through the medium of English, by developing **bilingual education**. The medium in lower primary is Malay; then supported English-medium education is gradually introduced in upper primary – English language and subject classes are combined with, for example, the teaching of English through geography. Similar developments can be found in Hong Kong, another location where English retains an important presence. However, for the majority of children wherever they live, English is still learnt as a subject in classes that focus on language learning itself.

Contexts in which English is taught and learnt

The examples below illustrate just some of the variety of contexts in which English is learnt. They paint a complex picture of English language teaching and its connections to the whole-school curriculum and to policy at national level.

France

In France most pupils study at least three to four hours of English a week from the age of 11. While most classes focus on the teaching of the language, there is a *classes européenes* scheme in some *lycées* in which English is learnt through subject content (i.e. taught through the medium of English). Since 1989 there have been schemes for introducing English at primary level: by 2005, according to Graddol (2006, p. 89), at least a third of French primary-school children were studying English.

Malaysia

Malaysia is a multilingual country. The main language groups include speakers of Malay, Chinese and Tamil. Bahasa Malaysia has been adopted as the country's official language, with English recognised as an important second language. Although English is a language used extensively for internal business, Chinese is an equally important trading language in the region. Because of the colonial history, English was for many years the medium of education; however, Bahasa Malaysia was gradually introduced into the system until, by 1983, it had replaced English as the medium of instruction from the primary school through to the university. This policy led to concern that university students no longer achieved the competence in English that they needed in order to work with the scientific and technical texts that were published mainly in English. Accordingly, since 1995 the national language policy has been modified to allow universities to teach scientific and technical subjects through the medium of English. In 2005, Nottingham University (UK) opened a new English-medium campus, Nottingham Malaysia.

Morocco

French remains the predominant foreign language taught in schools in Morocco, but a reading knowledge of English has become increasingly important at university level, even where courses are taught through the medium of Arabic or French. In addition, a new English-medium university has been opened – a development found in a growing number of countries. In 1993 the Minister of Education announced that 90 per cent of secondary students listed English as their preferred foreign language option. The focus has shifted from an emphasis on developing spoken English to attaching greater importance to the development of reading and study skills in English for academic success.

Teaching adults in Brazil

In addition to the teaching of English in the school system, there is a big demand for English for adult learners all over the world. In Brazil, for example, there are highly popular language schools run by both British and US cultural organisations. In addition, a huge number of registered private language schools teach English, and English language teacher training has a strong presence in the university system, which offers MAs for local teachers of English.

Students have the choice of learning British or US English, depending on which language school they go to. For some, socio-political considerations appear to determine the choice of school, alongside practical factors such as expense and convenience. While the US variety would appear to be the most relevant, given geographical location, some Brazilians choose British English because it seems to be more politically neutral in this context, or even to signal rejection of US power in the region.

Which variety of English?

As we have seen in the examples above, there is a huge variety of contexts and purposes for learning English. This raises the issue of which variety of English should be chosen to serve as a model in the classroom for which particular group of learners. There has been much debate over whether a variety of Standard English or a local variety of English would be the better goal for learners in different parts of the world. At the same time, while there is a greater recognition of local varieties, there is also awareness of the need for communication across the wider world through the introduction – alongside the local – of some form of international English. Factors such as age, background, national context, career ambitions and employment opportunities all need to be taken into account in selecting the appropriate target language variety for learners.

Politics also plays a part in such a choice. In most countries, as in the Brazilian case above, learners make a choice between US or British Standard English in deciding on a private language school. In south-east Asia, on the other hand, some teachers promote Australian or New Zealand norms of English. Analysis of international textbooks indicates that these tend to adopt a choice of either British or US Standard English (Dendrinos, 1992). However, these varieties are now generally labelled International English, a redefinition I find problematical because it makes a variety of English that is used by some appear to be the model of language for all. In practice, teachers in regions such as south Asia or Africa tend to adopt the variety of English that is in use among the elite in the English-speaking countries in their region, such as Singapore or Nigeria. Perhaps the solution is that learners' goals should include an ability to understand the range of varieties with which they are likely to come into contact (British/US/Australian/local varieties): to speak and write at least one variety, perhaps a local one initially, and then to take on more 'standard' varieties higher up the education system.

English language teaching: a global industry

In order to maximise profitability and hold down costs, the publishing industry attempts to produce English language teaching textbooks, audiovisual material and teacher training materials that will be acceptable across as many different countries as possible. Thus fashions and fads, and concerns about pedagogy in English-dominant countries, as well as carefully thought-through suggestions for effective English teaching, have swept around the globe through the medium of popular, best-selling language schemes, mainly based in the UK and the USA.

Private language schools, not tied to national syllabuses and often with unqualified teachers looking for guidance on teaching, have been prime customers for such English language textbooks. While private language schools tend to work with small classes, English teaching in state schools often involves large classes with few resources. Expectations of the sorts of activity that should take place in the school classroom are also likely to place great constraints on English teachers. Nevertheless, techniques and materials developed in the private language-school context have often been recommended as models for state school teachers by visiting teacher trainers. I look at some of these trends later in the chapter, and consider arguments that this practice constitutes a form of 'cultural colonisation' of other nations.

English as a second language

English as a second language (ESL) is the term traditionally used to refer to situations in which speakers of other home languages are learning English in a context in which English is the dominant language of public life. Others, particularly within the UK, prefer to use the term **English as an additional language (EAL)**, a term which explicitly recognises the benefits of bilingualism and the possibility of multilingualism.

ACTIVITY 6.1

Allow about
15 minutes

Read the following case studies adapted from Jordan (1992). Jot down the ways in which the language-learning needs of these people are likely to differ.

1   Rafiq, aged 11, can speak, read and write Bengali competently, having completed five years at school in Bangladesh before moving to England. He is now taking his first tentative steps in the use of English. In his school, English language support teachers work alongside subject teachers; they provide training and support in organising group work, and in planning lessons to give access to the curriculum for bilingual learners of English. Children like Rafiq, who need more support with reading and writing in English, also have extra small-group English literacy lessons.

2   Amina, aged 14, arrived in Australia as a refugee directly from Somalia, where she had seen her brother shot. She was clearly traumatised, depressed and frightened of crowds. Amina's school arranged for her to join a small and sheltered 'induction' class for some weeks to support her and to help her to understand her new environment. Her school also arranged for a Somali-speaking community volunteer to come to her lessons each week and to accompany her for professional counselling. Because of her age and the fact that her peers will soon be entering examination classes, Amina will probably attend English support classes for the rest of her time in school. These will not focus on English alone but will attempt to give access to the full curriculum and prepare Amina for making use of further education opportunities after she leaves school.

3   Lupita came to California from Mexico two years ago at the age of 7. She spoke no English but joined a school where over 90 per cent of the children and at least half of the staff were Spanish speakers. Lupita's parents were encouraged to place her in the 'bilingual' stream of the school. In the early years the curriculum here was mainly in Spanish, with classes in English as a second language. Just recently, the language balance of the class has begun to shift, with more and more work being done in English. By the time Lupita transfers to high school she will be working mainly in English, although she will also continue to improve her reading and writing in Spanish.

4   Leila is an adult political refugee to England from what she calls Turkish Kurdistan. She was a journalist there but, although she is a university graduate, she is now working as a clothes presser in a factory, where all her fellow workers are Turkish Kurds. Her original intention was to learn English quickly and become a journalist again, but she found she had to take a job for financial reasons, which limits time for study, and as she arrives tired for evening language classes her progress is disappointingly slow. She is trying to find an alternative job in a company which provides language support linked to skills training.

5   Thatch is from Cambodia. He was educated to primary level and worked as a driver there. On arrival in Australia he attended a short, intensive 'survival' English course in a reception centre. After several years in Australia he understands English well and can cope with everyday situations. He can read and write English a little. Many people he meets, however, still find his pronunciation of English unclear and sometimes do not understand him. As he was made redundant from his first job, he has time to go regularly to English classes to learn how to look for work and handle interviews, and to prepare for coping with specialist job training courses if he is fortunate enough to get a place on one. He particularly wants to improve his pronunciation.

6   Liu is a businessman working in a new Chinese 'joint enterprise'. He has been sent to Singapore for business studies as well as to seek new contracts and improve his English. He attends a twice weekly English course for businessmen in a private language school where he is taught one-to-one and in small group classes.

Comment

In the first three case studies the emphasis was on finding ways of supporting the development of English while giving the children access to the full educational curriculum. Rafiq, Amina and Lupita were lucky to go to school in areas that had built up their resources and developed expertise in working with bilingual children. This is certainly not the case everywhere, and learners of English can be left to sink or swim in a monolingual school curriculum.

In Amina's case, English was not the immediate priority compared to dealing with her traumatised condition, but it remained an important element in coming to terms with life in her new surroundings. Longitudinal research (e.g. Collier, 1987) has shown that, even with good teaching, it takes at least five years for a child to develop a new language to the level needed for cognitive/academic purposes. (Canadian researcher Jim Cummins termed this Cognitive Academic Language Proficiency or CALP, by contrast with BICS or Basic Interpersonal Communication Skills. See Cummins, 2000; 2003.) However, concepts established in a child's stronger language can easily be transferred into a second language as it develops. Children like those in the case studies cannot wait until they have learnt enough English before they acquire literacy skills, learn mathematics, history, etc. and join in other classes, or they will lose their entitlement to an education.

This is a powerful argument for at least transitional bilingual education such as Lupita's if full bilingual education is not possible or desired. However, the resources are not always available or the numbers of children speaking the same language may make such provision financially and organisationally impractical. Political policy decisions are involved here. Where the emphasis is on the integration of minority groups into the dominant society, provision for languages other than English may receive little attention. On the other hand, as in some states in the USA, political will and community activities may bring about provision for bilingual education like Lupita's where there are large groups of people sharing the same languages. In either context, special provision is likely to be made for some form of extra English language teaching, since most educationalists would accept that no child should be denied access to the language of the wider society and the power that goes with it.

It is important to remember the diversity of needs among English language learners such as these in English-dominant countries: they will have different prior experience of and access to English, different levels of education and literacy in their first languages, and different views of themselves as minority group members in the English-dominant society.

The three adults described in the case studies also have different needs from one another. Although the first two are both relative beginners in English, they look for different things in their classes. Leila would really like intensive English classes like the ones Liu receives, to take her to the high level she needs for journalism. However, she is willing to settle for English language development integrated into skills training in order to be paid while improving her English. Thatch also wants language linked to skills training but first needs help to handle the hurdle of job-finding and interviews. Again, his needs are pressing, and slow progress in English will lead to disillusionment. Liu's private classes allow him to work at his own level and pace, while working in an English-speaking milieu at the same time forces him to make use of all the English he knows and to build up fluency.

In making appropriate provision, teachers have to consider learners' needs and aspirations, the language skills they possess in both their languages, other skills they may make use of, and any barriers to learning and ways of overcoming them. Ideally, an analysis of this sort will lead to the planning and negotiating of an individual programme, drawing on the courses and study-centre facilities on offer.

6.3 How is English taught and learnt?

Although particular methods of English teaching have been fashionable at different periods, many of them survive to the present day, coexisting in a variety of guises and contexts even within the same classroom. With this in mind, let's consider some experiences of learning English. The two passages below suggest that learners can respond quite successfully to different strategies for learning English, especially when the content matches their interests.

ACTIVITY 6.2

Allow 10–15 minutes

If you have ever learnt English or another language as a foreign or second language, how did you go about it? Did you learn in class or informally?

Which strategies and activities seemed most useful to you inside and outside class? In what ways were your own interests engaged by the content?

Read through the quotations below about the strategies employed by two learners of English. The first, from *Quicksilver* by Marie Rambert, was first published in 1972 and the second, *Memories of Lenin* by Nadezhda Krupskaya, in 1930.

> He taught me from a book by a man named Robertson, and I can remember exactly how it was laid out. There would be a short passage of some six or seven lines of English. I remember one that began: 'We are told that the Sultan Mahmoud by his perpetual wars abroad, and his tyranny at home, had filled the dominions of his forefathers with ruin and desolation and had unpeopled the Persian Empire.' Underneath each word there would be its literal translation into French, thus: 'Nous sommes dit que ...' And finally there was the translation into good French: 'On nous dit ...'. Thus you had a clear idea of the relative construction of English phrases and French. It was a simple, but brilliant system. I was interested, and I learnt it all by heart in no time.
>
> (quoted in Brumfit, 1991, p. 30)

> We thought we knew the English language, having even translated a whole book (the Webbs') from English into Russian, when we were in Siberia. I learnt English in prison from a self-instructor, but had never heard a single live English word spoken ... When we arrived in London we found we could not understand a single word and nobody understood us. At first this was very comical, but although Vladimir Ilyich [Lenin] joked about it, he soon got down to the business of learning the language. We started going to all kinds of meetings. We stood in the front row and carefully studied the orator's mouth. We went fairly often to Hyde Park, where speakers harangued the passing crowds on diverse themes ... We were particularly keen on listening to one speaker of this kind. He spoke with an Irish accent, which was easier for us to understand ... We learnt a great deal by listening to spoken English.
>
> (quoted in Brumfit, 1991, p. 27)

Comment

Although I chose these passages to illustrate different methods of learning English, once I had brought them together I found it interesting to consider the *content* of the 'English lessons' they referred to. In one, English is used to learn about world history, although whether from an English or French perspective is unclear from the passage, while at the same time an explicit focus on the written language is provided. In the second, the emphasis is on learning the spoken language, and the vehicle is politics. I particularly enjoyed the reference to the Irish speaker as being 'easier to understand'. This contradicts the view that speakers of English as a first language need to learn one standard variety to be understood in the wider world!

Both of these experiences of learning English belong to an earlier period than the present, before an industry of English language teaching grew up, before there was easy access to English-teaching textbooks and before there were teacher-training departments established to research and disseminate specialised methods. Yet is it inconceivable that people might adopt similar approaches today? You may have begun to learn a language mainly through listening to speakers in an informal setting, or perhaps through watching films and TV, or through listening to popular music.

While it is usual to talk of changes in approaches to English teaching across the decades, when new trends appear they usually coexist with earlier approaches still in use in other classrooms or in other parts of the world. The **grammar translation method** of learning English used by Marie Rambert, for example, bears some resemblance to the extract from a Japanese textbook in Figure 6.1, which shows some study sentences that follow on from a reading passage in English containing new vocabulary and grammatical structures. As with Marie Rambert's approach, the text is (in this case partially) translated and accompanied by a number of exercises that focus on specific grammatical points from the passage. However, the content in the reading passage from the Japanese textbook is simplified and controlled, and appears less cognitively demanding than the one Rambert tackled. We will come back to the question of the content of English teaching later in this chapter.

In contrast to the emphasis on written English taken by the grammar translation method, another approach – one that made an impact on English language teaching from about the turn of the twentieth century until the 1970s – focused on teaching spoken English first, through intensive **oral pattern drilling**. English alone was to be used in the classroom. Translation was thought to be appropriate only at advanced levels. Illustrations, mime and other visual aids were used as clues to enable students to grasp meanings. There was an emphasis on pronunciation and grammatical form, rather than on meanings. The fictional example in the box, 'Language drill', illustrates how such drills could be put into practice.

FOR STUDY

---

〔１〕 現在完了進行形

現在完了進行形は〔have (*or* has)＋been＋現在分詞〕の形で，現在までの動作の継続，進行をはっきりと表す。

How long *have* you *been waiting* for me?

I *have been waiting* for you for a few hours.

He *has been staying* at this hotel since July 5.

cf. He *has stayed* at this hotel for a week.

〔２〕 **any** と **some**

Figure 6.1 Extract from a Japanese textbook on English (Ueyama and Tamaki, 1984, reproduced in Grant, 1987, p.47)

ACTIVITY 6.3

Allow about
5 minutes

In the extract below, from a work of fiction by Ngũgĩ wa Thiong'o, what do you think Njoroge is learning about his relationship with English and about being a learner of the language?

What do you think his teacher has learnt about being a teacher of the language?

Language drill

It was in Standard IV that they began to learn English.

Lucia, Mwihaki's sister, taught them. They all sat expectantly at their desk with eyes on the board. A knowledge of English was the criterion of a man's learning.

Stand = Rugama

TEACHER	I am standing up. What am I doing?
CLASS	You are standing up.
TEACHER	Again.
CLASS	You are standing up.
TEACHER	(pointing with a finger) You – no – you – yes. What's your name?
PUPIL	Njoroge.
TEACHER	Njoroge, stand up.

He stood up. Learning English was all right but not when he stood up for all eyes to watch and maybe make faces at him.

TEACHER   What are you doing?

NJOROGE   (thinly) You are standing up.

TEACHER   (slightly cross) What are *you* doing?

NJOROGE   (clears his throat, voice thinner still) You are standing up.

TEACHER   No, no! (to the class) Come on. What are *you, you* doing?

Njoroge was very confused. Hands were raised up all around him. He felt more and more foolish so that in the end he gave up the very attempt to answer.

TEACHER   (pointing to Mwihaki) Stand up. What are you doing?

MWIHAKI   (head bent on to one shoulder) I am standing up.

TEACHER   Good. Now, Njoroge. What is she doing?

NJOROGE   I am standing up.

The class giggled.

(Ngũgĩ wa Thiong'o, 1964, pp. 44–5)

Comment

Ngũgĩ's fictional incident is a sharp observation of once fashionable 'English only' language teaching methods, imposed on teachers through their training as the 'scientific' or 'correct' methods. Njoroge seems to be learning that speaking English is a source of great humiliation to him, and that his teacher for some reason refuses to help him understand what he's doing wrong. His teacher has presumably been trained to ignore her bilingual skills, when they might so easily have helped to sort out Njoroge's confusion.

At the same time, the extract indicates the fundamentally authoritarian nature of this drill approach. Ownership of the language is firmly in the hands of the textbook writer or curriculum planner. The teacher who is a non-native speaker simply has to manage the communicative event, and learners are discouraged even from using a dictionary to manage their own learning. Understanding the language becomes less important than producing it on demand.

Although less popular today, oral drills still have their place among other activities in many modern textbooks. Echoes of the approach are seen, too, in a tendency to frown on the use of the first language and translation methods in English classes, and in an emphasis on developing spoken before written English even in contexts where students' priorities are for reading English (for example university entrants who need to handle science texts published only in English in order to graduate in their first languages in their own countries).

However, just like the 'translation' methods which have been so strongly criticised, and yet which seemed to work for Rambert and Lenin (even though supplemented by Speakers' Corner!), drills may have worked well for some learners, providing them with a way into communication and an identity that suited them as English speakers.

A major reaction to the use of oral drills arose from an interest in **communicative competence**, a term – coined in the 1960s and widely disseminated in the 1970s – referring to acquiring everything a language user needs to know to communicate effectively. This embraced not only grammar, pronunciation and word meaning, but also knowledge of how to use language appropriately for different audiences, how to construct well-organised written texts or oral monologues, and how to integrate language with other appropriate communication systems – gesture, eye contact, and so on. In a famous phrase, communicative competence incorporated the 'rules of use without which the rules of grammar would be useless' (Pride and Holmes, 1972, p. 278).

Proponents of **communicative approaches** to language teaching suggested that 'errors' in early use of English were to be expected and welcomed as signs of the way the learner is hypothesising about how the language system works. Rather than becoming bad habits, 'errors' would be corrected gradually as the learner gained more experience of the system (see, for instance, Corder, 1974). There was a demand for more interactive classrooms where learners could use English (develop 'fluency'), as well as learn its grammar (develop 'accuracy').

In the USA Stephen Krashen (1981) went further, suggesting that learning a second language was very like learning the first, and proposing a 'natural approach'. He argued that learners should simply be encouraged to participate in plenty of easily comprehensible activities in the 'target language', absorbing English just as a child learns a first language, and not be required to produce English (the 'silent period') until ready to do so. The teacher's job should be simply to provide 'comprehensible input' and activities which would encourage learners to use English, with feedback focusing on meaning rather than form. Teaching that focused on grammar or structures would be of little use. While Krashen's extreme position was controversial, debate for some time centred on how to balance 'accuracy' and 'fluency' activities most effectively in the classroom.

With the establishment of oral drill methods of language teaching in the 1960s the ESL teaching tradition had begun to diverge strongly from the concerns of teachers in 'mother-tongue' contexts. Methods were so different that during periods of large-scale migration to English-speaking countries, new teachers were thought to be required for learners of English as a second language. These learners were also thought to need separate classes since the teaching methods were so different.

With the 'natural approach', mother-tongue and second language teaching came closer together, influencing each others' practice in interesting ways, especially in a new emphasis on literacy and wider educational outcomes for bilingual learners of English.

EFL textbooks have also responded to demands for communicative 'fluency' activities alongside models of grammatical 'accuracy'. Hutchinson and Torres (1994) compared textbooks of the late 1970s, which they say consisted almost entirely of texts, questions and substitution drills, with more recent successors, often by the same authors, which contained integrated video materials, problem-solving exercises, role play, songs, the development of reading, writing and listening skills, games, grammar summaries and transcripts.

Where the learning context is one in which there is less English in the environment to be absorbed, and classmates share another, stronger language, learning English is obviously less 'natural' than learning a first language, and communicative methods have to be planned with care if they are not to degenerate into trivial games as meaningless as the oral drill routines described so vividly by Ngũgĩ.

6.4 Who does what in English?

Communicative approaches to language teaching suggest that learners need to be taught not only language forms but also **language functions**. Indeed, within the European Union, there has been an attempt to codify the range of language functions that learners may need to operate at different levels in the form of a Common European Framework of Reference for languages (2006).

For instance, the sentence *Are those your books on the floor?* has an interrogative form. But functionally, it is ambiguous: it may be a question, seeking information; but it may also be an order (*Pick them up!*) or a complaint. Not all functions, however, are equally available to all speakers. As Foucault has written, 'We know very well that we are not free to say anything, that we cannot speak of anything when and where we like, and that just anyone, in short, cannot speak of just anything' (quoted in Sheridan, 1980, p. 122).

ACTIVITY 6.4

Allow about
10 minutes

How many different ways can you think of to ask somebody to open the window? Jot these down, and consider which ones you would teach to a beginner with little experience of English. Why?

Comment

You may have listed forms such as:

- Open the window please.
- Could you open the window, do you think?
- Would you mind opening the window?
- Excuse me, I wonder if you could possibly open the window?
- Do you think it's getting a bit stuffy in here?

Look at your list again. What sorts of relationship between speaker and hearer do the different forms imply? In my list the first, *Open the window please*, is a simple structure to teach a beginner and, indeed, orders and instructions of this form were present in early lessons in textbooks based on oral drills. However, this may be an inappropriate form to use in some situations, for example in British English you would probably be expected to use a more indirect request form to someone more powerful, such as your teacher.

This is why, although teachers ask questions (see Chapter 4), pupils learning English as a second language are generally not required to produce questions in school, but to give answers. However, one structure they are asked to produce from their earliest days in an English-speaking school is *May I go to ... please?* and *Can I have ... please?*

A student learning English is inevitably being positioned as a certain sort of English speaker within the social meanings of the text on offer. Learners may of course reject this positioning, but for the moment at least they must play along; as a consequence they may well (like Njoroge in the extract earlier) develop unfavourable attitudes towards the language and towards using the language. What sorts of function, then, are learners of English invited to perform through English teaching texts: what social positions may they take up in the new language?

First, let's look at an example from a general English course for beginners that was published in 1978. The cartoon and exercises in Figure 6.2 invite learners to take part in a rather typical EFL textbook situation. The participants want to meet people in some social gathering. Historically the role models in the textbooks were English 'mother-tongue' speakers indulging in 'typical' social practices, as in this illustration of what looks like a cocktail party. Speakers of other languages were often represented as stereotypes, as illustrated by the French man and the Japanese woman in Exercise 3 in the figure.

Figure 6.2   Learning to socialise in the 1970s (Hartley and Viney, 1978, pp. 1–2)

ACTIVITY 6.5

Allow about
30 minutes

Try to find some examples of contemporary general English courses, and look in particular at how the topic of social introductions is handled. In what ways, if at all, has the approach changed from the example in Figure 6.2?

Comment

Your own examples will provide the most persuasive evidence but, in general, more recent textbooks have attempted to show a multilingual context similar to that found in an EFL language school or in international gatherings – where English is the common medium of communication among speakers of many different languages.

Each textbook makes assumptions about its readers' lives and what they will need to do with English. While introductions are a feature of most general purpose courses, they do not feature in *High Season* (Harding and Henderson, 1994), a specialised English textbook for the hotel and tourist industry and an example of **English for specific purposes (ESP)**. The functions emphasised here are: listening carefully to others' requests, answering questions with factual information, describing rooms and facilities, understanding duties and undertaking routine procedures (reception, checking out). The workers' own personalities, wants and needs are absent. In Figure 6.3 the learner is shown the 'correct way' to handle complaints.

---

1 Listen to this conversation between a guest and a receptionist.

    a Make a list of the things the guest is complaining about.
    b What does she want to do?
    c What is the outcome?

2 Now listen to the second conversation. What is the outcome this time?

3 Listen to both conversations again. In what ways does the receptionist behave differently in the second conversation? What does she offer to do?

Responding to complaints

Look at this example of responding to a complaint.

Complaint	Apology	Action
▶ *This room is filthy!*	*I'm terribly sorry.*	*I'll send someone up to clean it immediately.*

Now respond to the following complaints in a similar way.

Complaint	Apology	Action
a This soup's disgusting!		
b I'm sorry to trouble you, but I don't seem to have any towels.		
c It's really noisy. Can't you do something about it?		
d The central heating's not working.		
e Look. Our sheets haven't been changed.		
f Sorry, but I ordered tea, not coffee.		
g I can't seem to get the shower to work.		

Figure 6.3   Learning to handle complaints (Harding and Henderson, 1994, pp. 79–80)

Compare this with the more powerful positioning of learners in *Business Opportunities* (Hollett, 1994) in Figure 6.4, where they are encouraged to make and justify their own choices of action among a range of alternatives.

Functions emphasised in this course include making arrangements and appointments, collecting information, asking for opinions, making suggestions and giving explanations.

LANGUAGE WORK

International meetings I

You are attending a two-day conference at the international headquarters of your company. Top managers from all over the world are attending, but you encounter a few problems. Decide what to do about them, and tick one of the boxes.

1 Before the conference, the organizers send you some working papers. You are short of time. Decide what to do with them.

☐ I'll make sure I study the papers thoroughly, even if I have to stay up all night.
☐ I'll have a quick look at them on the plane.
☐ I'll do something else. (What?)

2 Your Finance Director is supposed to attend the conference with you, but something important has come up and she can't. Decide what to do.

☐ I'll go alone.
☐ I'll see if her deputy can attend instead, even though he has a much lower status in my organization.
☐ I'll do something else. (What?)

3 This morning's meeting is supposed to be about next year's budget. However, you've had an idea about the distribution system that you'd prefer everyone to discuss. Decide what to do.

☐ I'll keep quiet and discuss the budget.
☐ I'll introduce the topic of the distribution system.
☐ I'll do something else. (What?)

4 The subject of this morning's meeting has little relevance to your area of work. You have a phone call to make and you'd like to leave half-way through. Decide what to do.

☐ I'll leave without saying anything.
☐ I'll wait until the meeting is over to make my call.
☐ I'll do something else. (What?)

5 The weather is very hot and the sun is beating through the meeting room windows. You are getting uncomfortable. Decide what to do.

☐ I'll remove my jacket and loosen my tie.
☐ I'll do nothing.
☐ I'll do something else. (What?)

6 You are sitting in a small meeting, listening to the Production Manager's report. You are not an expert on the subject of production but suddenly you have an idea. Decide what to do.

☐ I'll indicate I'd like to speak and tell everyone my suggestion.
☐ I'll keep quiet and speak to the Production Manager later.
☐ I'll do something else. (What?)

7 You are putting forward a proposal that several people at the meeting disagree with. You are absolutely sure that you are right and they are wrong. How will you handle this?

☐ I'll stick to my guns.
☐ I'll drop the proposal.
☐ I'll do something else. (What?)

Figure 6.4 Learning to make and justify changes (Hollett, 1994, p. 36)

Extending the contrast, a functional course for migrant learners of English as a second language, *A New Start* (Furnborough et al., 1980), offers students the following functions: saying *hello* and *goodbye*; simple transactions such as buying a ticket and paying in a supermarket; simple directions; 'insisting politely'; and making an apology. There is a great deal of emphasis on teaching the learner to follow instructions of various kinds. In *Business Opportunities*, however, it was the learner who was expected to give instructions and make explanations.

Some of the dangers of assuming particular needs for particular groups of language learners seem immediately apparent. Are learners offered the sort of English used by the powerful or by the powerless? Do they learn about the differences between the two? Do they discuss the social consequences of making choices? How far would a certain presentation of themselves (as taught in *Business Opportunities*, for example) be seen as legitimate or appropriate by those around them in their own work context? I have suggested that, as speakers of other languages enter into English, different positions are constructed for them – different things are judged possible and legitimate for them to say and do depending on their perceived age and social position.

Learners may be aware of this and so resist learning the English on offer. Others may welcome new positions offered to them by the new language – for example it may offer a new gender positioning which legitimates ways of speaking and acting that would have seemed impossible in the first language. Thus, for some, English may offer a vehicle for developing a new sort of identity (see, for example, the case studies in Kanno, 2003). But much still depends on whether or not the new English-speaking context the learner is attempting to enter will accept the sort of identity offered by the learner.

Tomic and Trumper (1992) have described their experiences as Chilean professional economists who fled to Canada as refugees (in a similar way to Leila, the journalist referred to in Activity 6.1). Tomic and Trumper felt they were repositioned by the Canadian immigration process as 'Third World working class', and not given opportunities to receive the English teaching they required to continue their professional lives and re-establish their identity as professionals. They write:

> Although race, colour, size, gender or age cannot be taken officially into account in a hiring process, it is accepted that a certain level of fluency is essential to work in certain jobs. Denying us access to language training made us ineligible for other than unskilled and poorly paid work.

> (Tomic and Trumper, 1992, p. 176)

The situation Tomic and Trumper outline is not confined to Canada. With reference to the English programmes run at the time by the USA for refugees in camps in south Asia, Pennycook (1989) suggests that there was a 'covert policy to ensure that immigrants will have enough English to perform adequately in minimum-wage jobs while avoiding any welfare dependency, yet not enough to move beyond these levels of employment' (Pennycook, 1989, p. 593).

In the UK this sort of challenge to ESL teaching has led some teachers to transfer their focus from the learners themselves to the wider context within which they must operate. Thus, in the 1970s, the National Centre for Industrial Language Training (NCILT) ran programmes aimed at restructuring workplace attitudes in multilingual contexts; more recently, school-based projects such as the Partnership Teaching Project (Bourne and McPake, 1991) have focused on ways of changing school structures and routine ways of working to make them more receptive to a diversity of needs, including those of developing bilingual learners.

Teachers have also sought to address the content of the English curriculum. For instance, Mukherjee (1985) recommends a language syllabus for minorities in English-dominant nations which is based on key concepts such as power and powerlessness, identity and rootlessness, equality and justice.

The question of developing serious content has also become important in English teaching outside English-dominant countries. Neville Grant, in Reading A, believes in introducing serious issues in real discussion as stimulus to a deeper engagement with the language, whatever the context for English teaching. However, in writing for countries other than his own, Grant is aware of the difficulties of providing appropriate stimulus material for an unknown audience 'within a vocabulary of 1,400 words' which also satisfies the political and cultural constraints imposed by government sponsors.

ACTIVITY 6.6

In this activity, you will be looking in more detail at these problems in the context of reading 'Dilemmas of a textbook writer' by Neville Grant (Reading A).

1   Before reading, make a short list of the cultural and moral issues you think you would need to consider in writing English teaching materials for use in a country other than your own.

2   As you read, note down the ways in which Grant addresses these issues. Does he identify any issues you had not thought of?

3   Why does Grant want 'to reflect national social and cultural aspirations' in his materials rather than teach about British or US culture? How successful do you think he is in this aim in the examples of material he gives?

Comment

As an educational writer specialising in syllabus design and materials development, some of the difficult questions on which Grant finds he has to take a personal stand include:

- the extent to which it is possible to teach and practise English without raising cultural and moral issues

- whether or not EFL materials are the right place to discuss such issues with learners
- whether there are some issues too sensitive to be touched on for cultural or other reasons (e.g. bride-wealth, arranged marriages, contraception, female circumcision)
- the extent to which authors can remain 'neutral' in introducing sensitive issues without compromising themselves.

The reading illustrates the tightrope that textbook writers walk in producing acceptable English materials for different countries. At its most basic this can mean appreciating that, for example, while a dog may be taken generally in the UK to have a positive image, as a pet, it may more frequently be interpreted as something potentially dangerous or unclean in the Middle East (Alptekin, 1993). Even the illustrations that are used to give clues to meanings in materials need to be carefully examined.

Grant shows that the EFL textbook writer is not usually the sole decision maker in terms of content. Local political control is maintained over the sorts of social, cultural and political meanings conveyed through teaching materials. EFL textbooks appear to be as much part of local control mechanisms (syllabuses, classroom methods, examinations) as they are Western exports.

Grant says that in China he was asked to provide a 'window on the world outside' through his materials, and to consider 'cultural differences'. In northern Europe it is generally seen as an important part of English classes for students to gain an awareness of life in English-speaking countries. The idea is that students need to learn how to operate with English speakers or in English-speaking countries – to become 'culturally competent' as well as communicatively competent. In contrast, in the African examples, where English has a local presence through a colonial history, the situation is more complicated. Grant uses English as a stimulus to get students talking about local issues. In his introduction he shows that he is anxious to avoid any charge of 'cultural imperialism and an unpleasant ethnocentrism', and to support 'native culture'. But in learning any language how far can or should issues of cultural differences be avoided? For example, Grant's choice of certain topics as 'controversial' itself indicates something of his own cultural perspective.

Grant himself asks whether the author is 'downloading cultural values or raising international issues in a relatively uncontroversial manner'. In addition to the text itself, it is worth considering the sorts of activity the textbook sets up. How far is the classroom in which students sit expressing and discussing their different opinions a product of a particular culture? Consider English teaching in China, where the practice of 'intensive reading', the careful analysis of written texts in English, is a valued method of study. What does Grant's invitation to students to 'form their own views' mean in this context? Pennycook (1994b) argues that teaching methods as well as content carry cultural messages. A further problem is the trivialising of issues through the holding of discussions apparently without purpose – this week freedom of the press, next week abortion.

6.5 The spread of English language teaching

The previous section dealt with the issue of values in English teaching in terms of the methods and materials used. I want now to explore English language teaching in its broader socio-political context.

Many of the issues we have looked at so far in this chapter cross the boundary between EFL and ESL teaching, with common problems in the selection of content and target language variety, and similar concerns regarding values. More generic terms used in this context to cover both EFL and ESL are **English language teaching (ELT)** and, particularly in the USA, **English to speakers of other languages (ESOL)**. In this section I consider whether, and under what conditions, ELT or ESOL can be a neutral activity, or whether it necessarily serves certain interests at the expense of others.

Where earlier advantages were gained for English by British colonial activity, political pressure was renewed during the twentieth century to enhance the pace of the spread of English. In the mid twentieth century the UK and the USA attempted to increase the global dominance of English as part of an effort to resist the threat of Hitler and any that might follow him. A new cultural body, the British Council, was set up by the British government in 1935 to promote Britain and the English language abroad. Routh (1941), an adviser to the British Council, wrote 'Every nation now being educated is also possessed by ideas, opinions, doctrines, and these have to be canalised, no less than economic resources ... We have to capitalise brains even more consistently than national debts' (Routh, 1941, pp. 15–16).

Routh argued that, around the world, there was an untapped desire to learn English and a need to create a new 'army of linguistic missionaries' to meet that demand. However, he warned that other nations 'will not want to be anglicised', nor to 'merge their national identity in an imported civilisation'. Britain in the world peace-keeping role he envisaged for it might not always be popular with those it intended to manage. The solution, he argued, was to present English as an international language. In the post war settlement:

> They may have to recognise the British Empire as a disciplinarian in disguise, but not as an instructor undisguised. So if they need our language it will not be as a cultured alternative to their own, but as a business-like amplification, a *lingua franca* ... our instructor must begin by learning submergence in the comity of nations. He is to diffuse not so much English but the language which the English originated.

(Routh, 1941, pp. 31–2)

In arguments such as this we can see the emergence of a concept of English as neutral and as an international possession, not 'ours' but 'all of ours'. The validity of the concepts of 'native' and 'non-native' speaker has been questioned in relation to expertise in using English, as has the validity of assessing English in relation to a British or American norm rather than, say, a local norm (e.g. Rampton, 1990) or an international non-native speaker norm (e.g. Seidlhofer, 2003), as embodied in the notion of **English as a lingua franca (ELF).**

Britain is not alone in the promotion of English around the world. Quite apart from the USA, there is increasing competition from other English-dominant nations such as Australia and the Republic of Ireland to export English language teaching overseas.

In addition, the promotion of English as an international language (as 'not ours but all of ours') is having a side effect. There is a growing confidence in local English teaching expertise on the part of many *non*-English-dominant countries, who no longer see themselves as needing outside 'experts', or, indeed, 'native speakers' of English as teachers. For what use is the concept of 'native speaker' when English is conceived of as an international language? Countries other than those that are English-dominant are beginning to export their own English-teaching expertise: the Scandinavian countries and Austria, for example, have well-established teacher training departments and developed methodologies, and are increasingly involved in teaching English to overseas students; and Singapore provides English language teaching for students from China and other parts of East Asia.

How are English-dominant countries responding to this competition in the market for teaching English? To take Britain as an example, there was a counter trend in the 1990s that played down the 'international' status of English. British providers became interested in developing 'British Cultural Studies' (Storey, 1994; Walker, 1994); some emphasised the importance of having native speaker teachers, establishing Standard (British) English norms (Quirk, 1989) and devising test materials to grade global English users against such norms.

The political and economic importance to Britain of English language teaching has been explicitly addressed in the policy statements of the British Council. Two of the main aims of the British Council project *English 2000* (Bowers, 1994) were: 'to assist in ensuring that English remains the preferred language for international communication' and 'to sustain and develop the global market for English goods and services'. Similar trends can be traced in other English-exporting countries, such as the USA and Australia, as they each try to carve out a distinct niche in the global market. (For a fuller discussion of trends in global English teaching, see Graddol, 1997; Block and Cameron, 2002; Graddol, 2006.)

There have been several responses to the global promotion of English language teaching. Phillipson (1992) saw this as an example of **linguistic**

imperialism, in which the exertion of power in favour of English has led to the neglect of other languages in national language policies and education systems. In summary, he claimed that attempts have been made to:

- persuade people of the superior merits of English (as the language of modernisation, social mobility, liberalism, international communication, science and technology, etc.) in comparison to what are presented as the failings of other languages (divisive, parochial, community, heritage, backward-looking);

- promise goods and services to those who use English (e.g. education, science, technology, progress, access to world markets);

- covertly support those people or issues that stigmatise or threaten local languages (e.g. internal divisions and conflicts over languages, resource costs, difficulties in learning English, problems in world markets).

Phillipson is not against the teaching of English, but argues that English should be in a position of equality with other languages in multilingual countries. It should be part of the available linguistic competence on which people may draw for their own purposes.

Bisong (1995) argued that in Nigeria, as in other countries, parents wish their children to learn English to open up new opportunities. But, he claimed, their aim is multilingualism: 'Why settle for monolingualism in a society that is constantly in a state of flux, when you can be multilingual and more at ease with a richer linguistic repertoire and an expanding consciousness?' (Bisong, 1995, p. 125). Rather than replacing the first language, it appears that Nigerian parents see the school as adding English to the child's language repertoire. The parent simply wants 'to ensure a good future for the child, to make certain that the child does not lose out on anything good that is going' (Bisong, 1995, p. 125).

A somewhat different position was taken by Annamalai (1986), who claims that English helps maintain divisions and hierarchies within a country: it is used for 'elite formation and preservation, intranational and international links between elites, and international identity' (Annamalai, 1986, p. 9). The introduction of English into schools works to exclude rather than include; it is yet another hurdle for children to jump in order to increase their life chances, providing a sorting and classifying mechanism for access to higher education. It legitimates differences in economic wealth through an appearance of providing equal opportunities, where in fact one class stands to gain from possessing the 'cultural capital' of easy access to English in the home and access to expensive extra English classes.

Rogers (1990) also argued that, whatever the multilingual ideal, teaching English in the context of developing economies simply does not work for the majority. Despite the enormous resources it diverts from other educational development possibilities, it actually achieves very little. For *most* children (outside English-dominant countries) it is not a passport to a better job: few jobs exist at the managerial, academic and technical levels for which fluency in English is required. Few will be required to communicate with English speakers or to use English as an international language or for higher education. Rogers claims that if the aim really is access to educational opportunity, progress is more likely to be achieved by education in local languages.

Writing from a later perspective, Graddol argues that 'the world has been changing so fast that it scarcely seems to be the same place as that of the 1990s' (Graddol, 2006, p. 10). The old issues, from the choice of methodology to the charge of cultural imperialism, have not gone away, he argues, but English has genuinely become a global language used for a range of purposes among non-native speakers. He envisages 'a new generation of English-knowing children' (Graddol, 2006, p. 101) around the world, for whom English represents a basic skill.

Multilingual language policies

Several national language policies have attempted to recognise the needs of bilingual and multilingual communities. For instance (as discussed more fully in Chapter 5), the South African constitution now recognises the principle of multilingualism and gives equal status to eleven official languages (Desai, 1995). However, the extent to which this intention has remained simply at the level of rhetoric is an area of contention in South Africa.

It is not impossible to conceive of a national language policy which does recognise multilingualism. Lo Bianco (1987) presented just such a new model for Australia, integrating proposals for: English for speakers of other languages; English as a first language; Aboriginal languages; and the 'other languages for, and of, Australians' (Lo Biance, 1987). These other languages included, for example: Italian as a 'heritage language' spoken by a large Australian community; Vietnamese, spoken in local communities as well as the language of an increasingly important trade partner in the region; and Chinese, the language of a nation of geopolitical and economic importance to Australia. The aim of the Lo Bianco policy was to make every child bilingual, if not multilingual. However, the policy was never fully implemented in Australia, and later government policies have given English renewed emphasis.

Struggles concerning the dominance of English continue in other parts of the world, too. The 'English only' movement, which aims to make English the official language of the USA, has already had an effect on the provision of bilingual education in schools across the different states. In contrast, in Hong Kong there has been ongoing debate about whether English should be replaced by Chinese.

Countries that depend on aid will continue to be heavily influenced by the decisions of international agencies such as the World Bank, who will decide what sort of educational initiatives to fund and the priority that should be given to English teaching in them.

Generally, among the aid agencies there has been a perceptible switch of resources away from English language teaching and towards wider educational projects, with higher priority being given to the use of the medium of the first language to raise attainment in learning, rather than on language learning per se. As the director of the UK's government aid agency asked English language teaching experts at a British Council seminar:

> What is the economic value of English teaching? ... Increasingly we see projects that aim to develop a range of key subjects and techniques ... it will be ever more important to be able to justify educational projects with an ELT element in them in terms of their economic productivity. In aid terms the teaching of English is simply not an end in itself.

(Iredale, 1991, pp. 8–9)

I began this chapter by discussing the range of contexts in which English is taught, and the range of methods that have been used to teach it. I then moved from questions of pedagogy in a fairly narrow sense to cultural and political dimensions of English teaching: to the values that seem necessarily to be associated with teaching materials and methods, and to broader political debates about the teaching of English in different parts of the world. Many of the researchers and commentators I have referred to in the last two sections have seen English teaching as a threat: English teaching has been seen by some as positioning individual learners in such a way as to disempower them and, at an international level, as bound up with 'linguistic imperialism'.

ACTIVITY 6.7

Allow about 30 minutes

Look back carefully at the various examples and arguments discussed in Sections 6.4 and 6.5, and try to evaluate them. Which do you agree with? How far, and in what ways, do you think it is possible, in Pennycook's words, to 'establish some way of teaching English that is not automatically an imperialist project' (Pennycook, 1994b, p. 69)?

Some current developments

The teaching of English to speakers of other languages is by no means a settled area; it continues to change in response both to changing social and political imperatives and to its practitioners' attempts to come to grips with some of the issues discussed in this chapter. Ongoing developments include diversification of the ELT curriculum, a broader educational remit for English teaching, and both critical and bilingual approaches.

Diversification of the ELT curriculum

There have been calls for diverse teaching approaches both within and between countries, for example: EFL combined with cultural studies;

'international' ESP linked to the training of engineers, doctors and tour guides; **English for academic purposes (EAP)** for people entering higher education or intending to study abroad; and balancing a focus on literacy skills or communicative oral skills for schoolchildren, depending on national educational goals.

A broader educational remit for English teaching

Teaching ESOL is now being seen as part of wider educational programmes. For instance, in Australia the focus is on providing children with access to the full school curriculum – on literacy development, on the development of study skills in English and, especially, on coming to understand the different sorts of text required for science, literature, history, etc. This approach is mirrored in the advice and materials developed as part of the national literacy strategies for England and Wales. At issue for the success of such approaches is whether students are really given access to powerful ways of writing, or simply coached to produce set forms or genres to pass examinations.

Critical approaches to language in society

Pennycook (1994a) argued that, even in classes that attempt to deal with serious topics, teachers 'have often failed to link the focus of these classes either to the language being learnt or to the lives of the students' (Pennycook, 1994a, p. 132). He argued that there is a difference between 'dealing with "serious issues"' and 'dealing with issues seriously'.

A critical approach to language in society has been taken in the South African context by Janks (1993), who explores what being a speaker of English might mean to students in the 'new' South Africa, and how the language has come to take on different social meanings before, during and after the apartheid era. Another example comes from Greece, where Prodromou, an English teacher, suggested taking as a classroom topic 'Grainglais': 'the English that Greeks see and hear all around them' (Prodromou, 1990, p. 37). This has two major aims: to improve students' competence in English and to increase their awareness of what happens when cultures come into contact. In this way they explore what it means to be a (bilingual) Greek user of English.

Bilingual approaches to language learning

Another kind of focus on the structure of English is made possible by bilingual linguists. It is becoming increasingly acceptable to focus on the *forms* (or grammar) of language in the classroom as well as on communicative activities *using* the language. In this context, work on the contrastive analysis of English and other languages seems to offer considerable potential for learners. For example, Tony Hung (1993) has suggested the examination of comparative phonology in English and Chinese to raise awareness of pronunciation patterns and avoid some of the communicative difficulties a Chinese learner of

English can face. Contrastive analysis may in time lead to experimentation and the development of more truly bilingual approaches to English teaching, including work on codeswitching and other forms of bilingual language behaviour relevant to many learners. Such approaches would also tend to recognise the expertise of local bilingual teachers.

Critical studies of how language works in society, including comparative analysis across languages and cultures, may offer a way in to developing an understanding of the kind of English that Michael Christie reports an Australian Aboriginal community as demanding for their children: 'We want them to learn English. Not the kind of English you teach them in class, but your secret English. We don't understand that English but you do. To us you seem to say one thing and then do another. That's the English we want our children to learn' (quoted in Christie, 1985, p. 50).

6.6 Conclusion

This chapter has emphasised the different contexts in which English is taught to speakers of other languages, and the varying needs of different learners. I have also tried to give a sense of the debates that surround the teaching of English in different contexts, and to encourage you to take part in these debates. There has been discussion about the particular variety of English that should serve as a model for learners; about the methods that should be used to teach English; about the content of English (the styles and functions that are made available to learners, and the topics covered in teaching materials); and about the extent to which English should be taught at all. Underlying such debates have been concerns about the social and cultural values that are bound up with English teaching, and the sorts of identities learners are invited to construct for themselves as English speakers.

READING A: Dilemmas of a textbook writer

Neville Grant
(Neville Grant is a professional textbook writer.)

Specially commissioned for Bourne (1996, pp. 275–82).

[At the time of writing in the mid-1990s,] I have been a writer of English language teaching/learning materials for over twenty years. I do this as a full-time occupation, although I also undertake some consultancy work and a certain amount of teacher training.

Members of my subgroup within the English language teaching (ELT) profession fall broadly into two categories. There are those writers who develop materials for 'global' markets. These are the writers who try to satisfy the inexhaustible demands of language schools from Montevideo to Mexico City to Madrid and Milan – as well as, these days, Moscow: they tend to produce materials for a kind of international middle class. Secondly, there are those who write for the school systems of particular countries – Italy, Mexico, Nigeria or Japan. These fall into two further subcategories – those who write English as a foreign language (EFL) materials and those who write English as a second language (ESL) materials. Much of the work I have done comes into this second category. I started off writing materials for countries where I had lived and which I knew fairly well – in East and West Africa. Later I was commissioned to write for other parts of the world where it was necessary for me to get to know the countries as well as I possibly could in as short a time as I possibly could. In all cases, I worked as a member of a team with local participants. Usually, I was the only full-time professional author.

It is widely thought that it is almost impossible to learn a language without undergoing some cultural change. But language teaching/learning programmes that are 'designed to encourage learners to "become American" for example, to adopt certain values and attitudes considered appropriate for immigrants, and to shift allegiance from their native culture to the dominant American culture' (Tollefson, 1991) are, to this writer at least, anathema. It is difficult to avoid the view that such programmes smack of cultural imperialism and an unpleasant ethnocentrism. Syllabus designers and curriculum workers in the countries in which English is learnt as a second language, such as Nigeria, Ghana, Kenya, South Africa or Botswana, would be aghast at suggestions that their language-learning syllabuses should in any way follow the 'integrative' line. It is hoped that the case studies below will give an insight into some of the cross-cultural issues raised in ELT.

All the work I have been involved in has been done against the background of education systems – the education systems of the target countries, including their teaching syllabuses and examination syllabuses. Materials that do not conform in detail to a national syllabus may not receive approval, and may therefore never be used within the education system for which they were devised, no matter how 'good' the materials. Similarly, materials that are not tailored to national examinations will also fail to be adopted. Such examinations are these days almost always set by national or regional examination boards. It is one of the professional hazards that such examinations may be overly influenced by educational considerations that are now considered out of date (updating examinations and/or education systems is extremely expensive). Such examinations may not be as closely tailored to economic strategies of development as may be thought desirable. Thus, some examinations may unduly reward accuracy in manipulating the forms of language at the expense of functions of language, which is a criticism that has been levelled at West African examinations; or they may seem unduly literary and elitist, a criticism that has been levelled at Caribbean examinations.

In all the materials development projects in which I have been involved, a priority has been to reflect national social and cultural aspirations. Thus, a course written for Kenya will give prominence to writing by Kenyan writers, of whom Ngũgĩ wa Thiong'o is the best known, whereas a course for Nigeria will contain a great deal of writing by such writers as Chinua Achebe, Buchi Emecheta or Wole Soyinka.

Case study 1: Nigeria

In order to accommodate syllabus changes I have recently been involved with rewriting and updating materials that I developed for Nigeria some years ago. (For an early account of this project see Grant, 1983.) The new syllabus highlights a number of lexical items that need to be taught, typically in the context of meaningful and relevant reading materials. Among these are terms concerned with marriage and weddings, including the term 'bride-price'.

It was decided to treat this topic in a four-pronged manner: (1) reading material (with comprehension and discussion questions); (2) vocabulary exercise; (3) debate; and (4) poem.

1 Reading material

One reading text, adapted for level and length, from Chinua Achebe's famous novel of 1958, *Things Fall Apart*, includes a description of some negotiations over a 'bride-price' between two families.

Bride-price

Just then, Akueke came in carrying a wooden dish with three kola nuts and pepper. She gave the dish to Machi, her father's eldest brother, and she stretched out her hand, very shyly, to her suitor and his relatives. She was about sixteen and just ripe for marriage. Her suitor and his relatives looked her over to make sure that she was beautiful and ready for marriage.

Akueke's hair was combed up into a crest along the middle of her head. Her skin smelt of scented wood. She wore a string of black beads around her neck. On her arms were red and yellow bracelets, and on her waist four or five rows of waist beads.

After she had held out her hand to be shaken, she returned to her mother's hut to help with the cooking.

The men in the hut were preparing to drink palm wine which Akueke's suitor had brought. Okonkwo could see that it was very good wine, for white bubbles rose and spilled over the edge of the pot.

'That wine comes from a good tree,' said Okonkwo, Obierika's friend.

The young suitor, whose name was Ibe, smiled broadly. He filled the first horn and gave it to his father, Ukegbu. Then he poured wine out for the others, starting with Akueke's father, Obierika. Okonkwo brought out his big horn from the goatskin bag, blew into it to remove any dust that might be there, and gave it to Ibe to fill.

As the men drank, they talked about everything except the thing for which they had gathered. After the pot had been emptied, the suitor's father cleared his voice and explained the reason for their visit.

(Achebe, 1958; adapted by Grant et al., 1995, p. 104)

The questions include the usual mandatory comprehension questions, plus 'Discussion and opinion' questions designed to encourage learners to give their own views. Included among these were the following questions:

- In this extract, women seem to take no part in the negotiations – and no one asked Akueke's [the bride's] opinion. Do you think that this is right?
- Some people say that paying bride-price is an out-of-date custom. What do you think?
- Chinua Achebe's book *Things Fall Apart* is set in the old days in Nigeria. Could the negotiations described in this extract still take place in a similar way today, do you think?

2 Vocabulary exercise

A follow-up vocabulary exercise is provided which mentions that 'bride-wealth' is in many ways a better term to use than bride-price. The exercise consists of a cloze (blank-filling) text which first briefly describes Western-style courtship patterns, and then proceeds:

> However, in many cases, marriage (in Nigeria) is definitely a family affair: it is seen as the joining together of two families rather than just two people, and an engagement is preceded by a period of ... (4) ... rather than courtship. In such situations ... (5) ... must be paid by the kin of the man to that of the woman. Once this has been given and received, it is seen as a sign that the ... (6) ... is taken very seriously.

3 Debate

A debate is suggested, with these motions:

1   Bride-wealth should be abolished.

2   Polygamy should not be encouraged.

4 Poem

At the end of the unit there is a poem by the Guyanese poet Grace Nichols, followed by a wide-ranging discussion which includes the interesting question 'What do you suppose Grace Nichols would think of the institution of bride-wealth?'

Holding my Beads

Unforgiving as the course of justice
Inerasable as my scars and fate
I am here
A woman ... with all my lives
strung out like beads before me.

It isn't privilege or pity
that I seek
It isn't reverence or safety
quick happiness or purity but
the power to be what I am/a woman
charting my own futures/a woman
holding my beads in my hand.

(Nichols, 1988)

Figure 1 A Nigerian bride

Discussion

In this unit an attempt is made to treat the subject of weddings and a very common Nigerian custom in a culturally sensitive and well-informed manner. No attempt is made to 'preach' to students; every attempt is made to encourage them to use English to think about the issue. An assimilationist model in the Nigerian context is clearly unthinkable. It is not for the writer of ELT materials to make value judgements, but merely to present ideas and activities that encourage learners to think, to learn, and to make up their own minds on the issues raised.

While on one hand it would appear that the writer of ELT materials adopts a neutral stance on issues such as the custom of bride-price, it might be argued that in opening a debate and possibly encouraging dissent, the writer is 'smuggling in' Western notions of self-expression associated with bourgeois liberal humanism. However, anyone who has worked in Nigeria, at least in the south, would acknowledge that enthusiastic controversy and argument, far from being a feature solely of Western democracy, is a prominent feature in Nigerian culture.

Case study 2: China

Between 1988 and 1992 I was involved in helping to develop a new course for the People's Republic of China, working for a project funded by UNDP (United Nations Development Project), and implemented by two publishers working together – the People's Education Press in Beijing, and Longman Group from the UK. This involved extended visits to Beijing and other cities, during which I worked closely with Chinese colleagues in the People's Education Press.

English was and is seen as an essential part of China's 'modernisation' programme. The development of the new course *Junior English for China* (Grant et al., 1991) was seen as a major curriculum development initiative, involving trialling in pilot schools in many parts of China, collecting feedback, and revising the materials accordingly. A detailed draft syllabus had been developed by the Chinese, but wisely remained in draft form until after the materials interpreting it had been developed, so that the syllabus itself could be fine-tuned in the light of the trialling of the materials. This might seem to be an odd way to approach curriculum development; in fact, it makes very good sense to combine top-down approaches in which working parties hammer out a draft syllabus with bottom-up approaches in which teachers in the classroom give feedback that can fine-tune, or even radically alter, the syllabus. (Curriculum development in the UK could have benefited from such a combined approach in recent years.)

From the outset it was made clear that the Chinese wanted to improve the students' ability to use the English language communicatively, and at the same time provide learners with a window on the world outside China. They were particularly interested in studying 'cultural differences'. This was all the more remarkable given that the project developed at a particularly difficult and sensitive period in China's history. However, 'knowing about' the world outside definitely did not mean 'identifying with' it, and reading passages used in the course were, not surprisingly, closely checked to ensure that what appeared conformed to the syllabus – that is, included the lexis and grammar specified in the syllabus – and contained nothing that was 'unsuitable' or politically controversial.

It is of course quite difficult to be controversial within a limit of some 1400 words (the number of words targeted by the syllabus). In the event, it is surprising what was included: the texts included fragments of British and American history (Abraham Lincoln is a firm favourite), and some references to modern culture (great interest evinced in fast food and fish and chips). Modern mores also played their part: the Chinese were interested in texts that highlighted cultural differences, for example the different way in which Europeans respond to compliments.

It may be imagined that it is not easy to generate interesting reading texts that have some intrinsic educational value within a very small vocabulary. No great claims are made on behalf of the text illustrated in the box other than to say that it was an attempt to break the cultural stereotype common in China that all British (English) are Caucasian and middle class, with 2.4 children, a Ford and a bowler hat. The text seeks to amuse, to treat certain target items of vocabulary, to indicate that the UK is a multicultural society and, last but not least, to address the issue of racism – which, by the way, European societies do not have a monopoly on.

> ## The queue jumper
>
> It was a cold spring morning in the city of London in England. The weather was very cold, and many people were ill. So there were many people in the doctor's waiting room. At the head of the queue was an old woman. The woman was a visitor. She did not live in London. She lived in the country. She was in the city to visit her daughter. She wanted to see the doctor because her back hurt.
>
> 'If I get there early, I can see the doctor quickly,' she thought. So she was first in the queue. She sat nearest to the doctor's door.
>
> An Indian came into the waiting-room, and walked quickly to the doctor's door. The old woman thought he was a queue jumper. She stood up and took his arm. Slowly, she said, 'We were all here before you. You must wait for your turn. Do ... you ... understand?'
>
> The Indian answered: 'No, madam. You don't understand! You're all after me! I'm the doctor!'
>
> Everyone laughed at the woman's mistake.
>
> (Grant et al., 1991, p. 91)

When I first presented this text in draft form to my colleagues they were pleased to see material about queuing – an important cultural feature. But they were also puzzled. 'Why is the doctor an Indian?' they asked. I explained about Britain being a multicultural society. 'Our teachers will find it difficult to understand what an Indian is doing in London. Why don't we make the doctor an Englishman?' [sic]. I agreed that this would be possible, but that it would rather destroy the point of the story. I indicated that there was a gentle anti-racist lesson in the story. This gave my colleagues some pause for thought. In the end, somewhat reluctantly, the story was included in the text.

Discussion

It might be thought that I had some hidden anti-racist agenda and was persuading my Chinese colleagues, perhaps against their better judgement, to include material which they would not ordinarily have chosen. Since my Chinese colleagues had veto powers, however, the question is rather whether or not a professional author is going beyond the call of duty to try to include educational values in the text. Would I have been failing in my duty not to present materials that might not ordinarily have been selected? In so doing was I downloading cultural values or raising international issues in a relatively uncontroversial manner? Should I instead have addressed the issue of racism in a much more controversial way and included (within a vocabulary of 1400 words) an account of race riots in Bristol or wherever? I have to confess that I avoided the latter, partly because of the technical problems of doing so within a restricted vocabulary, but partly also because my Chinese cultural antennae indicated that to describe a riot in a manner sympathetic to the victims might easily have been interpreted as a coded support for those who demonstrated in Tiananmen Square in 1989. Such interpretations could, conceivably, have ugly consequences for one's Chinese colleagues, and even for the whole project.

Case study 3: Tanzania

One of the most interesting problems arises in relation to the press. Not all the countries that one has to write for have a free press. The newspaper is the one publication most likely to be read by students in countries such as Nigeria or Tanzania where there is little tradition of reading more widely. I think it is important that the students are taught to read newspapers, and not necessarily to believe everything they contain!

Some years ago the magazine *Index on Censorship* carried an article by Graham Mitten on newspapers in the Third World.

> At a party in Dar es Salaam a few years ago three Tanzanian journalists argued fiercely about an important issue ... Reports were coming in of a village settlement scheme that had failed badly. Large sums of money had been lost ...
>
> The first journalist argued that they should ignore the story. The government ... had only just launched the policy of ujamaa villages, involving peasants in communal agriculture. It was a difficult policy to put over and [an unfavourable report now] would reinforce existing doubts and might well sway the undecided against the policy ...
>
> The second journalist disagreed ... the press was performing a public duty if it investigated and prevented the government from 'sweeping the whole story under the rug' ... The only way to be sure that government had sensible policies was to report everything connected with those policies ...
>
> The third journalist ... agreed that the press had to say something about the story ... [Not to report it would damage] the credibility of the press ... But everything should be written with great care. The Tanzanian journalist had to be conscious of the effects of what he wrote. Journalists had no business campaigning against elected governments [particularly in Third World countries where resources of all kinds were very limited] ... It was legitimate for the government of Tanzania to expect cooperation from the press.

(Mitten, 1977, p. 35)

This article (presented in a simplified form in Grant et al., 1980) generates great interest in all the classrooms where it has been tried. The book itself remains neutral on the issues raised – and leaves it to the students to be partisan, which, joyfully, they are.

Later in the unit there are two contrasting news reports, one attacking the Tanzanian government for the failure of the village settlement scheme, and one seeking to present the government's efforts in the best possible light. These news reports again generate great interest, and the students enjoy picking out examples of bias, misrepresentation and so forth.

However, the issue – for writer and publisher – arose: how would this article be received in Tanzania? Was the issue so politically sensitive that it might lead to the books not being ordered and used in Tanzania? Was this a good reason to impose self-censorship – a procedure far more common in the world than many of us realise? The material was sent to Tanzania for advice – and the message was relayed back that there was no problem. The then president of Tanzania, Julius Nyerere, welcomed frank discussions of important sensitive issues.

Conclusion

In all the case studies mentioned here there has been a common thread: materials that in some way or other seem to go against the grain – or at least someone's grain – are vetted for content, for cultural acceptability. Doubts are expressed about them, then either the doubts are allayed, or at least declared invalid, or the material is amended or discarded.

References for this reading

Achebe, C. (1958) *Things Fall Apart*, London, Heinemann.

Grant, N.J.H. (1983) 'Materials design for Nigerian secondary schools' in Brumfit, C.J. (ed.) *Language Teaching Projects for the Third World*, Oxford, Pergamon/British Council.

Grant, N.J.H., Olagoke, D.O. and Southern, K. (1980) *Secondary English Project*, Harlow, Longman.

Grant, N.J.H. et al., (1991) *Junior English for China: Students' Book 2*, Beijing, People's Education Press.

Grant, N.J.H. Olagoke, D.O., Nnamonu, S. and Jowitt, D. (1995) *Junior English Project* (for Nigerian Secondary Schools), Harlow, Longman.

Mitten, G. (1977) 'Tanzania – a case study', *Index on Censorship*, vol. 6, no. 5, p. 35.

Nichols, G. (1988) *I is a Long Memoried Woman*, London, Karnak House.

Tollefson, J.W. (1991) *Planning Language, Planning Inequality*, London, Longman.

Academic writing in English
Ann Hewings, Theresa Lillis and Barbara Mayor

7.1 Introduction

In this chapter we look at English as an academic language as it is used by lecturers, students and researchers in higher education in many parts of the world. Our main focus will be on academic writing, rather than speech, since this has been more extensively studied. The main questions that we address are:

- What is 'academic' English and how is its nature related to its functions?
- How does academic writing vary across disciplines?
- To what extent does academic writing vary across cultures and education systems across the world?
- How do students acquire academic literacy, and what does it mean to them to write in an 'academic' way?

7.2 English in the academic world

The use of English as an international academic language, among researchers as well as in teaching activities, has increased dramatically in recent years. In many parts of the former British Empire – in many African countries, India and Singapore, for instance – English has long been established as a medium of university education. Although in postcolonial times there have been some powerful political campaigns to encourage the greater use of other languages in academic settings (such as the pro-Mandarin campaign in Singapore in the 1980s, described in Pennycook, 1994b), many such countries continue to use English in their higher education systems. In Malaysia, the language of tertiary education has continued to be highly contested, with the teaching of some disciplines having moved from English to Malay and back again within the space of a decade. Such a trend is not limited to former colonial territories, however. In 1994 the government of the Netherlands seriously considered a proposal that all Dutch higher education should in future be conducted in English – although this particular proposal was rejected, many individual university courses across Europe are now offered in English.

A further reason for the increased use of English in higher education is that, as the most commonly learnt foreign language, English may function as a lingua franca for scholars of different language backgrounds. Thus, the official language of the European Association for Research in Learning and Instruction (EARLI) is English, even though the vast majority of its members have some other language as a mother-tongue. In the Europe of the Middle Ages, Latin had been the lingua franca of such academic communities. Against this background, the USA has taken a leading role in many academic fields of research, increasing academic publishing in English.

This spread of English in higher education has been at the expense of other languages, whose role in academic life is inevitably diminished. For example, though mathematics research was, before the Second World War, commonly published in international German-language journals, English-language journals now predominate. In an influential book called *Linguistic Imperialism*, British sociolinguist Robert Phillipson (1992) describes the process whereby a powerful language displaces others in some social functions, and in so doing assists the cultural influence of the nations which speak it. Support for the academic use of English throughout the world has been an element of British foreign policy, as both Phillipson (1992) and another British academic Alistair Pennycook (1994b) have shown. However, because English now has a status as a world language, its link with specific national cultures may be becoming less strong. In some multilingual academic settings, English may be attractive precisely because it is distinct from local or regional languages and cultures and therefore seen as more 'neutral' (e.g. Corson, 1994).

But to what extent is 'academic' English distinct from other types of English? Is it something that needs to be taught to students with English as a first language, or only to those with English as an additional language?

ACTIVITY 7.1

Allow about
5 minutes

Before reading on, you may like to make a note of your initial responses to the following questions, and set them aside to refer back to later:

- How would you describe 'academic' English?
- Why might it need to be specifically taught?

7.3 Disciplinary differences in academic writing

We will begin by looking at the purposes of academic writing, and the specific influences of the disciplinary context and audience. We go on to focus in greater depth on research studies into the types of features which differ across different disciplines.

The nature of academic English

Linguist John Swales (1990) has described academic life in terms of the activities of various disciplinary **discourse communities**, each focused on a particular academic subject or area of research. Such communities are often spread worldwide and depend heavily on written communications. It is common for scholars in each discipline to establish their own language

Figure 7.1 Becoming a member of an academic discourse community

conventions and practices which new members have to acquire, and there are consequently different varieties of academic English associated with different disciplines. The educational researcher Gordon Wells explains:

> Each subject discipline constitutes a way of making sense of human experience that has evolved over generations and each is dependent on its own particular practices: its instrumental procedures, its criteria for judging relevance and validity, and its conventions of acceptable forms of argument. In a word, each has developed its own modes of discourse. To work in a discipline, therefore, it is necessary to be able to engage in these practices and, in particular, to participate in the discourse of that community.

> (Wells, 1992, p. 290)

Linguist Michael Halliday (1994) suggested that one common feature in the creation of a suitable functional variety of language for a field of study is the creation of new words for referring to newly discovered or specially defined objects, processes, relationships and so on. Thus, in English language study, we find terms such as *phonological awareness* or *discourse community*, as opposed to, say, *metastasis* in medicine or *binary code* in computing.

Of course, academic discourse communities are not entirely distinct. Discourse communities can overlap, and members of some may use English in ways that are quite similar to others. The discourses of sociologists and historians, for instance, are more similar to each other than they are to the discourse of biologists, but historians of science use English in similar ways to both historians and biologists.

ACTIVITY 7.2

Allow about
20 minutes

Read the following examples of specialised academic discourse. All three are extracts from the introductory sections of articles in research journals. As you read, focus on the following linguistic features: lexis (the particular words used, any specialised terminology) and overall style (e.g. whether they represent formal or informal, personal or impersonal ways of using language). Then consider:

1 Which text is easiest for you to understand?
2 What does reading them reveal about your own relationship to academic discourse communities?
3 How do the texts differ?
4 What, if anything, do they have in common in terms of style?

Example 1

Written language like spoken language achieves communicative and conceptual goals by using a complex system of arbitrary symbols and conventional rules ... Writing however is a visible language, a graphic symbolic system whose roots we suggest lie in pictographic representation before links are established with spoken language. In this respect, development reflects evolution in that all writing systems which represent sounds of language evolved from pictorial representations rather than from spoken language.

(Martlew and Sorsby, 1995, p. 1)

Example 2

The attempt to give a comprehensive account of the many hundreds of differences between the 1608 (Pied Bull) Quarto of *King Lear* (Q) and the 1623 First Folio version (F), has occasioned a daunting amount of scholarly study, and the three hundred lines that appear in Q but not in F, and the hundred or so that are in F but not in Q, are an obvious focus for analysis and debate ... It is with F's 'omissions' that I shall mainly concern myself, in taking issue with the 'new revisionists' of the last fifteen years or so, who argue that F is the product of systematic authorial revision of *King Lear*, with Q (however imperfectly) representative of its unrevised state. My own observations will be made from the perspective of the theatre practitioner.

(Clare, 1995, p. 1)

Example 3

In earlier papers we have reported the excess volumes and viscosities of different binary mixtures containing N-methylmethanesulfonamide as one component. In view of the importance of alcohols as solvents, it was of interest to continue this work with an investigation of the properties of the (methanesulfonamide + an aliphatic alcohol). In this study we report the excess volumes for NMMSA + methanol, + propan-1-ol, + propan-2-ol, + butan-1-ol, and + 2-methylpropan-2-ol.

(Pikkarainen, quoted in Bhatia, 1993, p. 89)

Comment

Our guess is that most readers of this book found Example 1 or Example 2 the easiest to comprehend, and Example 3 the hardest. Possible reasons for this are:

1   The first example (which comes from the European journal *Learning and Instruction*) and the second (from *The Library: The Transactions of the Bibliographical Society*) include not only fewer specialised lexical items than the third (which is from the *Journal of Chemical Thermodynamics*) but also fewer whose meaning is completely impenetrable to any reader who is 'outside' the specialised academic community of discourse. The meaning of technical terms such as *symbolic system* and *pictographic* (in Example 1), could perhaps be guessed at by educated 'outsiders' to the discourse of language study, if they drew on their general knowledge of English. This might also be the case for terms like *Quarto* and *Folio* in Example 2; but it is not possible for many of the terms in Example 3. The third example even uses a specialised English morphology (for example, the numbers and dashes in 'propan-2-ol') and syntax (e.g. the use of plus signs in + *methanol,* + *propan-1-ol*) which render it even more code-like and incomprehensible to the uninitiated.

2   The first and second examples are both from fields of study (children's literacy development and published literary texts), which are relatively close to the subject matter of this book. Even if someone is not a 'full' member of the relevant research community, a reader of a book on the English language is more likely to have the kind of background knowledge required for making sense of an article on some aspect of literacy than for understanding the contents of the *Journal of Chemical Thermodynamics*.

3   The most obvious differences between the texts relate to their subject matter and the use of a different **specialised lexis**, or vocabulary of technical terms associated with a specific field of study. In addition, the author of Example 2 is alone in referring to himself individually (*I, myself, my*).

4   The use of a specialised lexis is itself a kind of similarity between the texts. But academic discourses have other characteristic features of style. One feature common to both Examples 1 and 3, which is typical of much writing in scientific research journals, is the lack of any overt reference to the authors as individuals; instead they refer to the collective *we*, or disguise their personal opinions or agency behind third person

formulations such as *it is likely* or *it was of interest*, thus offering (what appears to be) an objective account of their research.

In addition, the three abstracts have an obvious *functional* similarity: each is meant to introduce a report of a research study. Swales (1990) has suggested that the introductions to scientific research articles often have a common basic structure, which reflects the aim of authors to claim a niche for themselves in the research field in which they are involved.

What can we learn from research on disciplinary variation?

Disciplinary variation has been one of the key themes of research into academic writing in recent years, prompted on the one hand by a wish to understand what the disciplinary differences in writing can tell us about how different communities of scholars see knowledge and its creation, and on the other by a concern to help students understand the writing practices of the disciplines they are working within.

Researchers often group disciplines together according to whether they are perceived as 'hard' or 'soft' and 'pure' or 'applied'. Archetypally 'hard' disciplines are those which tend to build knowledge around a framework of shared assumptions over aims, methods of investigation and evaluation criteria. Archetypally 'soft' fields, in contrast, can be characterised as more subjective in their approach to research, encouraging a view of knowledge as a matter of interpretation. Applied fields which are practically orientated, such as engineering or nursing, are contrasted with 'pure' fields such as philosophy or mathematics. Tony Becher in studies of the 'tribes' of academia identified four broad disciplinary groupings:

Pure sciences	(e.g. physics)	hard-pure
Humanities and pure social sciences	(e.g. history) (e.g. anthropology)	soft-pure
Technologies	(e.g. mechanical engineering)	hard-applied
Applied social sciences	(e.g. education)	soft-applied

(adapted from Becher, 1994, p. 154)

The different approaches to knowledge highlighted by the hard–soft, pure–applied dimensions have effects that can be seen in the writing conventions and styles adopted in individual disciplines. Some of these are clearly visible as in, for instance, the genre of the laboratory report in the sciences or the practice notes in education or health care. These genres clearly arise from within the contexts of the disciplines concerned and from what the disciplinary practitioners deem important. So in science, for example, the laboratory report is indicative of the need for care over methods and observations, so that experiments can be replicated if necessary. A body of knowledge built up over the years is transmitted to the novice scientist, who then has to demonstrate the ability to apply that knowledge in the ways sanctioned by the scientific community. For the trainee teacher or health practitioner, practice notes and/or a diary serve to record what is done and how well objectives were achieved, as well as providing a vehicle for more personal reflections on one's own emotional responses and/or how practice could be improved. In such applied areas, students are being encouraged to become 'reflective practitioners', to stand back and constantly evaluate and innovate. Clearly the writing demands and the criteria for success will be different in these two polarised cases.

Writing for a particular discipline involves learning the technical language associated with that discipline and the genres associated with participation. Students of English language, for example, are likely to write notes, essays, linguistic analyses and, possibly, small-scale research projects. If you are studying at an institution you will be submitting some of these genres to the scrutiny of a more highly trained member of the discipline who will judge your writing against their experience of other examples of the disciplinary discourse. You are, in effect, being judged as a novice writer in the disciplinary discourse community of English language study.

Efforts to find out what it means to be a writer within a particular disciplinary community began in the 1970s and 1980s with analysis of research articles (RAs). This genre has become, arguably, the most significant for professional academics, particularly in the sciences. It is the way a person's work becomes known and evaluated by the disciplinary community and it is also key to promotion prospects within academia. The genre itself has recurrent features across disciplines, with most RAs showing a typical structure of Introduction, Methods, Results, Discussion (or IMRD) (Swales 1990). Closer textual analysis reveals that linguistic characteristics cluster around the distinctions between 'hard' and 'soft' disciplines discussed by Becher. Susan Peck MacDonald (1994), for instance, found that the types of item that appeared as the subject of sentences in psychology tended to be more abstract, as befits a scientific orientation, compared with those found in history or literature, which were more focused on particular people, places and events. William Vande Kopple (1986) also noted that scientifically oriented writing is characterised by complex noun phrases in subject position (as in the italicised segment of Example 4). He argues that such phrases allow scientists to condense information available in earlier works.

Example 4

The findings of ... Chase-Lansdale and Owen (in press), cited earlier, as well as those from other studies (e.g., Cochran & Robinson, 1983) indicate that boys might be particularly susceptible to any negative consequences of nonmaternal care in the first year.

(quoted in MacDonald, 1994, p. 162)

Another rhetorical or persuasive feature to come under close scrutiny is 'directives', utterances that instruct readers to perform an action or see things in a way determined by the writer. Ken Hyland (2002), for example, compared the use of directives in a 2.5 million word corpus of texts collected across eight disciplines and comprising three different genres as follows:

Research articles (RAs)	Textbooks (TBs)	Final-year undergraduate project reports* (SRs)
1.4 million words	481,000 words	628,000 words

* Reports written by students in Hong Kong with English as an additional language.

He examined three grammatical forms, which have the function of directing the reader (Hyland, 2002, pp. 216–7):

verbs in the imperative mood
(e.g. **Consider** *the Achilles paradox.*)

modal verbs of obligation addressed to the reader
(e.g. *Together, these acts produced a total speech act that **must** be studied in the total speech situation.*)

adjectives expressing the writer's judgement of necessity/importance followed by a complement to-clause
(e.g. *This means **it is essential to** characterize the large signal model of the HBT as a function of operating and ambient temperatures.*).

ACTIVITY 7.3

Now read the extract 'Rhetoric and reasoning: directives across disciplines' from Hyland's study of directives, which is reproduced as Reading A. Look carefully at Table 1 in the reading. Notice the difference in the use of directives in different genres and disciplines. What reasons can you think of for these differences?

Comment

You might have noticed that overall there are fewer directives in the reports genre than in RAs and textbooks. This could be because of the position of the student writer in relation to the likely expert reader. Students, as you will read later in this chapter, often have difficulties finding the right voice as they are learning to become members of the discipline. You may not feel able to direct your reader to do something or see something in a particular way if you are a relative novice in the field. The student writers were also not first language speakers of English and their own rhetorical traditions or those they had been taught are likely to have influenced their choices (a point we take up again in Section 7.4). However, it is interesting to note that even these students largely conform to the disciplinary preferences shown in the textbook and RA genres. They are already writing more like the experts in their chosen discipline than other novices in different disciplines.

Questioning the writing advice given to second language academic writers, Yu-Ying Chang and John Swales (1999) conducted research into informal elements of academic writing style which are sometimes deemed inappropriate by style manuals and writing guidebooks. They compiled a list of eleven grammatical features commonly associated with informality of style and examined their occurrence in a corpus of ten research articles from each of three disciplines: statistics, linguistics and philosophy. The features identified in order of frequency were:

> imperatives directed at the reader
>
> first person pronouns (*I*, *we*) used to refer to the author(s)
>
> broad reference using pronouns such as *this*, *that* and *those* to refer to lengthy and sometimes unspecified sections of earlier text
>
> split infinitives (e.g. *to* boldly *go*)
>
> beginning a sentence with a conjunction (e.g. *and*, *but*)
>
> ending a sentence with a preposition
>
> run-on sentences and expressions (such as ending a list with *etc.*)
>
> sentence fragments which do not contain vital elements such as a subject or verb
>
> contractions (*aren't, I'm, can't*)
>
> direct questions
>
> exclamations.

> (adapted from Chang and Swales, 1999, p.148)

Their findings were that philosophers used the range of informal features most frequently and that statisticians used them least frequently.

ACTIVITY 7.4

Allow about
5 minutes

Thinking about what you have read about disciplinary differences, what explanations can you come up with for this finding?

Comment

Chang and Swales suggest that the use of all the different features allows philosophers to achieve their intended rhetorical goals of arguing for a particular viewpoint in a discipline that does not have established ways of dealing with issues. Additions to knowledge are 'a matter of *conversation* between persons, rather than a matter of interaction with nonhuman reality' (Rorty, 1979, p. 157, quoted by Chang and Swales, 1999, p. 154). A conversational – in other words typically oral – style is generally less formal and more interactive than the traditional view of academic writing. In contrast:

> ... researchers in Statistics seem to continue to believe in the empiricist and positivist assumption that scientific studies are factual, and hence best designed to be faceless and agentless; their insistence on formal style thus still remains ... To be prudent scientists, the statisticians avoid using features which reveal personal involvement or emotion (e.g. *first person pronouns, direct questions* and *exclamations*)

> (Chang and Swales, 1999, p. 154).

This view of scientific knowledge as based on empirical, that is observational or experimental, data which needs no interpretation by the researcher is perhaps one of the fundamental differences between 'hard' and 'soft' disciplines. But detailed textual analysis of scientific writing has revealed not that scientists do not use language to persuade their discourse community to accept their claims, but that they use it differently because the shared understandings of what constitutes knowledge are different in different fields. For student writers this presents a challenge, particularly if they are working across different disciplinary areas. It does, however, start to explain why a student may be a successful writer for one of their courses, but deemed unsuccessful in another. Based on what we know of disciplinary discourse communities, it is unlikely that the writing practices associated with one discipline will transfer neatly across to another.

The increased awareness of the varieties of academic English associated with particular academic subjects has had profound implications for the teaching of English for academic purposes (EAP). EAP was traditionally regarded as a branch of teaching English as a foreign language (EFL). However, it is increasingly seen as having relevance for all students, whatever their first language.

7.4 Cultural differences in academic writing

We have seen some of the ways in which academic writing varies according to academic discipline. Alongside this, however, are literacy practices associated with the different linguistic and cultural communities to which writers belong. Indeed, a field of research known as **contrastive rhetoric (CR)** is devoted to exploring the ways in which linguistic resources and traditions may vary cross-culturally. (There is a good overview of this field in Connor, 1996.)

Some differences in literacy practices arguably derive from the different linguistic resources available in different languages. For example, some languages, such as Chinese, do not require the topic of each sentence to be explicitly restated if it can be deduced from what has gone before. Others, such as Arabic, use fewer conjunctions than English to signal logical connections between sentences or parts of sentences. (These and other cases are discussed at greater length in Baker, 1992.) Obviously, this does not imply that similar meanings are *incapable* of being conveyed through different languages, but rather that this is achieved in different ways. Such differences may occasionally lead student writers for whom English is an additional language to transfer inappropriate features into their English writing.

Others aspects of cultural difference, however, relate to the rhetorical styles and discourse structures that are traditionally valued within a culture, reflecting the different teaching and learning practices through which writers have been educated. Such differences may relate to the overall structure of a text: for example, not all cultural traditions teach that you should announce your topic directly in an introduction or use your conclusion merely to restate what has gone before. Other areas of difference include the extent to which logical relations are signalled between different parts of a text, (e.g. the use in English of 'linking' words or phrases such as *therefore* or *in summary*), or the extent to which figures of speech such as metaphor are conventionally employed. (Scollon and Scollon, 2001, provide a useful overview of such issues.)

It can of course be difficult to distinguish between an author's use of a style associated with a particular academic culture (say, a Chinese or French style of social scientific research, rather than a British one) and their use of a particular language. However, given the current role of English as a global language of academia, it has become possible to study the variation in writing in English within the same discipline across a range of different cultural contexts where English is used.

Differences in discourse structure and rhetorical style

According to Scollon and Scollon (2001, pp. 86–105), the model academic essay in English is characterised by a 'deductive' style of argument, which presents its main thesis before arguing its case. This approach, they argue, assumes a relationship of 'symmetrical solidarity' (Scollon and Scollon, 2001, p. 101) between reader and writer in the common pursuit of truth. Many students from non English-speaking backgrounds, however, are familiar with a rhetorical strategy which presents its rationale *before* advancing its thesis, an approach which Scollon and Scollon term 'inductive'. This kind of essay, they argue, assumes a hierarchical relationship between writer and reader: the person in the lower position in the social hierarchy (in this case the student writer) has no right to introduce his or her own topic without first convincing the person in the higher position (in this case, the teacher-reader) of the reasons for doing so. In ways such as these, they argue, the written relationship between teachers and learners in English is constrained by the specific resources of the language and the traditions of its speakers.

In different cultures, as indicated above, traditional literacy practices may vary considerably. Bloor and Bloor (1991, p. 10) comment on how academic writing in French is influenced by the ideal model for essay writing that is taught in French schools, in which argument is constructed through the consideration of a 'thesis' (one side of the argument) and an 'antithesis' (the other side of the argument), leading finally to a 'synthesis' (resolution). Chinese school writing, on the other hand, has been characterised, among other things, by use of the rhetorical question. The resultant tendency of Chinese students to argue via the use of questions even in their English writing has been noted by Thompson (2001, p. 74), as well as by Milton, who quotes evidence from a comparative corpus of student writing that 'Direct questions are used about 50% more frequently' by Hong Kong students than by UK students (Milton, 2001, p. 13). Bloor and Bloor (1991, pp. 7–9) also note that when personal opinions or disagreements are expressed in formal academic English, authors tend to use a polite and seemingly self-effacing style, with many 'hedged propositions' (such as *it would seem that* ... and *one possible interpretation of this finding might be* ...). They contrast this with a more direct, personal 'unhedged' style found in academic journals written in the Czech language.

Interpersonal relationship in English-language texts

As discussed elsewhere in this book, language is not simply used to express our thoughts and perceptions of the world; it also implies a communicative relationship between speaker and hearer or writer and reader. Halliday (1994) uses the terms 'ideational' and 'interpersonal' to refer to these two distinct linguistic functions. The interpersonal function is most evident in written texts through the use of personal pronouns and in expressions of emotion, judgement or modality (indicating relative certainty or tentativeness). All of these may serve to draw the reader into a particular perspective or call on them to respond in some way, implying that writer and reader are engaged on a common journey. It follows that part of the goal of writing in English is to 'second-guess the kind of information that readers might want or expect to find at each point in the unfolding text, and proceed by anticipating their questions about or reactions to what is written' (Thompson, 2001, p. 58). However, for novice academic writers, particularly those whose previous education has not been through the medium of English, this crucial sense of audience may be lacking, in other words the student writer may lack a clear notion of the reader's expectations. This is not just a matter of what ideational knowledge can be taken for granted. As Hyland and Milton caution, 'To be effective, writers need to make claims and assertions ... which reflect appropriate social interactions', and this means that 'differences [in the rhetorical practices of different languages and cultures] can make NNSs [non-native speakers] vulnerable to the risk of violating communicative norms' (Hyland and Milton, 1997, pp. 183, 186). Thus, it seems to be impossible to write in English without subtly positioning oneself relative to the reader in a position of solidarity, equality or hierarchy.

Differences in the use of personal pronouns

A particularly salient way of constructing a sense of common purpose between writer and reader is through the use of personal pronouns and possessives: either the first person plural *we/our,* implying shared understanding or responsibility, or pseudo-dialogue involving the use of *I/my, you/your,* etc. Contrary to popular wisdom, and some style manuals, interpersonal reference of this kind is also a common feature of academic writing. As a consequence, it is one of the most extensively researched features (see, for example: Ivanič, 1998; Tang and John, 1999; Hyland, 2001; Thompson, 2001).

Research conducted by two of the present authors (Mayor, 2006; Mayor et al., 2006) on student academic writing for the International English Language Testing System (IELTS) test, revealed that candidates from Chinese language backgrounds used the first person singular (*I/me/my*, etc.) four times more than the average for professional academic prose (according to Biber et al., 1999), surpassing even the levels for the most self-referential academic discipline, philosophy (according to a study by Hyland, 2001). Moreover, according to Hyland (1999, pp. 118–9), the principle way in which first person reference (both singular and plural) is used in texts by professional academics is to introduce or discuss research activities, followed by organising arguments/structuring texts and, finally, indicating attitudes to findings or aligning oneself with theoretical positions. Among the Chinese IELTS candidates in our study, on the other hand, it was the expression of personal attitude or commitment that predominated. It is inevitable that there will be differences between professional academic writing and that of students writing under test conditions. However, it would seem that these novice writers were either reproducing a style that was closer to popular journalism than academic writing, or transferring valued features from their first language education.

Consistent with their higher use of rhetorical questions, the Chinese candidates in our study also used the second person (*you/your*, etc.) to directly address the reader over six times more often than the average for professional academic prose, coming closer to the levels identified as typical of everyday conversation (according to Biber et al., 1999). According to Milton, who compared texts written in English by Hong Kong Chinese and UK students, 'not a single question in 500,000 words of the UK students' texts contains the second person pronoun', whereas 'almost all ... questions in HK students' texts are [the kind of rhetorical questions] that demand an affirmative response' on the part of the reader (Milton, 2001, p. 13).

Of course, interpersonal reference is not the only means of creating an impression of shared perspective through language. This may also be achieved by representing certain practices as 'normal' or readily understandable, whereas others are carefully explained, or when an assumption is made that readers will share the writer's response, as in *This is not such an unusual example as may appear* .... In a global context, however, such appeals to a common perspective may not be tenable.

Differences in choice of reporting verbs

Despite its reputation for objectivity, academic writing in English includes many subtle indications of the **authorial stance** of the writer. (For a good overview of this, see Hunston and Thompson, 2000.) In particular, academic discourse often requires a distinction between the writer's evaluations of facts and those of the primary researchers being discussed. One way in which this can be managed in English is through the use of a reporting verb, as in *Chomsky **claimed** that humans produce an infinite variety of sentences.* Even though the subject of the verb *claim* is Chomsky, the selection of reporting verb is that of the writer. One key distinction with regard to reporting verbs is between those which are 'factive' (implying the truth of the statement following) and those which are 'non-factive' (suggesting that the truth of the following statement is, or could be, in question). A factive version of the sentence above might be *Chomsky **discovered** that humans produce an infinite variety of sentences.* The strength of a claim can also be signalled through the use of some other phrase which modifies the verb, as in *Chomsky **supposedly** discovered ...* or ***According to some commentators**, Chomsky discovered ....* In ways such as this, the reader is called upon to enter into the world view of the writer.

However, there are important cross-cultural differences with regard to these features, even within English-medium texts. According to a study one of us conducted into course materials and student work from various open learning institutions (Graddol and Mayor, 1996), texts from The Open University

(UK) – by the use of non-factive verbs such as *appears* and *suggests* – tended to present knowledge not as something fixed and absolute, but as something which is produced and evaluated through institutionalised processes of research. On the other hand, the preference in texts from Indira Gandhi National Open University (IGNOU) in India was for factive verbs such as *found* and *revealed*. A predominance of past tense verbs also reinforced the impression of factivity. Not surprisingly, students from the two institutions were socialised into the use of such attitudinal markers and their underlying value systems, with the result that something of this difference was also reflected in their assessed work.

The challenge for global English-medium education is to decide to what extent these kinds of difference in rhetorical style actually matter.

ACTIVITY 7.5

Now read 'Culture in rhetorical styles: contrastive rhetoric and world Englishes' by Yamuna Kachru (Reading B). Use the following points and questions to guide your reading.

- Kachru uses the terms *inner circle* and *outer circle* to refer to two groups of English speakers in the world today. How does she see CR research as discriminating against academic writers in the outer circle?
- What are some of the differences she identifies, in the ways texts are organised and arguments are presented by inner circle academic writers, compared with those from an outer circle country such as India?
- What might be the consequences of Kachru's arguments for the way academic English is defined and taught?

Are there limits to diversity in academic English?

The nature of academic English, in any of its varieties, is shaped by its various social and cultural functions as the language of academic communities of discourse. In Reading B, Kachru attempts to show that some established styles of English academic writing other than those conventionally used in 'inner circle' countries are legitimate and valuable, representing different but not inferior ways of thinking and presenting knowledge.

However, as we have seen in the previous section, academic English, even across disciplines, is characterised by some common stylistic features. According to linguist Bhatia (1993), there is a common expectation in academic discourses across the world that writers should make their reasoning explicit in the text, so that other researchers can evaluate that reasoning. Although Kachru argues for more cultural flexibility in upholding the conventions of academic 'Englishes', she is not necessarily arguing against the desirability of maintaining that expectation. Rather, she is suggesting that there is more than one valid, culturally based way of making such reasoning explicit in English.

The analysis of academic varieties of English – their nature and function, the styles to which students are meant to conform and the justifications for upholding and enforcing conventions – is bound eventually to bring us up against some profound and difficult questions. Is the truth or validity of a piece of academic work determined by the language used? Is academic English a necessary counterpart of 'rigorous thinking', or merely a superficial aspect of style? There are no firm answers to these questions. Some of the accepted conventions or ground rules of academic writing have been brought under critical scrutiny (Sheeran and Barnes, 1991; Bhatia, 1993). Alongside this, the disciplinary ground rules are themselves continuing to evolve, as can be seen by comparing styles of writing in academic journals over the past century. As disciplinary areas themselves evolve and cross-fertilise, so do the associated literacy practices, along with the relationships to knowledge that they embody.

Vassileva (2001, p. 88) has argued that those writing in a second language may 'try to preserve their cultural identity ... irrespective of the language they use' by the retention of certain pragmatic features in the discourse. Given the growing role of English as an international medium of education (see Mayor and Swann, 2002, pp. 111–30), it may be that rhetorical norms from other cultures will gradually become more embedded within Anglophone writing practices, to the extent that there will be a range of legitimate academic English*es*.

Support for this view is offered by Canagarajah in reflecting on his own experience as an academic who writes in several languages and in different rhetorical traditions.

> I find that being caught between conflicting and competing writing traditions, discourse, or languages is not always a 'problem'. These tensions can be resourceful in enabling a rich repertoire of communicative strategies. The conflicts I have faced as I shuttled between my native community and Western academic community generated many useful insights into the ideological and rhetorical challenges in academic communication. ... It was probably a blessing that I was an outsider in both the center and the periphery academic communities!
>
> (Canagarajah, 2001, pp. 36–7)

Currently, however, most students in Anglophone higher education are confronted by a set of institutional practices which judge their writing according to a more fixed, and often unspoken, set of norms. It is to the experience of the student writers that we now turn.

7.5 Identity and 'voice' in student academic writing

Finally, we focus on student writers, and in particular, the importance of identity in student academic writing. 'Identity' refers both to how one sees one's own position in the world and how one is 'identified' by others. The relationship between identity and language use has been explored in many ways: sociolinguists in particular have shown that there are not only differences between the ways in which groups of people speak – relating to geography, social class, ethnicity, gender, age – but that people use language to signal who they are and who they want to be identified with (and, as importantly, who they don't want to be identified with). It may seem surprising to consider that similar influences are at work in academic writing. This may be because academic writing is often considered to be 'impersonal' or 'objective', as somehow separate from the person or people writing. Yet, as we have already seen in this chapter, the considerable variety in genres and discourses across disciplines, and within and across cultural and linguistic contexts, is closely associated with particular groups and communities, each with its particular kind of identity. Thus, a clear marker of writing – and hence the writer – in the natural sciences is its apparently impersonal nature (although, as we have seen, an angle on the message may be achieved in more subtle ways). Hyland in Reading A refers to this as writers in the hard sciences 'playing down their role', by not explicitly referring to themselves or their views on a topic. This stands in contrast to writing in philosophy which involves writers overtly referring to themselves and their views and, moreover, explicitly seeking to persuade the reader to share such views.

Students writing in higher education are not only *writing about* particular areas of knowledge but they are also learning to *write themselves into* existing areas of knowledge which involve particular ways of approaching knowledge making. In a sense, they are learning to 'be' particular types of knowledge makers: to write as a scientist, a psychologist, a philosopher and so on. Indeed, this can happen almost imperceptibly and without anybody consciously deciding to do so. Bartholomae, a US academic and writing teacher, talks of students having to 'invent the university' as they sit down to write, that is to write like academics often before knowing what is involved: 'The student has to learn to speak our [academics'] language, to speak as we do, to try on the peculiar ways of knowing, selecting, evaluating, reporting, concluding and arguing that define the [various discourses] of our community' (Bartholomae, 1985, p. 134).

ACTIVITY 7.6

Allow about
30 minutes

Read the extracts below from four students' academic writing and consider the following questions:

- Which disciplines or areas of study do you think the students are writing in? (Are they 'hard' or 'soft' disciplines? Is it possible to identify a specific discipline?)
- What features in the text indicate this? (Consider the lexis, the type of verbs used, whether first person pronouns – *I, we* – are used, whether there are statements, questions or directives.)
- What kind of writer identity is evident in the extracts? (Do they, for example, represent themselves as impartial observers or as personally involved in the topics they discuss?)

Example 5: Sara (undergraduate year 1)

Corsaro (1985, as cited by Miel, 1990) used observational methods to study children's conversations with friends in their natural environments at nursery and home. ... It was discovered that children's views on friendship and social behaviour were complicated and became apparent through their use of language. Corsaro found that friendship was used as a tool to gain access to groups of children, to strengthen groups performing the same activity, and to exclude children outside of the group. The result supports Selman's findings at stage 0 where children only see friendship being formed during mutual activity.

(quoted in Lillis, 2003, p. 201)

Example 6: Mary (undergraduate year 1)

Although ethnic minorities do represent an underclass in relation to what has been discussed above. They have made a significant contribution to the culture of British society despite all the negative research concerning their social restrictions in society. For example, during the 60's when the 'flower power' movement emerged, this was popular culture amongst the white middle class youth. ... Their pursuance of Asian philosophy, a doctrine which preached 'peace and love' brought about political radicalism. ... Black youth culture has also had a dramatic effect upon white youths, especially through the influence of music.

(quoted in Lillis, 2003, p. 200)

Example 7: César (year 1 masters)

The line transect methods basically involve the recording of the length of random-spaced parallel lines that are intercepted by plants or sessile animals. Line intercept transect (LIT) are used to assess the sessile benthic community in coral reefs. The community is characterized using life-form categories that provide a morphological description of the reef community.

(quoted in Ivanič and Camps, 2001, p. 12)

Example 8: Evodia (year 1 masters)

Whether entrepreneurial literacy is a viable alternative to organise humanised modes of production, how is the conscientization component introduced, in order to motivate people to transform the world? These questions are formulated based upon an important issue that concerns this author: environmental education rarely blends with development initiatives.

(quoted in Ivanič and Camps, 2001, p. 12)

Comment

All four extracts are from 'essays' – that is, extended writing in response to a question set by tutors – but they clearly reflect different disciplinary interests. You may have spotted clues as to their specific discipline in some of the words and phrases in each extract: the use of *observational methods, natural environments, Corsaro found* and *Selman's findings* in Example 5 contrasts strongly with *underclass, British society, social, political radicalism* and *youth culture* in Example 6. Example 5 is from psychology and Example 6 from sociology. Likewise, the specialist discourse evident in Examples 7 and 8 signals their disciplinary differences: wordings such as *line transect methods, sessile animals* and *benthic community* are being used for writing on a course on biodiversity; just as *entrepreneurial literacy* and *conscientization* n Example 8 are in this student's writing on education and development.

Examples 5 and 7 are more towards the 'hard' sciences end of the knowledge continuum as is evident in their emphasis on reporting rather than offering opinions or views on a topic. This is reflected in the verbs they use: in Example 5 the simple past *used, was discovered* and *found* and in Example 7 the simple present *involve, are, used* and *is characterised*. In Examples 5 and 7 the writer's identity or 'voice' is one of a dispassionate reporter of events which is very much in line with a notion of knowledge as something that is objective and universally true; what is crucial is that methods and procedures used are appropriate and valid (hence the attention paid to methods in both extracts).

In contrast, Examples 6 and 8 are from the 'soft' end of the continuum. Here, rather than acting as a reporter or observer, the writers engage in arguments about a topic by making claims, as in Example 6, and raising questions, as in Example 8. In both Examples 6 and 8 there is a stronger impression of the writers' personal 'voice' than in Examples 5 and 7: in Example 6 the writer makes a strong evaluative claim about the contribution of 'ethnic minorities': *They have made a significant contribution to the culture of British society;* and in Example 8 the writer's 'voice' is most explicitly signalled where she actually refers to herself as *this author* (albeit still in the third person, rather than as *I*) and points to her personal involvement and interest in specific questions. This is in line with a notion of knowledge as something that is socially constructed, by interested parties in specific socio-historical contexts, and prominent in social (as compared with natural) sciences.

As you were reading the examples (which are of course extracts from longer texts), you may have formed a view about the quality of the students' writing: perhaps you were concerned about the lack of referencing of sources in Examples 6, 7 and 8; or maybe you were critical of the use of a full stop rather than a comma in the first sentence of Example 6. What does seem clear, however, is that all the students have been successful in producing written texts which are, to a greater or lesser extent, in line with the discourse norms of the specific discipline they are studying within. As Ivanič and Camps observe, 'In this way, they are locating themselves firmly in the culture of people who are interested in these sorts of things, who engage in research of this sort' (2001, p. 13). In fact César (author of Example 7), specifically acknowledges that 'I learnt these types of sentence ... I try to write in the way or style that is written in scientific articles and technical reports' (Ivanič and Camps, 2001, p. 13).

The extent to which different student writers are comfortable with these norms – relating to content, style and voice in their writing – is an issue we return to below.

Voices in the text

We referred above to the writer's 'voice'. Voice is used in a number of ways in discussions about identity and academic writing. Here, we are using 'voice' to refer to the impression the writer gives in the text of their position on, or relationship to, a particular topic. As discussed above, one way in which this may be done is by adopting a disciplinary position – a writer may represent themselves as a scientist or an educationalist through the kinds of language they use. But they can also of course represent themselves as a particular *kind* of scientist or educationalist with specific views on a subject through the specific textual choices that they make.

In the boxed extract below, Ivanič and Camps analyse another section of a text written by Evodia (author of Example 8), focusing on how different features in her text help to construct a particular kind of voice.

Values and beliefs in academic writing

Values, beliefs, and preferences are carried by choice of classificatory lexis, generic reference, evaluative lexis, and syntax. For example, [the extract below] contains noun phrases, adjectives, and verbs that carry Evodia's value judgments on the topics she is discussing.

> *[Extract] from the 'Conclusion' of Evodia's dissertation on an MEd in Adult Education and Literacy for Rural Social and Community Development*
>
> To untangle the complexities of an unsustainable present, it was imperative to look at its roots in the dominant economic ideology. A competitive, efficiency-based development model has not considered the rate at which natural resources are being exploited. In the search for avenues shared by environmental care and economic justice, a reflection was made upon the role of education in the lives of economically poor people. On the side of economy, real alternatives to the dominant economic system were found; likewise ecological economics and the Theory of Organisation. On the side of environmental care, it was observed that the predominant Western-rooted environmental education model does not generate significant changes in the relationship between rural cultures and the environment.

An example of classificatory lexis that positions the writer is Evodia's choice of the term *rural cultures* for referring to people living in country areas. Had she chosen a term such as 'primitive people' instead of 'rural cultures', she would have projected an entirely different stance towards what she was talking about. Evodia used the generic noun *people* in the expression 'economically poor people'. Had she used the male-specific word 'men' instead of 'people' here, it would have suggested a very different position on gender issues. This choice may have been influenced by translation from Spanish [Evodia's first language], or it may have been made on political grounds, but this does not affect the way in which the writer is positioned in the mind of the reader. The adjectives *unsustainable* to modify 'present', *dominant* to modify 'economic ideology', *predominant Western-rooted* to modify 'environmental education model', and the verb *exploited* are all lexical choices that, we suggest, carry Evodia's value judgments on the issues she is discussing, conveying a strong indication of her stance, even to a reader who does not know her. ...

It is not only lexical but also syntactic choice that aligns writers with particular stances. ... the verb phrase *being exploited* carries Evodia's position not only through the connotations of the word 'exploited' but also because of its passive form. If Evodia had used an active verb such as 'are disappearing' in the same place in the sentence, it would have had a very different effect. By choosing a passive verb, Evodia is implying the responsibility of some (unnamed) agents for what is happening to natural resources. It is perhaps significant that [this extract] is the final paragraph of the final piece of work Evodia wrote as a Masters student. By this time, she had become more self-confident in her views and experienced in choosing how to express them.

(Ivanič and Camps 2001, pp. 13–14)

ACTIVITY 7.7

Allow at least 30 minutes

At this point you may find it interesting to look at one or two examples of your own academic writing, possibly from different stages in your life. Consider in particular the lexical and syntactic choices you made. Is it possible to identify a particular 'voice' in your writing? There may be more than one voice – perhaps at one point you seem to adopt an impersonal, objective stance and at another you may have made your own commitment or values very clear. Are there any voices that surprise you? Are there any that you would prefer to change?

Whose voices are in academic writing?

Figure 7.2   Developing an academic voice

Some students may find it relatively straightforward to adopt the voices most strongly associated with their particular discipline and adapt these according to their specific interests: in this way they can be seen to be developing their 'own' particular voice in their academic writing. However, research exploring student experiences of academic writing suggests two things. First, many students struggle to find out and learn what the 'rules of the game' are – that is, the academic and discipline-specific conventions tutors expect them to follow (Lea and Street, 1998; Lillis, 2001). Second, and of particular relevance to our discussion here, some students feel that the kind of voice or identity they are expected to adopt in their writing differs fundamentally from their own sense of 'real' self. This feeling of dislocation has been described in a number of ways: feeling like an 'outsider', 'on the margins', 'on the boundary' or as a 'stranger in strange lands' (Elbow, 1991; Rose, 1989; Lu, 1992; Villanueva, 1993; Belcher and Connor, 2001). Lillis (2001; 2003) illustrates this by summarising the experiences and perspectives of Mary (see box on 'Mary's experience').

Mary's experience: 'It's not me at all'

Mary is a Black working-class student [in the UK] who left school with few formal qualifications and, after a number of different jobs and courses, began her studies in higher education at the age of 21. ...

Mary has a strong sense that being at university is particularly difficult because of who she is, a Black working-class woman. Language is central to her concerns and raises particular issues for her when she sits down to write. In a discussion about writing in academia she compares the difficulties she faces to that of a white middle class student in the same course:

> He doesn't have to make a switch. It's him you see. Whereas when I'm writing I don't know who it is *[laughs]*. It's not me. And that's why I think it's awful, I think it's awful you know. It's not me at all. It's like I have to go into a different person. I have to change my frame of mind and you know, my way of thinking and everything. It's just like a stranger, it's like I've got two bodies in my head, and two personalities and there's conflict.

[Elsewhere Mary links the kind of language she is expected to use with her general sense of unease and distance from the world of academia:] 'I don't think it's important at all *[laughs]*. But you have to do it? It's like I'm imprisoned, honest to God *[laughs]*.

(Lillis, 2001, pp. 202, 85).

There are risks, then, in making choices about the kinds of language that students use, which are powerfully bound up with their sense of who they are. A black student in a study by Shelby Steele said 'he was not sure he should master standard English because he "wouldn't be black no more"' (Steele, 1990, p. 70; quoted in Lu, 1992, p. 909).

The examples above suggest that the convention of using a formal *style* in academic writing is uncomfortable for some students. Other students point to conventions surrounding the *content* of what they can write as being problematic because of their sense of who they 'really are'. Sara for example, as can be seen from Example 5 above, is successful in her academic writing in psychology. However, she feels dissatisfied because it doesn't allow her to explore other dimensions and voices which she feels are relevant:

> There's two sides to me, there's the theoretical side and the very spiritual side. Two of me you see, and I was thinking, my God, I could link this into psychology, cause it's *(referring to a book on spirituality)* talking about the self, the true you in other words. And I thought, my God, I'm studying the self at the moment, you know, from childhood and there's so many things. And I thought, I could bring them together, you know, they sort of intertwine and I thought, it's so interesting. And I thought, if I put that in my assignment [same essay as Example 5], they'll think *(laughs)* what's she talking about, this woman? ... They'll think I'm crackers. They'll think *(pause, lowers tone of voice)* 'fail'. So I think I can't put that in then.

(quoted in Lillis, 2003, pp. 203–4)

The extent to which a range of 'voices' are allowed in academic writing clearly varies across disciplines – consider the explicit self-reference in Example 8 – but is also linked to the kind of authority that writers can claim. Student writers, because of their status as 'students' or novices, can generally claim comparatively little authority in their texts: they are typically writing for a reader who is considered to be both more experienced and more knowledgeable in their field and who, to a large extent, is reading in order to see whether the student can conform to established conventions regarding content and style.

Voices, control and plagiarism

In talking about 'voices' in the text, we may have implied that it is relatively straightforward for writers to take control over the voices in their texts – by, for example, deciding to take on a particular disciplinary voice or by deciding which voices should or should not be in their texts. However, this is often not the case.

Whenever any of us write an academic text, we draw on a wide range of resources – most obviously other academic texts, lecture notes, discussions in classes, informal chats with friends, professional experience, activities outside of academia – only some of which we may consciously be using. Moreover, language itself is 'multivoiced' and, as Bakhtin points out, is not necessarily easy to control: 'Language is not a neutral medium that passes freely and easily into the private property of the speaker's intentions; it is populated – overpopulated – with the intention of others. Expropriating it, forcing it to submit to one's own intentions and accents, is a difficult and complicated process' (Bakhtin, 1981, p. 294). We glimpsed some of this difficulty above in Mary's struggle in the use of a more formal style which she did not associate with her sense of who she really was.

Taking conscious control over and signalling the voices in texts is not only difficult for writers, it presents real problems for tutors as they read and assess student writers' work. Such difficulties have come to the fore in discussions about 'plagiarism' in student academic writing. Many institutions have a policy on plagiarism, warning students of the severe penalties that they may incur if they are found 'guilty'. The Open University (UK), for example, defines plagiarism as follows: 'If you submit an assignment that contains work that is not your own, without indicating this to the marker (acknowledging your sources), you are committing "plagiarism"' (The Open University, 2006).

The key way in which sources are acknowledged in academic writing is through the convention of citation; however, many students struggle to understand this convention and to put it to use in their writing. For example, César (author of Example 7) commented that, 'As it [the assignment] is based on one book, I couldn't obviously quote the author all the time, but there are some phrases I took but ... I changed what followed, but I guess there are some textual phrases [that I have taken from the source]' (Ivanič and Camps, 2001, p. 13).

Moreover, Pennycook (1996) argues that plagiarism is a far from straightforward phenomenon, and that notions of plagiarism are related to contemporary Western conceptions of creativity and originality in writing – which, ironically, are belied by the routine borrowing of ideas, words and phrases that is practised by all writers. There is a particular problem for student writers who, while they are constantly being told they must put things in their 'own words', are also 'required to acquire a fixed canon of knowledge and a fixed canon of terminology to go with it' (Pennycook, 1996, p. 213). This may be more problematical for students whose own prior learning experiences have emphasised the accurate reproduction of ideas. Pennycook argues that teachers need to take account of different types of textual borrowing, different cultural meanings ascribed to the appropriation of words and ideas from authoritative texts, and students' own differing understandings of what they are doing as they incorporate others' words into their writing.

Issues surrounding the use and identification of voices in students' writing are of growing relevance, given that higher education sectors around the world are international in nature and increasingly global in reach. Most obviously, it is not possible to assume (if it ever was) that tutors and students will share similar backgrounds or that they will establish a relationship whereby the tutor is in a position to evaluate the voices in a text against his or her sense of the identity of the 'real' student. Caution is therefore needed when making assumptions about who writers are and the extent to which voices in their texts reflect their knowledge, understandings and positions. The notion of a 'novice to expert' trajectory, whilst useful in thinking about the ways in which some students come to be inducted into specific disciplinary practices in higher education, may be problematic in a context where increasing numbers of adult students with considerable previous and ongoing experience are taking part in higher education. They may be 'new' in academia, but they may or may not be novices in particular areas of knowledge and expertise.

7.6 Conclusion

Study in higher education requires a special kind of competence in English, which may be just as unfamiliar to monolingual speakers of English as to those whose previous education has been through another language. 'Academic English' is a collection of genres of English, each of which is shaped by the functional requirements and social conventions of academic communities of discourse. Familiarity with the conventions or ground rules which apply to any genre of academic English is an important factor in a student's progress. However, the conventions of academic disciplines will continue to evolve, especially as new interdisciplinary areas emerge and new modes of global communication become widespread.

READING A: Rhetoric and reasoning: directives across disciplines

Ken Hyland
(Ken Hyland is Professor in the Centre of Academic and Professional
Literacies at the London University Institute of Education.)

Source: Hyland, K. (2002) 'Directives: argument and engagement in academic writing', *Applied Linguistics*, vol. 23, no. 2, pp. 230–9.

The use of directives varies enormously across the disciplines. In some fields they represent a major rhetorical resource, a way of setting out arguments and interacting with readers which have become regular practices, ... In other fields they do not routinely figure as patterns of reasoning and interaction. [Table 1] shows frequencies ranging from over 55 per 10,000 words in the mechanical engineering and physics textbooks down to only 10 in sociology ... Overall, the hard science texts contained almost twice as many directives per 10,000 words, and over 65 per cent of directives in both textbooks and student reports occurred in the science and engineering texts. ...

Table 1 Disciplinary variations in use of directives (per 10,000 words)

Field: Textbooks [TBs]		Field: Articles [RAs]		Field: Reports [SRs]	
Mechanical Eng	55.6	Electronic Eng	29.0	Info Systems	24.4
Physics	50.9	Philosophy	27.3	Mechanical Eng	23.7
Biology	46.8	Physics	21.1	Biology	11.8
Electronic Eng	36.3	Mechanical Eng	19.6	TESOL	9.2
Philosophy	24.1	App Linguistics	19.5	Economics	8.9
Marketing	22.0	Sociology	16.1	Social Sciences	7.7
App Linguistics	13.8	Marketing	12.6	Marketing	3.9
Sociology	10.1	Biology	12.3	Pubic Admin	3.3
[Average]	31.7	[Average]	19.1	[Average]	10.5

[The following abbreviations are used later in this reading: AL = Applied Linguistics; Bio = Biology; EE = Electrical Engineering; ME = Mechanical Engineering; Mkt = Marketing; Phil = Philosophy; Phy = Physics; Soc = Sociology.]

... While I acknowledge there may be numerous reasons for disciplinary variations, I will try to show that such preferred uses can be seen, in part, as reflecting the broad areas of inquiry associated with the hard and soft fields. I will focus on typical writer–reader engagement practices, conventions of dialogic positioning, and the meanings attached to succinctness and precision.

Directives and reader engagement

One reason for the heavy use of directives in the hard disciplines may be that this is one of the few rhetorical devices that scientists use with any regularity to explicitly engage their readers. Writers' attempts to invoke reader participation take a number of forms and can include personal pronouns, questions, digressions, hedges, and emphatics. These conventions of personality however have been shown to differ across disciplines and are particularly low in science and engineering papers (Swales 1990; Hyland 1999, 2000). This is in part because of very different ways of conducting research and of persuading readers to accept results.

Generally speaking, hard science writers are attempting to establish empirical uniformities through research practices which typically involve familiar procedures, broadly predictable outcomes, and relatively clear criteria of acceptability (Becher 1989; Whitley 1984). As a result, they can rhetorically purge their authorial presence in the discourse, playing down their role to strengthen the objectivity of their interpretations and replicability of procedures while highlighting the phenomena under study. Scientific writing is therefore often informally regarded as impersonal, as writers commonly avoid projecting themselves into their discourse to take an explicit stance towards their topic and findings. Instead, they often prefer to locate their interpretations in the results of statistical or laboratory analyses. All writing, however, needs to solicit reader collusion: it must work to draw an audience in, carry it through an argument, and lead it to a particular conclusion. Directives enable writers in the hard sciences to do this without expressing a clear rhetorical identity [Example 1].

EXAMPLE 1:	
Note the transverse stress acts to fracture the monolith along the flow, direction.	(ME RA)
... *compare* lanes 1 in Fig. 3A and B.	(Bio RA)
The analysis given in our paper *should be* considered in the context of a more general problem of nonstationary phenomena ...	(Phy RA)
It is necessary to take into account the dT'/dUp derivative when calculating	(EE RA)

Directives in the science and engineering subjects can therefore help writers to maintain the fiction of objectivity by avoiding explicit attitudinal signals while simultaneously allowing them to adopt an authoritative command of their data and their audience ...

Directives, in other words, permit authorial intervention in a discourse. They offer a means to directly address readers, particularly by selectively focusing their attention on an aspect of research procedure or instructing them to interpret an argument in a certain way, without personalizing the dialogue.

Positioning and attention

... perhaps the most imposing use of directives involves positioning readers, directing them to some cognitive action by requiring them to *note, concede,* or *consider* some aspect of an argument. Typically these directives lead readers towards the writer's conclusions by setting up premises [Example 2] or emphasizing what they should attend to in the argument [Example 3] ... :

EXAMPLE 2:

Suppose we have two explananda, E1 and E2.	(Phil RA)
Consider a sequence of hatches in an optimal schedule. *Suppose* there is a non-full batch in the k-th position.	(EE RA)
Think about it. What if we eventually learn how to communicate with ...	(Soc TB)

EXAMPLE 3:

... *mark that* it is possible to interpret the larger symmetry in terms of supersymmetric quantum mechanics.	(Phy RA)
In cluster analysis *it is important to remember* that there is no single solution; only solutions that are more or less useful for a particular context.	(Mkt RA)
Please *note that* gender is not specifically discussed here, because ...	(Soc RA)

This kind of explicit manipulation of the reader clearly carries risks however (as the politeness marker used to mitigate the last example suggests) and is rarely found in the student texts.

As I have noted, while such reader positioning occurs in all disciplines, it is mainly a feature of the hard sciences. Maintaining an effective degree of personal engagement with one's audience is an equally valuable strategy in the soft disciplines of course, but there it contributes to a very different authorial persona. Because the variables that soft fields deal with are often less precisely measurable, and their practices are more explicitly interpretive than in the hard sciences, persuasion may depend to a larger extent on an ability to invoke a credible and engaging persona (Hyland 2000). So while the ability to rhetorically construct an appropriate degree of confidence and authority is an important part of effective communication, this is tempered with respect for the possible alternative views of readers and their right to hold these views. As a result, the writer's ability to manipulate an audience's reading of a text through directives, so invoking an implied authority, is perhaps more circumscribed, as both the applied linguist and marketing respondent observed:

> You take control with imperatives, you tell them what to think, and I don't think that will always go down too well. (Mkt interview)

> I am aware of the effect that an imperative can have so I tend to use the more gentle ones. I don't want to bang them over the head with an argument. I want them to reflect on what I'm saying. I use 'consider' and 'let's look at this' rather than something stronger. (AL interview)

... Philosophy is an exception to the other soft-knowledge research papers, with only a quarter of the directives in articles leading the reader to references and virtually none in textbooks. Here rhetorical and elaborative cognitive forms made up 68 per cent of all devices in the articles and 74 per cent in the textbooks, working to direct the reader to understand the exposition in a certain way. This strategy combines with a heavy use of features such as boosters, first person pronouns, and inclusive *we* in philosophy, all of which contribute to a high degree of personal involvement to create a sense of communal intimacy [Example 4].

EXAMPLE 4:

Suppose we consider that there is a finite basis for our reasonable beliefs. *Let us assume*, for the sake of argument, ...

Suppose now, that – as I think – at the end of our story, the ship of Theseus and the ship of Stathis share the same parts. ...

We must consider the semantic justification of the rule of adjunction.

Philosophical discourse differs from many other disciplines in that it does not seek to accomplish 'closure' by reaching consensus on a particular interpretation of an issue. Reading philosophy involves following a path without end where the writer's argument does not settle matters but simply contributes to a continuing conversation. Participation in this discourse, and the addition of an elegant argument, are central to being a philosopher ... Relationships are accomplished by way of a highly intrusive stance to create, or appeal to, a world of shared understandings and the sense of a closely-knit community of peers. Directives in philosophy, then, appear to help reduce the distance between participants and to stress participation in a shared journey of exploration, but it is always clear who is leading the expedition.

Succinctness and precision

A major distinction between hard and soft knowledge areas is the extent to which succinctness and precision are valued, or even possible. Because of the linear, problem-oriented nature of natural sciences, research tends to be highly focused, with heavy investments in equipment and expertise devoted to specific goals. Consequently much research occurs within an established framework of theoretical knowledge and routine practices which means writers can presuppose a certain amount of background, argument, and technical lexis in their writing (Bazerman 1988). ... hard knowledge research papers are typically half the length of those in the soft disciplines, and there are clear reasons for economy of expression in these fields.

Directives offer writers this kind of economy (cf. Swales *et al.* 1998) and devices such as *consider, suppose, let* statements, and so on allow them to cut to the heart of an argument without more space consuming locutions. ... In contrast, knowledge making in the humanities often needs to be accomplished with greater elaboration, its more diverse components reconstructed for a less cohesive readership. Time and space constraints are less urgent and directives perhaps less necessary to preserve them.

Related to this apparent preference for economic and straightforward argument style in the hard fields is a strong need for precision, particularly to ensure the accurate understanding of procedures. Hard knowledge research typically involves the precise application of specific methodologies in seeking to solve particular disciplinary problems and 93 per cent of all research focus directives occurred in the hard sciences. Respondents frequently mentioned that the manipulation and measurements of materials had to be systematic and exact, and writers had little hesitation in instructing readers exactly how these procedures should be carried out, particularly through the use of modal [verbs, as in Example 5].

EXAMPLE 5:

... the above definitions for the B2 index *should be* multiplied by a factor of 0.83.	(ME RA)
... attention *must be* paid to the standard membrane microstrip and for low free-space radiation loss.	(EE TB)

[Conclusion]

To sum up, the hard knowledge fields not only contained far more directives, but these were also more likely to function as a means of guiding readers through a procedure and to the conclusions of the writer. Both these frequencies and more impositional functions are partly influenced by traditions of precision, tight space constraints, and highly formalized argument structures in the hard fields. These features, in turn, are related to their sources in mathematics, shared research practices and understandings, and the rapid growth of scientific knowledge. It can also be surmised, however, that conventions of impersonality, which focus readers on the text not the writer, also contribute to engagement styles which allow writers to interact with readers while stressing the phenomena rather than their textual personalities. In other words, some fields permit greater authorial presence than others and the use of directives emphasizes that social relationships within discourse communities exercise strong constraints on a writer's representations of self and others.

References for this reading

Bazerman, C. 1988. *Shaping Written Knowledge*. Madison: University of Wisconsin Press.

Becher, T. 1989. *Academic Tribes and Territories: Intellectual inquiry and the cultures of disciplines*. [Buckingham]: SRHE/OUP [The Society for Research into Higher Education/Open University Press].

Hyland, K. 1999. 'Disciplinary discourses: writer stance in research articles', in C. Candlin and K. Hyland (eds) *Writing: Texts, processes and practices*. London: Longman, pp. 99–121.

Hyland, K. 2000. *Disciplinary Discourses: Social interactions in academic writing*. London: Longman.

Swales, J. 1990. *Genre Analysis: English in academic and research settings*. Cambridge: Cambridge University Press.

Swales, J., Ahmad, U., Chang, Y-Y., Chavez, D., Dressen, D. and Seymour, R. 1998. 'Consider this: the role of imperatives in scholarly writing,' *Applied Linguistics*, 19/1: 97–121.

Whitley, R. 1984. *The Intellectual and Social Organisation of the Sciences*. Oxford: Clarendon Press.

READING B: Culture in rhetorical styles: contrastive rhetoric and world Englishes

Yamuna Kachru
(At the time of writing, Yamuna Kachru was Professor of Linguistics at the University of Illinois at Urbana Champaign, USA.)

Specially commissioned for Hoadley-Maidment and Mercer (1996, pp. 305–14). (Revised by the book editors.)

In this reading, [as in Kachru (1995a)], I propose to look at the research area of [contrastive rhetoric (CR), the study of how language is used in writing in different cultural settings], in the context of the multilingual and multicultural users of world Englishes. ... The discussion takes the CR hypothesis out of the realm of English as a second language (ESL) and looks at the wider world of cross-linguistic and cross-cultural writing in general.

[The myth of an 'inner circle' norm]

B.B. Kachru (1985) divides the English-using world into three concentric circles. The *inner circle* consists of the native English speaking countries (e.g. Australia, Canada, New Zealand, the UK and the USA). The *outer circle* comprises the former colonies or spheres of influence of the UK and USA (e.g. India, Kenya, Nigeria, the Philippines, Singapore). In these countries, nativised varieties of English have achieved the status of either an official language or of a language widely used in education, administration, the legal system, etc. The *expanding circle* consists of countries where English is fast becoming a dominant second language in the domains of education, science and technology (e.g. China, Japan, Taiwan, Thailand and the countries of Europe).

The major claim of the CR hypothesis is that writers of English from the 'outer' and 'expanding' circles employ 'a rhetoric and a sequence of thought which violate the expectations of the native [inner circle] reader' (Kaplan, 1980 [1966]). Hence their writing is perceived as 'out of focus', 'lacking organization', or 'lacking cohesion' (Kaplan, 1980 [1966]). This claim is based on the assumption that there is a clearly established inner circle norm of writing in English, and its effect is to devalue rhetorical patterns which do not conform to the expectations of readers from the inner circle.

...

Two sets of CR findings are relevant for our purposes: one related to inner circle writing and the other to writing across languages. Contrary to the myth of a well-established inner circle norm for academic writing, Americans,

Australians, Britons and New Zealanders have been shown to differ significantly from each other in their rhetorical styles (e.g. Connor and Lauer, 1985; Vähäpässi, 1988; see also Hoey, 1983, p. 68; Smith and Liedlich, 1980, p. 21). Clear differences have been found even within one particular variety. It seems reasonable to conclude that writing in other languages has been and is being compared with some idealised notion of writing in English based on style manuals and textbooks for teaching rhetoric.

Cross-linguistic CR studies have shown that languages such as Arabic, Chinese, German, Hindi, Japanese, Korean, Marathi and Persian have their characteristic rhetorical organisations of expository and argumentative prose not shared by the native varieties of English (Eason, 1995; Kachru, 1995b; Martin, 1992 [and Connor, 1996] contain extensive bibliographical references). ... Additionally, it is doubtful that there are well-defined text types such as 'expository' and 'argumentative prose' in English (Biber, 1989; Grabe, 1987) which form the basis of CR research. Such genre distinctions may be 'foreign' to some literate cultures at least.

Literacy [in different communities]

Work on the acquisition of literacy in different communities has shown that even within a developed industrial society such as the USA communities may differ in terms of the functions, domains, roles and value of literacy in their lives (Heath, 1983). That communities which belong to different societies will show greater variation in their literacy practices is therefore not surprising (Scribner and Cole, 1981). Access to a writing system, or printing, or other devices to produce and reproduce written texts can be used to support a wide variety of literacy practices.

Ancient India had an advanced writing system probably by 500 BC (MacDonell, 1968 [1900], p. 17), in addition to well-developed traditions of creative literature (both prose and poetry), arithmetic, algebra, astronomy, grammar, logic and philosophy. However, there is no evidence that written texts played an important role in the transmission of this body of knowledge. Thus the claim in CR literature that western rhetoric is a result of the development of writing and, subsequently, of printing and the rapid diffusion of literacy following the industrial revolution, needs to be further examined.

Furthermore, perspectives such as Kaplan's (1966; and reproduced 1980) fail to acknowledge the ideological nature of *fact* and *truth* as widely discussed in philosophical, social scientific and humanistic (including linguistic) literature. Foucault, for example, says that:

> ... Each society has its régime of truth, its 'general politics' of truth: that is, the types of discourse which it accepts and makes function as true; the mechanisms and instances which enable one to distinguish true and false statements, the means by which each is sanctioned; the techniques and

procedures accorded value in the acquisition of truth; the status of those who are charged with saying what counts as true.

(Foucault, 1980, p. 131)

Truth or fact, whether transmitted orally or in writing, is always to some extent both socially constructed and mutable. ...

Writing in English in the outer circle

The history of writing in English in the outer circle indicates that cultural considerations play a role in the development of linguistic structures and discourse patterns (Kachru, B.B., 1992). Some of the discourse features that occur in Indian English academic writing, for example, are the following: nonlinear macro structure; global introductions rather than just the relevant background of the topic under discussion; more than one topic in a single paragraph; cyclical sequencing of components such as initiation, problem, elaboration, solution, evaluation, etc.; and use of ornate language. [These characteristics] can be illustrated by the following [essay] written by a second year BA student in an Indian college. (Paragraph numbers have been added for use in analysis.)

'Dowry System' in India

1   Growing up is a discarding of dreams and a realisation of the various facts of life. A general awareness creeps in. It is a process of *drinking deep the spring of knowledge* and perceiving the different facets of life. Life is panorama of events, moments of joys and sorrows. The world around us is manifested by both, good and evil.

2   Dowry system is one of the prevalent evils of today. *Like a diabolic adder it stings* the life on many innocent people and is the burning topic of discussion. Looking down the vista of years, we find that it has permeated gradually into the fabrics of our customs and has acquired a prodigious form lately. Marriage which is supposed to be a sacred ceremony is made sour and becomes like any other business transactions. The extracting of money from the bride's family is ridiculous, attracious [sic] and above all sacrilegious.

3   It is truly said that making somebody happy is a question of give and take. Human beings by instinct show their concern and love by giving gifts. This even holds true for a bride's father. All fathers have a penchant to give something to their daughters. It is a propensity of human nature to see their daughters well settled. But this exchange of gifts should be a willing gesture and not an imposed cannon [sic]. The money and affluence becomes an asset to start a settlement in life. But it should be considered a

crime if the money is taken from someone who is left financially crippled. Each one should learn to lay the bricks of her own house herself.

4   Dowry system is *biting into the very vitals* of the Indian society. There are many evidences of burning of the bride, and disparages in matches because of this root cause. To eradicate this will be to *clear the weeds of our society*. There are many laws passed on this issue but still it needs to be dealt by delving deeper. It is said that 'Eclipses stain both moon and sun'. The custom of dowry is the biggest flaw and *a scar which mars the beauty of a sacred union.*

5   Various endeavours are being made to eradicate this. But what is necessary, that it should be the loudest cry of each person! Someone has to take a firm stand and the first step so that it benefits mankind. Everything can be cured and *all evils can be purged.* After all Raja Ram Mohan Roy did succeed in abolishing Sati system, Lord William Bentick worked to elevate the position of women. *To wipe out this will be like a rise from a stagnant, putrid pool to the great height of perfection. Living will be a bliss!*

As far as linguistic competence is concerned, the writer of this essay is obviously highly competent. The grammatical and spelling errors may be attributed to the pressure of time (Kachru, Y., 1995c). As regards the conventions of language use, however, the text exhibits all the characteristics of Indian writing mentioned above. In view of limitation of space, I can comment on only some of the characteristics of the text. The CR hypothesis would suggest that the macrostructure of the text (the organisation of the text as a whole and the contents of the paragraphs) will violate the expectations of inner circle readers. The sequence of problem–elaboration in paragraph 2, elaboration–solution in paragraph 4, and the occurrence of comment in paragraphs 3 and 5 ('comment' provides more historical background or expresses the writer's hopes and wishes) are worth noting. This is a perfect example of the spiral or circular rhetorical pattern that is found in Indian writing in general. (I am using 'circular' and 'spiral' as purely descriptive terms, with no implication that they are either 'illogical' or unfit for scientific/ technical discussions). The first paragraph is a good example of the global introduction phenomenon mentioned above and the italicised parts throughout illustrate the use of ornate language, but such usage is not uncommon and does not make Indian English readers uncomfortable. ...

Implications for research

... A study of the traditions of writing in different cultures is necessary to establish clear criteria for comparability across genres and registers, since (1) there may be genres which are unique to a language and culture, and (2) there may be different rhetorical patterns associated with different genres. ... In academic writing, there is a text type in Hindi that is labelled 'deliberative' (*vicaratmak* in Hindi), which is not necessarily equivalent to the Anglo-American 'argumentative' essay. In an argumentative text the goal is to prove that the view put forward in the text is right and that all competing opinions are wrong. In the deliberative text, however, the points in favour as well as those opposed to a particular position are put forward so that readers are informed on all facets of an issue, and the decision as to which one of the positions presented is right or wrong is left to the reader. The writer, however, is free to indicate [their] preference, if [they] so desire.

An example of specific rhetorical patterns associated with particular genres is the circular or spiral rhetorical pattern of expository prose in Hindi (Kachru, Y., 1983, 1988). Such non-linear patterns may have a social meaning. Hinds (1987) suggests that the non-linear pattern of Japanese expository prose is in harmony with the expectation that the listener/reader has the primary responsibility for effective communication. This contrasts sharply with the expectation in US English that the primary responsibility for effective communication lies with the speaker/writer. Hinds then goes on to suggest a typology of listener/reader versus speaker/writer responsibility in different languages. ...

The framework of CR must take into account one important component of sociocultural meaning, that of the intertextuality of texts, since all texts derive their meaning from others in the tradition too. For instance, the texts in the Indian tradition derive their meaning from the classical Sanskrit or Perso-Arabic tradition, in addition to the (partially, via English) shared Graeco-Roman tradition. In the genres of literary criticism, philosophy and grammar, for instance, a Hindi text may refer to the works of Panini (seventh century BC) and Bhartrihari (early sixth century AD) just as easily as to Aristotle, Humboldt or de Saussure.

Coming back to the social context, it has been observed that writers from several parts of the world, including China and India, give too much background information without relating it directly to the topic under discussion. The social meaning behind what appears to be a redundant amount of background information is related to the notion of politeness in these cultures. In most interactional contexts, directness is not as polite as indirectness. Instead of coming directly to the point, giving a great deal of background information allows readers to draw their own conclusions with regard to the topic being discussed. The reader responsibility phenomenon that Hinds (1987) mentions may be related to the East Asian notions of politeness too, in that the texts in these traditions give readers choices, instead of attempting to bring them round to the writer's point of view.

Conclusion

The teaching and evaluation of academic writing seem to involve an idealised notion of what an English paragraph or composition is, while most real texts, even within the inner circle, exhibit variation from the idealised pattern(s). If academic writing in general is not to become a sterile, formula-oriented activity, we have to encourage individual creativity in writing. It is the tension between received conventions and the innovative spirit of the individual that produces good writing in academic disciplines as well as in creative literature. Moreover, a narrow view of what constitutes good writing may bar a large number of original studies from publication and dissemination, since most of the information technology is under the control of the inner circle English-speaking world. Any view of rhetoric that shuts out a majority of people from contributing to the world's knowledge base, and legitimises such exclusion on the basis of writing conventions, hurts not only those who are excluded but also those who would benefit from such contributions.

References for this reading

Biber, D. (1989) 'A typology of English texts', *Linguistics*, no. 27, pp. 3–43.

Braddock, R. (1974) 'The frequency and placement of topic sentences in expository prose', *Research in the Teaching of English,* no. 8, pp. 287–302.

Connor, U. and Lauer, J. (1985) 'Understanding persuasive essay writing: linguistic/rhetoric approach', *Text*, vol. 5, no. 4, pp. 309–26.

Connor, U. (1996) *Contrastive Rhetoric: Cross-Cultural Aspects of Second-Language Writing*, Cambridge, Cambridge University Press.

Eason, C. (1995) 'Argumentative essay written by native speakers of Chinese and English: a study in contrastive rhetoric', PhD dissertation, Urbana, IL, University of Illinois.

Foucault, M. (1980) *Power/Knowledge: Selected Interviews and Other Writings (1972–1977)*, (ed. C. Gordon), New York, Pantheon.

Grabe, W. (1987) 'Contrastive rhetoric and text type research' in Connor, U. and Kaplan, R. (eds) *Writing across Languages: Analysis of L2 Text*, Reading, MA, Addison-Wesley.

Heath, S.B. (1983) *Ways with Words: Language, Life and Work in Communities and Classroom*, Cambridge, Cambridge University Press.

Hinds, J. (1987) 'Reader versus writer responsibility: a new typology' in Connor, U. and Kaplan, R. (eds) *Writing across Languages: Analysis of L2 Text*, Reading, MA, Addison-Wesley.

Hoey, M. (1983) *On the Surface of Discourse*, London, Allen & Unwin.

Kachru, B.B. (1985) 'Standards, codification and sociolinguistic realism: the English language in the outer circle' in Quirk, R. and Widdowson, H. (eds) *English in the World*, Cambridge, Cambridge University Press.

Kachru, B.B. (ed.) (1992) *The Other Tongue: English across Cultures* (2nd edn), Urbana, IL, University of Illinois Press.

Kachru, Y. (1983) 'Linguistics and written discourse in particular languages: contrastive studies: English and Hindi', *Annual Review of Applied Linguistics*, no. 3, pp. 50–77.

Kachru, Y. (1988) 'Writers in Hindi and English' in Purvis, A. (ed.) *Writing across Languages and Cultures: Issues in Contrastive Rhetoric*, Newbury Park, CA, Sage.

Kachru, Y. (1995a) 'Contrastive rhetoric in world Englishes', *English Today*, vol. 11, no. 1, January, pp. 21–31.

Kachru, Y. (1995b) 'Cultural meaning and rhetorical styles: toward a framework for contrastive rhetoric' in Seidlhofer, B. and Cook, G. (eds) *Principle and Practice in Applied Linguistics: Studies in Honour of H.G. Widdowson*, London, Oxford University Press.

Kachru, Y. (1995c) 'Language and cultural meaning: expository writing in South Asian English' in Baumgardner, R. (ed.) *South Asian English: Structure, Use and Users*, Urbana, IL, University of Illinois Press.

Kaplan, R.B. (1966) 'Cultural thought patterns in inter-cultural education', *Language Learning*, 16, pp. 1–20.

Kaplan, R.B. (1980) 'Cultural thought patterns in inter-cultural education' in Croft, K. (ed.) (1980) *Readings on English as a Second Language for Teachers and Teacher Trainees*, Cambridge, MA, Winthrop.

MacDonell, A.A. (1968 [1900]) *A History of Sanskrit Literature*, New York, Haskell House.

Martin, J.E. (1992) *Towards a Theory of Text for Contrastive Rhetoric: An Introduction to Issues of Text for Students and Practitioners of Contrastive Rhetoric*, New York, Peter Lang.

Scribner, S. and Cole, M. (1981) *The Psychology of Literacy*, Cambridge, MA, Harvard University Press.

Smith, W.F. and Liedlich, D. (1980) *Rhetoric for Today*, New York, Harcourt Brace Jovanovich.

Vähapässi, A. (1988) 'The problem of selection of writing tasks in cross-cultural study' in Purves, A. (ed.) Writing across Languages and Cultures: Issues in Contrastive Rhetoric, Newbury Park, CA, Sage.

References

ACCAC (2000) *Exemplification of Standards in English Key Stage 3, Levels 1 to 3: Speaking and Listening, Reading, Writing, and Levels 4 to 8: Reading and Writing*, Welsh Assembly Government, Thames Ditton, ACCAC Publications.

Adamson, L.B. (1995) *Communication Development during Infancy*, Madison, WI, Brown & Benchmark.

Aldridge, M. (1991) 'How the language grows up: an outline of how children acquire English as a mother tongue', *English Today*, no. 25, pp. 14–20.

Al-Khatib, H. (2003) 'Language alternation among Arabic & English youth bilinguals: reflecting or constructing social realities', *Bilingual Education and Bilingualism*, vol. 6, no. 6, pp. 409–22.

Alptekin, C. (1993) 'Target-language culture in EFL materials', *ELT Journal*, vol. 47, no. 2, pp. 136–43.

Anderson, A.H., Clark, A. and Mullin, J. (1991) 'Introducing information in dialogues: forms of introducing chosen by young speakers and the responses elicited from young listeners', *Journal of Child Language*, no. 18, pp. 663–87.

Annamalai, E. (1986) 'A typology of language movements and their relation to language planning' in Annamalai, E. and Rubin, J. (eds) *Language Planning*, Mysore, Central Institute of Indian Languages.

AQA (2004) *English (Specification A) Paper 2 Foundation Tier (3702/2F)*, Manchester, Assessment and Qualifications Alliance, GCSE November 2004.

AQA (2006) *English Specification A (3702/2F)*, GCSE 2004 November Series: Specimen Paper and Mark Scheme, Manchester, Assessment and Qualifications Alliance, http://www.aqa.org.uk/qual/gcse/qp-ms/AQA-3702H2-W-MS-nov04.pdf (Accessed 17 April 2006).

Arthur, J. (1992) *Talking Like Teachers: Teacher and Pupil Discourse in Standard Six Botswana Classrooms*, Working Paper no. 25, Centre for Language in Social Life, University of Lancaster.

Australian Education Council (1994) *A Statement on English for Australian Schools: A Joint Project of the States, Territories and Commonwealth of Australia*, Carlton, Victoria, Curriculum Corporation.

Baker, M. (1992) *In Other Words: A Coursebook on Translation*, London, Routledge.

Bakhtin, M. (1981) 'Discourse in the novel' in Holquist, M. (ed.) *The Dialogic Imagination: Four Essays by M.M. Bakhtin* (ed. M. Holquist, trans. C. Emerson and M. Holquist), Austin, University of Texas Press.

Baldauf, R. (1990) 'Education and language planning in the Samoas' in Baldauf, R. and Luke, A. (eds) *Language Planning and Education in Australasia*, Clevedon, Multilingual Matters.

Ball, S., Kenny, A. and Gardiner, D. (1990) 'Literacy, politics and the teaching of English' in Goodson, I. and Medway, P. (eds) *Bringing English to Order*, London, Falmer Press.

Bancroft, D. (1985) 'The development of temporal reference', PhD thesis, University of Nottingham.

Barnes, D. (1976) *From Communication to Curriculum*, Harmondsworth, Penguin Education.

Barnes, D. and Todd, F. (1995) *Discussion and Learnings Revisited: Making Meaning through Talk*, Portsmouth, NH, Heinemann.

Barnes, D., Britton, J. and Rosen, R. (1969) *Language, the Learner and the School*, Harmondsworth, Penguin Education.

Barrett, M., Harris, M. and Chasin, J. (1991) 'Early lexical development and maternal speech: a comparison of children's initial and subsequent use of words', *Journal of Child Language*, no. 18, pp. 21–40.

Bartholomae, D. (1985) *When a Writer Can't Write*, New York, Guildford Press.

Barton, D. (1994) *Literacy*, Oxford, Blackwell.

Barton, M.E. and Tomasello, M. (1994) 'The rest of the family: the role of fathers and siblings in early language development' in Gallaway, C. and Richards, B.J. (eds) *Input and Interaction in Language Acquisition*, Cambridge, Cambridge University Press.

Becher, T. (1994) 'The significance of disciplinary differences', *Studies in Higher Education*, vol. 19, no. 2, pp. 151–61.

Belcher, D. and Connor, U. (eds) (2001) *Reflections on Multiliterate Lives*, Clevedon, Multilingual Matters.

Benedict, H. (1979) 'Early lexical development: comprehension and production', *Journal of Child Language*, no. 6, pp. 183–200.

Berko Gleason, J. (1973) 'Code switching in children's language' in Moore, T.E. (ed.) *Cognitive Development and the Acquisition of Language*, London, Academic Press.

Bhatia, V.K. (1993) *Analysing Genre: Language Use in Professional Settings*, London, Longman.

Biber D., Johansson, S., Leech, G., Conrad, S. and Finegan, E. (1999) *Longman Grammar of Spoken and Written English*, Harlow, Pearson Education.

Bisong, J. (1995) 'Language choice and cultural imperialism: a Nigerian perspective', *ELT Journal*, vol. 49, no. 2, pp. 122–32.

Bissex, G. (1984) 'The child as teacher' in Goelman, H., Oberg, A. and Smith, F. (eds) *Awakening to Literacy*, London, Heinemann Educational.

Block, D. and Cameron, D. (eds) (2002) *Globalization and Language Teaching*, London, Routledge.

Bloom, L. (1973) *One Word at a Time*, The Hague, Mouton.

Bloor, T. and Bloor, M. (1991) 'Cultural expectations and socio-pragmatic failure in academic writing' in Adams, P., Heaton, B. and Howarth, P. (eds) *Socio-Cultural Issues in English for Academic Purposes* (British Association of Lecturers in English for Academic Purposes conference papers), London, Modern English Publications/British Council.

Blunkett, D. (2004) 'Integration with diversity: globalisation and the renewal of democracy and civil society' in Griffith, P. and Leonard, M. (eds), *Reclaiming Britishness*, London, The Foreign Policy Centre, http://fpc.org.uk/articles/182 (Accessed 15 January 2006).

Bourne, J. (1996) 'English for speakers of other languages' in Mercer, N. and Swann, J. (eds) *Learning English: Development and Diversity*, London, Routledge/Milton Keynes, The Open University.

Bourne, J. and McPake, J. (1991) *Partnership Teaching: Co-operative Teaching Strategies for Multilingual Schools*, London, HMSO.

Bowers, R. (1994) *English 2000*, Manchester, British Council.

Brumfit, C. (ed.) (1991) *Literature on Language: An Anthology*, London, Macmillan.

Bruner, J. (1986) *Actual Minds, Possible Worlds*, Harvard, MA, Harvard University Press.

Bryant, P. (1994) 'Literacy and phonological awareness', *The Encyclopedia of Language and Linguistics*, Oxford, Pergamon, vol. 4, pp. 2246–7.

Burling, R. (1978) 'Language development of a Garo and English-speaking child' in Hatch, E.M. (ed.) *Second Language Acquisition*, Rowley, MA, Newbury House.

CAHSEE (2005) 'Appendix: English-language Arts practice test', *Preparing for the California High School Exit Examination: An English Language Arts Study Guide*, Californian Department of Education, cde.ca.gov/ta/tg/hs/documents/eng05s.pdf (Accessed 17 April 2006).

Cambourne, B. and Turbill, J. (1987) *Coping with Chaos*, Rozelle, NSW, Primary English Teaching Association.

Cameron, D. and Bourne, J. (1988) 'No common ground: Kingman, grammar and the nation', *Language and Education*, vol. 2, no. 3, pp. 147–60.

Camilleri, A. (1994) 'Talking bilingually, writing monolingually', paper presented at the *Sociolinguistics Symposium*, University of Lancaster, March.

Canagarajah, S.A. (2001) 'The fortunate traveler: shutting between communities and literacies by economy class' in Belcher, D. and Connor, U. (eds) *Reflections on Multiliterate Lives*, Clevedon, Multilingual Matters.

CCEA (2004) *Northern Ireland Curriculum Key Stage 1 and 2: Curriculum Support,* Council for the Curriculum, Examinations and Assessment, http://www.rewardinglearning.com/development/ks1_2/ni_curriculum/ ni_curriculum _support/docs/emuguide.pdf (Accessed 13 April 2006).

Celce-Murcia, M. (1978) 'The simultaneous acquisition of English and French in a two-year-old child' in Hatch, E.M. (ed.) *Second Language Acquisition*, Rowley, MA, Newbury House.

Chang, Y.-Y. and Swales J.M. (1999) 'Informal elements in English academic writing: threats or opportunities for advanced non-native speakers?' in Candlin, C.N. and Hyland, K. (eds) *Writing: Texts, Processes and Practices*, London, Longman.

Cheshire, J. (1982) 'Linguistic variation and social function' in Romaine, S. (ed.) *Sociolinguistic Variation in Speech Communities*, London, Edward Arnold.

Chomsky, N. (1965) *Aspects of the Theory of Syntax*, Cambridge, MA, MIT Press.

Christie, M. (1985) *Aboriginal Perspectives on Experience and Learning: The Role of Language in Aboriginal Education*, Deakin, Victoria, Australia, Deakin University Press.

Clare, R. (1995) '"Who is it that can tell me who I am?" The theory of authorial revision between the quarto and folio texts of King Lear', *The Library: The Transactions of the Bibliographical Society*, Oxford, Oxford University Press.

Cleghorn, A., Merrit, M. and Obagi, J.O. (1989) 'Language policy and science instruction in Kenyan primary schools', *Comparative Education Review*, vol. 33, no. 1, pp. 2–39.

Collier, V. (1987) 'Age and rate of acquisition of second language for academic purposes', *TESOL Quarterly,* no. 21, pp. 617–41.

Common European Framework of Reference (2006) http://culture2.coe.int/ portfolio/documents_intro/common_framework.html (Accessed 28 February 2006).

Connor, U. (1996) *Contrastive Rhetoric: Cross-Cultural Aspects of Second-Language Writing*, Cambridge, Cambridge University Press.

Corder, S.P. (1974) 'The significance of learners' errors' in Richards, J. (ed.) *Error Analysis: Perspectives on Second Language Acquisition*, London, Longman.

Corder, S.P. (1978) 'Language-learner language' in Richards, J. (ed.) *Understanding Second and Foreign Language Learning: Issues and Approaches*, Rowley, MA, Newbury House.

Corson, D. (1994) 'Don's diary', *Times Higher Education Supplement*, 9 December, p. 14.

Cox, B. (1995) *The Battle for the English Curriculum*, London, Hodder & Stoughton.

Craik, D. (2005) 'Is this OK 4 U?', *Guardian Unlimited*, 7 March, http://jobsadvice.guardian.co.uk/officehours/story/0,,1431762,00.html (Accessed 12 April 2006).

Crystal, D. (1986) *Listen to your Child: A Parent's Guide to Children's Language*, Harmondsworth, Penguin.

Crystal, D. (1995) *The Cambridge Encyclopedia of the English Language*, Cambridge, Cambridge University Press.

Cummins, J. (2000) 'BICS and CALP' in Byram, M. (ed.) *Encyclopedia of Language Teaching and Learning*, London, Routledge.

Cummins, J. (2003) 'BICS and CALP: origins and rationale for the distinction' in Paulston, C.B. and Tucker, G.R. (eds.) *Sociolinguistics: The Essential Readings*, London, Blackwell.

de Villiers, P.A. and de Villiers, J.G. (1979) *Early Language*, London, Open Books.

DEET (1991) *Australia's Language: The Australian Language and Literacy Policy*, Companion volume, Canberra, Australian Government Publishing Service.

Dendrinos, B. (1992) *The EFL Textbook and Ideology*, Athens, Grivas.

Desai, A. (1995) 'The evolution of a post-apartheid language policy in South Africa: an ongoing site of struggle', *European Journal of Intercultural Studies*, vol. 5, no. 3, pp. 18–25.

Deterding, D.H. (1984) 'A study of the ways in which a two-year-old bilingual child differentiates between his two languages', MPhil dissertation, University of Cambridge Department of Linguistics.

Deuchar, M. and Quay, S. (1998) 'One vs. two systems in early bilingual syntax: two versions of the question', *Bilingualism: Language and Cognition*, vol. 1, no. 3, pp. 231–43.

DfES (2001) *Framework for Teaching English Years 7, 8 and 9*, London, Department for Education and Skills, www.standards.dfes.gov.uk/keystage3/respub/englishframework/foreword/ (Accessed 13 April 2006).

DFEWO (1995) *English in the National Curriculum*, Department for Education and Welsh Office, London, HMSO.

Dillon, J.J. (ed.) (1988) *Questioning and Discussion: A Multidisciplinary Study*, London, Croom Helm.

Dixon, J. (1975) *Growth through English* (3rd edn), Oxford, Oxford University Press.

Dobson, J.L. (1984) 'The interpretation of statistical data on the levels of literacy in nineteenth-century England and Wales' in Brooks, G. and Pugh, A.K. (eds) *Studies in the History of Reading*, Reading, University of Reading Centre for the Teaching of Reading and UK Reading Association.

Dombey, H. (1992) 'Lessons learnt at bedtime' in Kimberley, K., Meek, M. and Miller, J. (eds) *New Readings: Contributions to an Understanding of Literacy*, London, A & C Black.

Downing, J. (1973) *Comparative Reading*, New York, Macmillan.

Downing, J. and Leong, C.K. (1982) *Psychology of Reading*, New York, Macmillan.

Dulay, H.C. and Burt, M.K. (1976) 'Creative construction in second language learning and teaching' in Brown, H.D. (ed.) *Language and Learning* (papers in second language acquisition, proceedings of the Sixth Annual Conference on Applied Linguistics), University of Michigan, Special Issue no. 4, January.

Edwards, A.D. (1976) *Language in Culture and Class*, London, Heinemann.

Edwards, A.D. (1992) 'Teacher talk and pupil competence' in Norman, K. (ed.) *Thinking Voices: The Work of the National Oracy Project*, London, Hodder & Stoughton.

Edwards, J.R. (1979) 'Social class differences and the identification of sex in children's speech', *Journal of Child Language*, no. 6, pp. 121–7.

Edwards, V. and Sienkewicz, T. (1990) *Oral Cultures Past and Present: Rappin' and Homer*, Oxford, Blackwell.

Eisikovits, E. (1989) 'Girl-talk/boy-talk: sex differences in adolescent speech' in Collins, P. and Blair, D. (eds) *Australian English: The Language of a New Society*, Queensland, University of Queensland Press.

Elbow, P. (1991) 'Reflections on academic discourse: how it relates to freshmen and colleagues', *College English*, vol. 53, no. 2, pp. 135–55.

Fantini, A. (1985) *Language Acquisition of a Bilingual Child: A Sociolinguistic Perspective*, San Diego, College Hill.

Fillmore, L.W. (1979) 'Individual differences in second language acquisition' in Fillmore, C., Kempler, D. and Wang, W. (eds) *Individual Differences in Language Ability and Language Behaviour*, New York, Academic Press.

Franklin, M.B. and Barten, S.S. (eds) (1988) *Child Language: A Reader*, Oxford, Oxford University Press.

Furnborough, P., Cowgill, S., Greaves, H. and Sapin, K. (1980) *A New Start: A Functional Course in Basic Spoken English*, London, Heinemann Educational.

Genesee, F. (2000) 'Early bilingual language development: one language or two' in Li Wei (ed.) *The Bilingual Reader*, London, Routledge.

Gillen, J. (2003) *The Language of Children*, London, Routledge.

Gilligan, C. (1995) 'The centrality of relationship in psychological development: a puzzle, some evidence, and a theory' in Holland, J. and Blair, M. (eds) *Research and Feminist Pedagogy*, Clevedon, Multilingual Matters.

Goffman, E. (1981) *Forms of Talk*, Oxford, Blackwell.

Goodman, K., Goodman, Y. and Burke, C. (1978) 'Reading for life: the psycholinguistic basis' in Hunter-Grundin, E. and Grundin, H. (eds) *Reading: Implementing the Bullock Report*, London, Ward Lock Educational.

Goodman, Y. (1984) 'The development of initial literacy' in Goelman, H., Oberg, A. and Smith, F. (eds) *Awakening to Literacy*, London, Heinemann Educational.

Goodwyn, A. (2003) 'We teach English not Literacy: growth pedagogy under siege in England' in Doecke, B., Horner, D. and Nixon, H. (eds) *English Teachers at Work: Narratives, Counter Narratives and Arguments*, Kent Town, The Australian Association for the Teaching of English (AATE).

Goodwyn, A. and Findlay, K. (1999) 'The Cox models revisited: English teachers' views of their subject and the national curriculum', *English in Education*, vol. 33, no. 2, pp. 19–31.

Goswami, U. (2002) 'Rhymes, phonemes and learning to read: interpreting recent research' in Cook, M. (ed.) *Perspectives on the Teaching and Learning of Phonics*, Leicester, University of Leicester, United Kingdom Literacy Association.

Graddol, D. and Mayor, B.M. (1996) 'Knowledge and modality in academic discourse', paper presented to English Language Teaching and Learning Research Group, Centre for Language and Communications, Milton Keynes, The Open University.

Graddol, D., Leith, D., Swann, J., Rhys, M. and Gillen, J. (eds) (2007) *Changing English*, London, Routledge/Milton Keynes, The Open University.

Graddol, D. (1997) *The Future of English?: A Guide to Forecasting the Popularity of the English Language in the 21st Century*, London, The British Council.

Graddol, D. (2006) *English Next: Why Global English may mean the End of 'English as a Foreign Language'*, London, The British Council.

Grant, N. (1987) *Making the Most of Your Textbook*, London, Longman.

Graves, D. (1983) *Writing: Teachers and Children at Work*, London, Heinemann.

Gregory, E. (1992) 'Learning codes and contexts: a psychosemiotic approach to beginning reading in school' in Kimberley, K., Meek, M. and Miller, J. (eds) *New Readings: Contributions to an Understanding of Literacy*, London, A & C Black.

Gupta, A.F. (1994) *The Step Tongue: Children's English in Singapore*, Clevedon, Multilingual Matters.

Hakuta, K. (1986) *Mirror of Language: The Debate of Bilingualism*, New York, Basic Books.

Hall, N. (1987) *The Emergence of Literacy*, Sevenoaks, Hodder & Stoughton.

Halliday, M.A.K. (1978) *Language as Social Semiotic: The Social Interpretation of Language and Meaning*, London, Edward Arnold.

Halliday, M.A.K. (1985) *Spoken and Written Language*, Geelong, Australia, Deakin University Press.

Halliday, M.A.K. (1994) *An Introduction to Functional Grammar* (2nd edn), London, Edward Arnold.

Halliday, M.A.K. and Martin, J.A. (1993) *Writing Science*, Brighton, Falmer.

Harding, K. and Henderson, P. (1994) *High Season: English for the Hotel and Tourist Industry*, Oxford, Oxford University Press.

Harness-Goodwin, M. (1990) *He-Said-She-Said: Talk as Social Organization among Black Children*, Bloomington and Indianapolis, Indiana University Press.

Harrison, G.J. and Piette, A.B. (1980) 'Young bilingual children's language selection', *Journal of Multilingual and Multicultural Development*, vol. 1, no. 3, pp. 217–30.

Harste, J., Burke, C. and Woodward, V. (1981) *Children, their Language and World: Initial Encounters with Print*, National Institute of Education, Bloomington, Indiana University Press.

Hartley, B. and Viney, P. (1978) *Streamline English: Departures*, Oxford, Oxford University Press.

Hatch, E.M. (ed.) (1978) *Second Language Acquisition*, Rowley, MA, Newbury House.

Heath, S.B. (1982a) 'Protean shapes in literacy events: ever-shifting oral and literate traditions' in Tannen, D. (ed.) *Spoken and Written Language*, Norwood, NJ, Ablex.

Heath, S.B. (1982b) 'Questioning at home and at school: a comparative study' in Spindler, G. (ed.) *Doing the Ethnography of Schooling*, New York, Holt, Rinehart & Winston.

Heath, S.B. (1983) *Ways with Words: Language, Life and Work in Communities and Classrooms*, Cambridge, Cambridge University Press.

Heller, M. (1992) 'The politics of code-switching and language choice', *Journal of Multilingual and Multicultural Development*, vol. 13, no. 1, pp. 123–42.

Hilton, M. (2001) 'Are the Key Stage 2 reading tests becoming easier each year?' *Reading*, vol. 35, no. 1, pp. 4–11.

HMSO (1921) *The Teaching of English in England* (The Newbolt Report) London, His Majesty's Stationery Office.

HMSO (1963) *Half our Future* (The Newsom Report), London, Her Majesty's Stationery Office.

HMSO (1975) *A Language for Life* (The Bullock Report), London, Her Majesty's Stationery Office.

Hoadley-Maidment, E. and Mercer, N. (1996) 'English in the academic world' in Mercer, N. and Swann, J. (eds) *Learning English: Development and Diversity*, London, Routledge/Milton Keynes, The Open University.

Hollett, V. (1994) *Business Opportunities*, Oxford, Oxford University Press.

Holmes, J. (1992) *An Introduction to Sociolinguistics*, London, Longman.

Horgan, D. (1981) 'Learning to make jokes: a study of metalinguistic abilities', *Journal of Child Language*, no. 8, pp. 217–24.

Huang, J. and Hatch, E.M. (1978) 'A Chinese child's acquisition of English' in Hatch, E.M. (ed.) *Second Language Acquisition*, Rowley, MA, Newbury House.

Hull, R. (1985) *The Language Gap*, London, Methuen.

Hung, T. (1993) 'The role of phonology in the teaching of pronunciation to bilingual students', *Language, Culture and Curriculum*, vol. 6, no. 3, pp. 249–56.

Hunston, S. and Thompson, G. (2000) (eds) *Evaluation in Text: Authorial Stance and the Construction of Discourse*, Oxford, OUP.

Hunter-Grundin, E. (1997) 'Are reading standards falling', *English in Education*, vol. 31, no. 3, pp. 40–4.

Hutchinson, T. and Torres, E. (1994) 'The textbook as agent of change', *English Language Teaching Journal*, vol. 48, no. 4, pp. 315–28.

Hyland, K. (1999) 'Disciplinary discourses: writer stance in research articles' in Candlin, C.N. and Hyland, K. (eds) *Writing: Texts, Processes and Practices*, London, Longman.

Hyland, K. (2001) 'Humble servants of the discipline? Self-mention in research articles', *English for Specific Purposes,* no. 20, pp. 207–26.

Hyland, K. (2002) 'Directives: argument and engagement in academic writing', *Applied Linguistics*, vol. 23, no. 2, pp. 215–39.

Hyland, K. and Milton, J. (1997) 'Qualification and certainty in L1 and L2 students' writing', *Journal of Second Language Writing*, vol. 6, no. 2, pp.183–205.

Hymes, D.H. (1972) 'On communicative competence' in Pride, J.B. and Holmes, J. (eds) *Sociolinguistics: Selected Readings*, Harmondsworth, Penguin Education.

Ingram, D. (1989) *First Language Acquisition: Method, Description, and Explanation,* Cambridge, Cambridge University Press.

Iredale, R. (1991) 'The economic benefits of English language teaching', *Dunford Seminar Report: The Social and Economic Impact of ELT in Development*, Manchester, British Council, pp. 8–9.

Ivanič, R. (1998) *Writing and Identity: The Discoursal Construction of Identity in Academic Writing,* Amsterdam, John Benjamins.

Ivanič, R. and Camps, D. (2001) 'I am how I sound. Voice as self representation in L2 writing', *Journal of Second Language Writing,* vol. 10, no. 1–2, pp. 3–33.

Janks, H. (1993) *Language and Position*, Johannesburg, Hodder & Stoughton.

Johnson, R.K. and Lee, P.L.M. (1987) 'Modes of instruction: teaching strategies and students' responses' in Lord, R. and Cheng, H. (eds) *Language Education in Hong Kong*, Hong Kong, Chinese University Press.

Jordan, J. (1992) *An Introduction to ESOL Teaching*, London, Adult Learning and Basic Skills Unit (ALBSU).

Kamwangamalu, N.M. (1992) 'Multilingualism and social identity in Singapore', *Journal of Asian Pacific Communication*, vol. 3, no. 1, pp. 33–47.

Kanno, Y. (2003) *Negotiating Bilingual and Bicultural Identities: Japanese Returnees betwixt Two Worlds*, Mahwah, NJ, Lawrence Erlbaum.

Kenner, C. (2004) *Becoming Biliterate: Young Children Learning Different Writing Systems*, Stoke-on-Trent, Trentham Books.

Krashen, S. (1981) *Second Language Acquisition and Second Language Learning*, Oxford, Pergamon.

Kress, G. (1994) *Learning to Write*, London, Routledge.

Kress, G. (1995) *Writing the Future*, Sheffield, National Association for the Teaching of English (NATE).

Kress, G. (2003) 'Perspectives on making meaning: the differential principles and means of adults and children' in Hall, N., Larson, J. and Marsh, J. (eds) *Handbook of Early Childhood Literacy*, London, Sage.

Labov, W. (1964) 'Stages in the acquisition of Standard English' in Shuy, R.W. (ed.) *Social Dialects and Language Learning*, Champaign, Illinois, NCTE.

Labov, W. (1972) *Language in the Inner City: Studies in the Black English Vernacular*, Oxford, Blackwell.

Lankshear, C. and Knobel, M. (2003) *New Literacies: Changing Knowledge and Classroom Learning*, Buckingham, Open University Press.

Lathey, G. (1992) 'Talking in your head: young children's developing understanding of the reading process', *English in Education*, vol. 26, no. 2, pp. 71–82.

Le Page, R.B. and Tabouret-Keller, A. (1985) *Acts of Identity: Creole-based Approaches to Language and Ethnicity*, Cambridge, Cambridge University Press.

Lea, M. and Street, B. (1998) 'Student writing in higher education: an academic literacies approach', *Studies in Higher Education*, vol. 11, no. 3, pp. 182–99

Leavis, F.R. (1948) *Education & the University: A Sketch for an 'English School'* (3rd edn), London, Chatto & Windus.

Levitt, A.G. and Utman, J.G.A. (1992) 'From babbling towards the sound systems of English and French: a longitudinal two-case study', *Journal of Child Language*, no. 19, pp. 19–49.

Li Wei, (1994) *Three Generations, Two Languages, One Family*, Clevedon, Multilingual Matters.

Lillis, T. (2001) *Student Writing: Access, Regulation, Desire*, London, Routledge.

Lillis, T. (2003) 'An "academic literacies" approach to student writing in higher education: drawing on Bakhtin to move from "critique" to "design"', *Language and Education*, vol. 17, no. 3, pp. 192–207.

Lin, A. (1988) 'Pedagogical and para-pedagogical levels of interaction in the classroom: a social interactional approach to the analysis of the code-switching behaviour of a bilingual teacher in an English language lesson', *Working Papers in Linguistics and Language Teaching*, no. 11, University of Hong Kong Language Centre.

Lo Bianco, J. (1987) *National Policy on Languages*, Canberra, Commonwealth Department of Education.

Lu, M. (1992) 'Conflict and struggle: the enemies or pre-conditions of basic writing?', *College English*, vol. 54, no. 8, pp. 887–913.

Luke, A. and Freebody, P. (1999) 'A map of possible practices: further notes on the four resources model', *Practically Primary*, vol. 4, no. 2, pp. 5–8.

Macaulay, R.K.S. (1978) 'Variation and consistency in Glaswegian English' in Trudgill, P. (ed.) *Sociolinguistic Patterns in British English*, London, Edward Arnold.

MacDonald, S.P. (1994) *Professional Academic Writing in the Humanities and Social Sciences*, Carbondale and Edwardsville, Southern Illinois University Press.

Magalhaes, M.C.C. (1994) 'An understanding of classroom interactions for literacy development' in Mercer, N. and Coll, C. (eds) *Teaching, Learning and Interaction: Explorations in Socio-Cultural Studies*, no. 4, Madrid, Infancia y Aprendizaje.

Malcolm, I. (1982) 'Speech events of the Aboriginal classroom', *International Journal of the Sociology of Language*, no. 36, pp. 115–34.

Marenbon, J. (1987) *English our English: The New Orthodoxy Examined*, London, Centre for Policy Studies.

Marshall, B. (1997) 'The Great Education Debate?' *Critical Quarterly*, vol. 39, no. 1, pp. 111–18.

Marshall, B. (2000) 'A rough guide to English', *English in Education,* vol. 34, no. 1, pp. 24–41.

Martin, J.A., Christie, F. and Rothery, J. (1987) 'Social processes in education: a reply to Sawyer and Watson (and others)' in Reid, I. (ed.) *The Place of Genre in Learning: Current Debates*, Deakin, Australia, Centre for Studies in Literacy Education, Deakin University.

Martin, J.R. (1985) *Factual Writing: Exploring and Challenging Social Reality*, Deakin, Victoria, Australia, Deakin University.

Martin-Jones, M. (1995) 'Code-switching in the classroom' in Milroy, L. and Muysken, P. (eds) *One Speaker, Two Languages: Cross Disciplinary Perspectives on Code-switching*, Cambridge, Cambridge University Press.

Martlew, M. and Sorsby, A. (1995) 'The precursors of writing: graphic representation in preschool children', *Learning and Instruction*, vol. 5, no. 1, pp. 1–19.

Maybin, J. (1994a) 'Children's voices: talk, knowledge and identity' in Graddol, D., Maybin, J. and Stierer, B. (eds) *Researching Language and Literacy in Social Context*, Clevedon, Multilingual Matters.

Maybin, J. (1994b) 'Teaching writing: process or genre?' in Brindley, S. (ed.) *Teaching English*, London, Routledge.

Maybin, J. (2000) 'The canon: historical construction and contemporary challenges' in Davison, J. and Moss, J. (eds) *Issues in English Teaching*, London, Routledge.

Maybin, J. (2007) 'Everyday talk' in Maybin, J., Mercer, N. and Hewings, A. (eds) *Using English,* London, Routledge/Milton Keynes, The Open University.

Mayor, B. (1996) 'English in the repertoire' in Mercer, N. and Swann, J. (eds) *Learning English: Development and Diversity*, London, Routledge/Milton Keynes, The Open University

Mayor, B.M. (2006) 'Dialogic and hortatory features in the writing of Chinese candidates for the IELTS test', *Journal of Language, Culture and Curriculum,* vol. 19, no. 1, pp. 1–18.

Mayor, B.M. and Swann, J. (2002) 'English language and global teaching' in Lea, M.R. and Nicoll, K. (eds) *Distributed Learning: Social and Cultural Approaches to Practice,* London, Routledge, Falmer.

Mayor, B.M., Hewings, A., North, S., Swann, J. and Coffin, C. (2006) 'A linguistic analysis of Chinese and Greek L1 scripts for IELTS Academic Writing Task 2', *Studies in Language Testing*, no. 19, UCLES/CUP, pp. 250–313.

McClure, E. (1977) 'Aspects of code-switching in the discourse of Mexican-American children' in Saville-Troike, M. (ed.) *Linguistics and Anthropology*, Georgetown, WA, Georgetown University Press.

Mehan, H. (1979) *Learning Lessons: Social Organization in the Classroom,* Cambridge, MA, Harvard University Press.

Mercer, N. (1995) *The Guided Construction of Knowledge: Talk amongst Teachers and Learners*, Clevedon, Multilingual Matters.

Mercer, N. (2000) *Words and Minds: How We Use Language to Think Together*, London, Routledge.

Mercer, N. and Barnes, D. (1996) 'English as a classroom language' in Mercer, N. and Swann, J. (eds) *Learning English: Development and Diversity*, London, Routledge/Milton Keynes, The Open University.

Mercer, N., Dawes, R., Wegerif, R. and Sams, C. (2004) 'Reasoning as a scientist: ways of helping children to use language to learn science', *British Educational Research Journal*, vol. 30, no. 3, pp. 367–85.

Milton, J. (2001) 'Elements of a written interlanguage: a computational and corpus-based study of institutional influences on the acquisition of English by Hong Kong Chinese students', *Research Reports,* 2, Language Centre, Hong Kong University of Science and Technology, http://hdl.handle.net/1783.1/1055 (Accessed 18 April 2005).

Mitchell-Kernan, C. and Kernan, K.T. (1977) 'Pragmatics of directive choice amongst children' in Ervin-Tripp, S. and Mitchell-Kernan, C. (eds) *Child Discourse*, New York, Academic Press.

Moore, A. (1995) 'The academic, linguistic and social development of bilingual pupils in secondary education: issues of diagnosis, pedagogy and culture', PhD thesis, Milton Keynes, The Open University.

Mukherjee, T. (1985) 'ESL: an imported new empire' in North London Community Group (eds) *Language and Power: Dynamics of Change and Control*, London, North London Community Group.

Mullis, I.V.S., Martin, M.O., Gonzalez, E.J. and Kennedy, A.M. (2003) *2001 International Report: IEAs Study of Reading Literacy Achievement in Primary Schools in 35 Countries*, PIRLS, Boston, MA, Boston College, International Study Centre.

Murray, L. and Andrews, L. (2000) *The Social Baby*, Richmond, Children's Project Publishing.

Myers-Scotton, C. and Bolonyai, A. (2001) 'Calculating speakers: codeswitching in a rational choice model', *Language in Society*, vol. 30, no. 1, pp. 1–28.

Nation, K. and Snowling, M.J. (2004) 'Beyond phonological skills: broader language skills contribute to the development of reading', *Journal of Research in Reading*, vol. 27, no. 4, pp. 342–56.

National Writing Project (1989) *Becoming a Writer*, Walton-on-Thames, Thomas Nelson.

National Writing Project (1990) *A Rich Resource: Writing and Language Diversity*, Walton-on-Thames, Thomas Nelson.

Ngũgĩ wa Thiong'o (1964) *Weep Not, Child*, Oxford, Heinemann.

Norman, K. (ed.) (1992) *Thinking Voices: The Work of the National Oracy Project*, London, Hodder & Stoughton.

Ofsted (2003) *The National Literacy and Numeracy Strategies and the Primary Curriculum*, London, Ofsted, www.ofsted.gov.uk (Accessed 13 April 2006).

Ofsted (2005) *English 2000–05: A Review of Inspection Evidence* (HMI 2351), London, Ofsted, www.ofsted.gov.uk (Accessed 13 April 2006).

Ong, W. (1982) *Orality and Literacy*, London, Methuen.

Paradise, R. (1996) 'Passivity or tacit collaboration: Mazahua interaction in cultural context', *Learning and Instruction* (special edition on cooperation and social context in adult–child interaction), vol. 6, no. 4, pp. 379–89.

Payne, A. (1980) 'Factors controlling the acquisition of the Philadelphia dialect by out-of-state children' in Labov, W. (ed.) *Locating Language in Time and Space*, New York, Academic Press.

Pennycook, A. (1989) 'The concept of method, interested knowledge, and the politics of language teaching', *TESOL Quarterly*, vol. 23, no. 4, pp. 589–618.

Pennycook, A. (1994a) 'Incommensurable discourses?', *Applied Linguistics*, vol. 15, no. 2, p. 132.

Pennycook, A. (1994b) *The Cultural Politics of English as an International Language*, London, Longman.

Pennycook, A. (1996) 'Borrowing others' words: text, ownership, memory and plagiarism', *TESOL Quarterly*, no. 30, pp. 201–30.

Phelps, G. (1949) 'English and the Classics', *English in Schools*, vol. 2, no. 9, pp. 156–62.

Philips, S. (1972) 'Participant structures and communicative competence' in Cazden, D., John, V. and Hymes, D. (eds) *The Functions of Language in the Classroom*, New York, Teachers College Press.

Phillipson, R. (1992) *Linguistic Imperialism*, Oxford, Oxford University Press.

Poplack, S. (1980) 'Sometimes, I'll start a sentence in Spanish y termino en espanol (sic)', *Linguistics*, no. 18, pp. 581–618.

Preyer, W. (1889) *The Mind of the Child*, New York, Appleton.

Pride, J.B. and Holmes, J. (eds) (1972) *Sociolinguistics: Selected Readings*, Harmondsworth, Penguin.

Prodromou, L. (1990) 'English as cultural action' in Rossner, R. and Bolitho, R. (eds) *Currents of Change in ELT*, Oxford, Oxford University Press.

Pye, C. (1986) 'Quiché Mayan speech to children', *Journal of Child Language*, no. 13, pp. 85–100.

QCA (2004) *Introducing the Grammar of Talk*, London, Qualifications and Curriculum Authority.

QCA (2006) 'About English', English subject home page, www.qca.org.uk/7898.html (Accessed 13 April 2006).

Quirk, R. (1989) 'Separated by a common dilemma', *Times Higher Education Supplement*, 10 February, pp. 15, 18.

Rampton, B. (1995) *Crossing: Language and Ethnicity among Adolescents*, London, Longman.

Rampton, B. (1996) 'Youth, race and resistance: a sociolinguistic perspective', *Linguistics and Education*, vol. 8, no. 2, pp. 159–74.

Rampton, M. (1990) 'Displacing the "native-speaker": expertise, affiliation and inheritance', *ELT Journal*, vol. 44, no. 2, pp. 97–101.

Rashid, R. (1993) *A Malaysian Journey*, Kuala Lumpur, 15 Larong 1412C, 46100 Petaling Jaya, Selangor Darul Ehsan.

Ravem, R. (1974) 'The development of *wh*- questions in first and second language learners' in Richards, J. (ed.) *Error Analysis: Perspectives on Second Language Acquisition*, London, Longman.

Redlinger, W.E. and Park, T.-Z. (1980) 'Language mixing in young bilinguals', *Journal of Child Language*, vol. 7, no. 2, pp. 337–52.

Reid, E. (1978) 'Social and stylistic variation in the speech of children: some evidence from Edinburgh' in Trudgill, P. (ed.) *Sociolinguistic Patterns in British English*, London, Edward Arnold.

Rogers, J. (1990) 'The world for sick proper' in Rosner, R. and Bolitho, R. (eds) *Currents of Change in English Language Teaching*, Oxford, Oxford University Press.

Rojas-Drummond, S. and Mercer, N. (2004) 'Scaffolding the development of effective collaboration and learning', *International Journal of Educational Research*, no. 39, pp. 99–111.

Romaine, S. (1975) 'Linguistic variability in the speech of some Edinburgh schoolchildren', MLitt thesis, University of Edinburgh.

Romaine, S. (1984) *The Language of Children and Adolescents*, Oxford, Blackwell.

Romaine, S. (1995) *Bilingualism* (2nd edn), Oxford, Blackwell.

Rose, M. (1989) *Lives on the Boundary,* New York, Penguin.

Routh, H. (1941) *The Diffusion of English Culture Outside England: A Problem of Post-War Reconstruction*, Cambridge, Cambridge University Press.

Sahni, U. (1992) 'Literacy for empowerment', paper presented at the First Conference for Socio-cultural Research: a research agenda for educational and cultural change, Universidad Complutense de Madrid, October.

Sanders, E.K. (1961) 'Where are speech sounds learned?', *Journal of Speech and Hearing Disorders*, no. 37, pp. 55–63.

Saxena, M. (1993) 'Literacies among the Panjabis in Southall' in Hamilton, M., Barton, D. and Ivanič, R. (eds) *Worlds of Literacy*, Clevedon, Multilingual Matters.

Schieffelin, B. and Cochran-Smith, M. (1984) 'Learning to read culturally: literacy before schooling' in Goelman, H., Oberg, A. and Smith, F. (eds) *Awakening to Literacy*, London, Heinemann Educational.

Scollon, R. and Scollon, S.W. (2001) *Intercultural Communication: A Discourse Approach*, Oxford, Blackwell.

Seidlhofer, B. (ed.) (2003) *Controversies in Applied Linguistics*, Oxford, Oxford University Press.

Sheeran, Y. and Barnes, D. (1991) *School Writing: Discovering the Ground Rules,* Buckingham, Open University Press.

Shelley, P.B. (2006 [1821]) *A Defence of Poetry*, http://www.gutenberg.org/dirs/etext04/adpoel0.txt (Accessed 16 January 2006).

Sheridan, A. (1980) *Michel Foucault: The Will to Truth*, London, Tavistock.

Shuy, R. (1978) 'What children's functional language can tell us about reading or how Joanna got herself invited to dinner' in Beach, R. (ed.) *Perspectives on Literacy: Proceedings of the 1977 Perspectives on Literacy Conference*, Minneapolis, University of Minnesota.

Sinclair, J. and Coulthard, M. (1975) *Towards an Analysis of Discourse: The English used by Teachers and Pupils*, Oxford, Oxford University Press.

Smith, F. (1978) *Reading*, Cambridge, Cambridge University Press.

Solsken, S. (1993) *Literacy, Gender and Work in Families and in School*, Norwood, NJ, Ablex.

Steele, S. (1990) *The Content of our Character: A New Vision of Race in America*, New York, St Martin's.

Storey, J. (1994) 'Mapping the popular: the study of popular culture within British cultural studies', *The European English Messenger*, vol. 3, no. 2, pp. 47–59.

Street, B. (1997) 'The Implications of the New Literacy Studies for Literacy Education', *English in Education*, vol. 31, no. 3, pp. 44–55.

Swain, M. (1972) 'Bilingualism as a first language', PhD dissertation, Irvine, University of California.

Swales, J.M. (1990) *Genre Analysis: English in Academic and Research Settings*, Cambridge, Cambridge University Press.

Talbot, G.B. (1940) 'English in the Technical School', *English in Schools*, vol. 1, no. 4, pp. 82–4.

Tang, R. and John, S. (1999) 'The "I" in identity: exploring writer identity in academic writing through the first person pronoun', *English for Specific Purposes*, no. 18 (Supplement), S23–S39.

Taylor, D. (1983) *Family Literacy: Young Children Learning to Read and Write*, Exeter, NH, Heinemann.

Teale, W. and Sulzby, E. (1988) 'Emergent literacy as a perspective for examining how young children become writers and readers' in Mercer, N. (ed.) *Language and Literacy from an Educational Perspective, Volume 1 Language Studies*, Milton Keynes, The Open University.

Temple, C.A., Nathan, R.G. and Burris, N.A. (1982) *The Beginnings of Writing*, Boston, MA, Allyn & Bacon.

The Open University (1991) *Talk and Learning 5–16: An In-service Pack on Oracy for Teachers*, Milton Keynes, The Open University.

The Open University (2006) 'Plagiarism', http://www3.open.ac.uk/our-student-policies/pdf/plagiarism.pdf (Accessed 17 March 2006).

Thompson, G. (2001) 'Interaction in academic writing: learning to argue with the reader', *Applied Linguistics*, vol. 22, no. 1, pp. 58–78.

Tomasello, M. and Bates, E. (2001) 'General introduction' in Tomasello, M. and Bates, E. (eds) *Language Development: The Essential Readings*, Oxford, Blackwell.

Tomic, P. and Trumper, R. (1992) 'Canada and the streaming of immigrants: a personal account of the Chilean case' in Satzewich, V. (ed.) *Deconstructing a Nation: Immigration, Multiculturalism and Racism in '90s Canada*, Halifax, NS, Fernwood.

Trevarthen, C. and Aitken, K.J. (2001) 'Infant intersubjectivity: research, theory and clinical applications', *Journal of Child Psychology and Psychiatry*, vol. 42, no. 1, pp. 3–48.

Trudgill, P. (1986) *Dialects in Contact*, Oxford, Blackwell.

Twist, L., Sainsbury, M., Woodthorpe, A. and Whelan, C. (2003) *Reading All Over the World: Progress in International Reading Literacy Study*, PIRLS, National Report for England, Slough, National Federation for Educational Research (NFER).

Ueyama, M. and Tamaki, D.C. (1984) *Chuo English Studies*, Tokyo, Chuo Tosho.

Vande Kopple, W.J. (1986) 'Given and new information and some aspects of the structures, semantics, and pragmatics of written texts' in Cooper, C.R. and Greenbaum, S. (eds) *Studying Writing: Linguistic Approaches*, London, Sage.

Vassileva, I. (2001) 'Commitment and detachment in English and Bulgarian academic writing', *English for Specific Purposes*, vol. 20, no. 1, pp. 83–102.

Victorian Curriculum and Assessment Authority (CAA) (1999) *English/English as a Second Language: Study Design*, Unit 4, Board of Studies, Carlton, Victoria, Australia, www.vcaa.vic.edu.au/vce/studies/english/englisheslsd.pdf (Accessed 1 April 2006).

Villanueva, V. (1993) *Bootstraps: From an American Academic of Color*, Urbana, IL, NCTE.

Walker, R. (1994) 'Back to basics: the revival of British studies', *International Association for Teachers of English as a Foreign Language (IATEFL) Newsletter*, no. 123, pp. 9–10.

Wells, G. (1986) *The Meaning Makers: Children Learning Language and Using Language to Learn*, London, Hodder & Stoughton.

Wells, G. (1992) 'The centrality of talk in education' in Norman, K. (ed.) *Thinking Voices: The Work of the National Oracy Project*, London, Hodder & Stoughton.

Willes, M. (1983) *Children into Pupils: A Study of Language in Early Schooling*, London, Routledge & Kegan Paul.

Wood, D. (1992) 'Teaching talk' in Norman, K. (ed.) *Thinking Voices: The Work of the National Oracy Project*, London, Hodder & Stoughton.

Yoshida, M. (1978) 'The acquisition of English vocabulary by a Japanese-speaking child' in Hatch, E.M. (ed.) *Second Language Acquisition*, Rowley, MA, Newbury House.

Youssef, V. (1991) 'The acquisition of varilingual competence', *English World-Wide*, vol. 12, no. 1, pp. 87–102.

Zentella, A.C. (1981) 'Ta'bien, you could answer me in cualquier idioma: Puerto Rican code-switching in bilingual classrooms' in Duran, R. (ed.) *Latino Language and Communicative Behavior*, Norwood, NJ, Ablex Press.

Acknowledgements

Grateful acknowledgement is made to the following sources:

Text

Pages 38–40: Adamson, L.B. (1995). 'Understanding Words', *Communication Development during Infancy*, pp. 176–9, Brown and Benchmark, Wm. C. Brown Communications, Inc.; pages 102–8: Kenner C., (2004), 'Living In Simultaneous Worlds', *Becoming Biliterate*, Trentham Books Limited; pages 108–14: Reprinted by permission of Sage Publications Ltd from Beard, R., 'Perspectives on Making Meaning', Hall, N. et al. (eds), *Handbook of Early Childhood Literacy*, Copyright (© Roger Beard, 2003); pages 253–8: Hyland, K. (2002) 'Directives: Argument and Engagement in Academic Writing', *Applied Linguistics*, Vol. 23 (2), extracts from pp. 230–6, by permission of Oxford University Press.

Figures

Pages 81 and 94: From: Becoming a Writer – The National Writing Project 1989, Central Project Team – School Curriculum and Assessment Authority. By kind permission of QCA (previously SCAA); pages 96 and 97: Reprinted by permission of Sage Publications Ltd, Thousand Oaks, London and New Delhi, 2003; Kress, G. (2002) 'Perspectives on Making Meaning', *Early Childhood Literacy*, Nigel Hall et al., pp. 160–2, © Gunther Kress 2003; pages 102 and 105: Kenner C., (2004), 'Living In Simultaneous Worlds', *Becoming Biliterate*, Trentham Books Limited; page 185: Robben Island Museum, http://www.robben-island.org.za; page 199: Ueyama, M. and Tamaki, D.C. 1984, *Chuo English Studies Book 1*, Chuotosho, Japan; page 204: Reproduced by permission of Oxford University Press from Streamline English-Departures by Hartley and Viney © Oxford University Press 1978; page 205: Harding, K. and Henderson, P. 1995, *High Season*, © Oxford University Press; page 206: Hollett, V. 1994, *Business Opportunities*, © Oxford University Press. Reprinted by permission of Oxford University Press; page 229: The Learning Workshop, Centre for Higher Education and Access Development, University of North London.

Tables

Page 9: Adamson, L.B. (1995). *Theoretical Foundations, Communication Development during Infancy*, p. 17, McGraw-Hill Inc.; page 13: Sanders, E.K. 1961, 'Where are speech sounds learned?', *Journal of Speech and Hearing Disorders*, pp. 55–63, Figure 1, American Speech-Language-Hearing Association; page 20: Ingram, D. 1989, *First Language Acquisition*, p. 142, Table 6.1, Cambridge University Press; page 136: Adapted from Zentella, 1981.

Illustrations

Page 31: © Belinda Lawley.

Index